D0845897

Rape

Rape

From Lucretia to #MeToo

Mithu Sanyal

VERSO
London • New York

The translation of this work was funded by Geisteswissenschaften International – Translation Funding for Work in the Humanities and Social Sciences from Germany, a joint initiative of the Fritz Thyssen Foundation, the German Federal Foreign Office, the collecting society VG WORT and the Börsenverein des Deutschen Buchhandels (German Publishers & Booksellers Association)

This English-language edition published by Verso 2019
Originally published in German by Editions Nautilus as
Vergewaltigung: Aspekte eines Verbrechens, 2016

1 3 5 7 9 10 8 6 4 2

Verso
UK: 6 Meard Street, London W1F 0EG
US: 20 Jay Street, Suite 1010, Brooklyn, NY 11201
versobooks.com

Verso is the imprint of New Left Books

ISBN-13: 978-1-78663-750-5
ISBN-13: 978-1-78663-752-9 (UK EBK)
ISBN-13: 978-1-78663-753-6 (US EBK)

British Library Cataloguing in Publication Data
A catalogue record for this book is available from the British Library

Library of Congress Cataloging-in-Publication Data
A catalog record for this book is available from the Library of Congress

Typeset in Sabon LT by Hewer Text UK Ltd, Edinburgh
Printed and bound by CPI Group (UK) Ltd, Croydon, CR0 4YY

Contents

Introduction

I'm not defined by my scars but by my incredible ability to heal.
—Lemn Sissay

When I give talks on the topic of this book, I am often asked to give what is commonly known as a "trigger warning." The aim of such warnings is to protect traumatized people from being retraumatized, and I agree that this is important. At the same time, I feel uncomfortable treating people who have been victims of violence as if they've also lost the ability to read. The title of this book (and my talks) is *Rape*. There is little that a warning could tell you that the title has not already, and I trust that if you are reading this, you are prepared to read a book about the charged issue of rape.

And make no mistake, rape is a charged issue for all of us, with far more impact on our lives than any other crime. Rape informs our mental maps, and determines where many of us go, at what times and (more importantly) where we don't.[1] Moreover, the information we get about rape isn't just information about rape; it's also about gender, the relationship of the sexes to each other, and even sexuality. And none of this information is pleasant.

Many people have been fighting so hard and for so long to have sexual assaults recognized as crimes and not just high spirits, that questioning the political convictions that have achieved so much carries the risk of playing into the hands of those who wish to relativize sexual violence. But knowledge is not absolute, and what was right and important forty years ago may have changed. Therefore it is necessary to reconcile our views with the new realities.

More importantly, to question something doesn't mean to reject it. In the words of legal and political scholars Wendy Brown and Janet

Halley, "The aim of critique is to reveal subterranean structures or aspects of a particular discourse, not necessarily to reveal the truth of or about that discourse. What critique promises is not objectivity but perspective."[2] Accordingly, this book is not—and cannot be—a comprehensive cultural history from the first documented rape to the present day, but an attempt to trace narratives and make visible the lines of connection. It examines some of our basic convictions that have hardened into consensus truths, to probe whether they are still useful for us today. In other words: This is a book about what we talk about when we talk about rape.

This is obviously easier said than done, because rape is a veritable hall of mirrors of expectations and discourses, and each sentence is followed by ten unspoken ones. I call this a *cultural sore spot.* Like sore spots on the body, cultural sore spots indicate something that needs our attention but that we are afraid to touch. It is little wonder that this book has encountered more resistance than any of my other texts. My first publisher was delighted when I told them I was working on my second book—until I told them what it was about. My first book, a cultural history of the vulva, has become a standard work in Germany and publishers were queuing up to do my next book only to bail out at the last minute.[3] Only Nautilus, in Germany—and now Verso Books—dared to do it, and my inner censor, too, had never been so shrill, nor had the knots in my brain ever been so tightly wound. That meant that this book took a lot longer to see the light of the bookshop than I'd anticipated. This turned out to be an advantage. So much happened during that time that could be included in these pages: the mass sexual harassment on New Year's Eve 2015–16 in Cologne, legal reforms in Germany, Title IX complaints on American campuses, Donald Trump's pussy-grabbing comments, and the allegations against Harvey Weinstein and #metoo.

It should be self-evident that not everyone has to share my conclusions, but rape is a topic where nothing is self-evident. So I'll give it to you in writing: Do what you will with this book. Give it to your best friend, use it as a coaster for your coffee cup, throw it against the wall—just please, please don't let it tell you that your feelings are wrong.

But this is exactly what is happening to lots of people. They are being told what to think and how to feel. My aim is to start a discussion and open up new ways to speak about rape, prevention, and healing, as individuals and as a society. One of the main problems is that rape is usually discussed as if it is a reality hewn into granite. But, as the historian Joanna Bourke, whose book *Rape: A History from 1860 to the Present* has been an invaluable tool in writing this book, puts it so concisely, rape "varies between countries; it changes over time. There is nothing timeless or random about it . . . On the contrary, rape and sexual violence are deeply rooted in specific political, economic and cultural environments."[4] Since political, economic, and cultural environments change, so too must sexual violence and our perception of it.

Despite the fears of many event organizers that my talks would trigger trauma in the audience, I regularly encounter the complete opposite. As if a dam were breaking, there is often a palpable relief. Listeners tell me personal stories during the lecture, and even more afterward, and the overwhelming feeling is that this subject was just waiting to be pulled out of the closet, dusted off, and reexamined. After all—and I only noticed it at this point—here was something I only ever talked about with friends as something abstract and theoretical, usually when a prominent case was in the media. Any connection to our own lives seemed to be carefully avoided—except our fear of dark streets at night.

This lack of language is usually interpreted as shame: that our experiences are too painful and embarrassing to share outside protected spaces. But how did that correlate with the complete strangers—of all sexes—who came to me after each lecture and talked to me about what I could not talk about with my friends?

Hardly any subject is as full of contradictions as rape. What other fear lurks behind every corner yet is at the same time supposed to be as rare as being hit by lightning? Where can you encounter so many crude and anachronistic concepts of human beings that don't resemble the human beings you know? Intimate spaces collide with political constructs, and the general uncertainty is only too palpable. That's not surprising in view of all the double binds that entwine the subject as if it were a castle tower with a perfect, beautiful virgin sleeping behind the thorns.

Rape is not just a word, it is a whole story—with a beginning and a tragic ending, part cautionary tale, part sensational literature. Just the sound of the word makes one want to put this book down and read something else. It's important to break with that narrative as well. Just because rape is such a depressing subject, this doesn't have to be a depressing book. Hacking through the thorns, I have done my best to make this book as liberating and empowering as I could. After all, it is a reappropriation of how we think and act. And the way we think and act has consequences: changing how we imagine something can change the way it has power over us.

Gender's Dark Doppelgänger

Being warned of rape is still an inextricable part of initiation into the world of gender. Most girls are told to be careful before they are told anything else about sex—usually without further information on how to do so. Sexual violence is often referred to not as a specific crime but as an inherent risk of being a woman. And the rape script knows only two sexes: perpetrators and victims. When we say *rape* we think of aggressive men and fearful women, of penises as weapons and vaginas as unprotected doorways into equally unprotected bodies—or, to drop the military metaphors, of men who think they have a "right" to female bodies.

The discourse around rape is one of the last bastions and breeding grounds for gender stereotypes we wouldn't dare to think, let alone say out loud—and that goes for all political camps and social strata. Communication in this context couldn't be more dysfunctional. The caricatures we encounter in speaking about rape resemble gender stereotypes in such an exaggerated form that it's hard to recognize them as members of the same species. As soon as we use the r-word, back go the clocks and it is forever 1955. The propaganda in the cold war of the sexes states that female sexuality is an area under threat and must be protected and defended—rather than explored and enjoyed. A little further under the radar, but just as influential, are the messages about male sexuality, which is appraised as a destructive force that must be mastered and controlled—rather than explored and enjoyed. Author Katie Roiphe has called this the "vampire model of male sexuality."[5]

Biologists Randy Thornhill's and Craig T. Palmer's book *A Natural History of Rape* (2000), reminds us that these discourses very much followed us into the new millennium. They attempt to explain rape in terms of evolutional biology, founded on the theory that men are genetically programmed to rape in order to improve their evolutionary prospects—by impregnating women who would've otherwise been way out of their league. Anthropologists, psychologists, and sociologists from all over the world point out that it isn't just women of childbearing age who are raped; that the probability of becoming pregnant as the result of rape is statistically lower than that of consensual sex—erectile dysfunction and lack of ejaculation are the rule rather than the exception in rape; that many pregnancies from rape are not carried to term; and that the evolutionary advantages of being born under such stressful circumstances are questionable anyway.[6]

But most of all, sex offenders must have been stunned when they learned of this supposed reason for their crimes. The inconvenient fact that "most male criminals do not cite reproductive success as a motive for their crimes" needn't stand in the way of this reproduction-by-rape thesis claim sociologists Sotoshi Kanazawa and Mary C. Still: "Psychological mechanisms usually operate at the unconscious level." They contended that it is "the evolved psychological mechanism that predisposes all men to seek reproductive success. The men are completely unaware of the evolutionary logic behind their motives."[7] This sounds uncannily like the cliché of the rapist who whispers in his victim's ear, "I know you want it too"—only, in this case, it's "science" that knows what the rapist wants.

Thornhill and Palmer didn't understand the outcry that followed their book's publication and justified their position by arguing, "People everywhere understand sex as something females have that males want."[8] They suggested an anti-rape program for schools that would train young men to diligently control their evolutionary urge to rape.

In plain language: When you know how dangerous something—meaning yourself—is, you restrain yourself accordingly. "Restrain? Is it that bad?"[9] sociologist Michael Kimmel asked cynically. How about "expressing" their equally evolutionary biological drive to experience pleasure, mutuality, and fun? Might we not be "hard-wired" for that as well? Education for restraint is one of the most politically bankrupt policy initiatives around—and utterly ineffective.

Apart from the fact that "rape is in your genes" is a devastating message for an adolescent, how are boys supposed to develop a healthy relationship with their own sexuality if they are supposed to fight against it at the same time, like a recovering alcoholic fighting their desire for liquor? Following that logic, the only safe place for sexuality would be behind locked doors. There must be friendlier and more humane theories (and thus friendlier and more humane solutions) for the rape enigma.

Kimmel proposes one such playful intervention: the "splash guard" that a colleague of his produced for their university's "Rape Awareness Week." (A splash guard is a plastic grate placed in public urinals that prevents splatter.) Kimmel's colleague had thousands made, printed with a simple, hopeful slogan: "You hold the power to stop rape in your hand."[10] This suggestion is, at least, charming and takes into account the human ability to change and to choose. However, it's also based on the gender dichotomy of men as perpetrators and women as victims.[11] But can it really be so simple?

According to police statistics around the world, men are 150 percent more likely to become victims of violent crimes than women. (Unless they're men of color; then the risk goes through the roof.[12]) The more brutal the crime, the more likely the victim is male. Women are not only safer outside the home than in, but also safer than men. So why don't we warn our sons when they leave the house that the world out there is too dangerous for delicate creatures like them? We're told it's because about 90 percent of the perpetrators of violent crimes are also male and about 90 percent of the victims of rape are female. (We will return to these figures later.)

This answer is as plausible as it is wrong. It doesn't explain why we care so much less for our sons—after all, all violence is horrible even when it doesn't involve sex—nor why we measure rape with a different scale from those we use for almost anything else. When we look at the murder statistics, for example, we find that two-thirds to four-fifths of the victims are male[13]—yet no one jumps to the conclusion that only men can be murdered.

In the case of rape, however, this conclusion is apparently the rule. Until very recently, the US Federal Bureau of Investigation (FBI) defined rape as "the carnal knowledge of a female forcibly and against her will."[14] British law necessitates penetration by a penis as part of its definition of rape. Until 1997, Germany shared the view that to be a rapist one needed a penis, but added that rape could only happen to "a female person to whom he was not married." By law and by common consensus, this meant that only women could be raped and only men could be rapists—as long as they weren't married to their victims. In 1997 that law was amended to recognize the existence of rape within marriage, penalize not only penetration but also "similar sexual acts," and change "female person" into "person." That meant that, for the first time in German history, men could also be considered victims of sexual violence. But only just.

The trailblazer for making rape law gender-neutral was Sweden, which did so in 1984. In England, the Sexual Offences Act was changed in 2003 to include men and trans people as possible victims. South Africa followed in 2007, Scotland in 2009, the FBI in 2012, and China in 2015. While in Switzerland you still need to "force a person of female gender to endure sexual intercourse," otherwise rape is not a rape.[15]

But even the "gender-neutral" wording of the Sexual Offences Act in England, like the FBI definition in America, is only neutral in regard to the victim. It still requires a penis as a prerequisite for recognizing a person as a perpetrator. Even though there are exceptions (which we will return to later), the general rule is: no penis, no rapist. This is not, as one might think, an anachronistic remnant of the old wording but the result of a Home Office debate from 2000, deciding that rape "as commonly understood" involves "forced penetration by a penis."[16] While the vagina and anus, as rapeable orifices, have now been supplemented with the mouth because forced fellatio is regarded "as horrible, as demeaning, and as traumatizing as other forms of forced penile penetration," the corresponding sexual transgression when perpetrated by the vagina is obviously not "horrible and demeaning" or "traumatizing" enough, especially if the victim is a man. "The offence of penile penetration was of a particularly personal kind," the Home Office explained, as it "carried risks of pregnancy and disease transmission."[17] But pregnancy is a highly unlikely result of forced fellatio or forced anal penetration, and sexually transmitted diseases can be just as easily transmitted by a vagina. Still the notion persists that the female body is particularly vulnerable, particularly to sexual acts that is, while at the same time lacking the power to violate—and not only in English legislation. In Germany, for example, if you take your clothes off in public you are only liable for exhibitionism if you inhabit a male-identified body.[18] The female body is not regarded as dangerous, and the law is just starting to grapple with the possibility of more than two kinds of bodies.[19]

"Rape is an 'essentially contested category' infused through and through with political meaning,"[20] writes Bourke. This doesn't mean that men are the "real" victims, but that rape is the most gendered of all crimes. It's also the crime that genders us the most. The way we think about rape is intricately and disturbingly related to the way we think about sex—and that encompasses the meaning of sexuality and of gender, in equal measure.

Given that genitals, chromosomes, and hormone levels are insufficient to determine gender, and a study at the University of Tel Aviv has put an end to the myth of male versus female brains (shockingly, we all have human brains), it would be extremely surprising if the true gender difference turned out to be a disposition to sexual violence.[21] What does it say about our culture that it's so hard for us to speak about rape other than as a crime that *only* men do to *only* women—even though that's not the whole story?

1

Sex: No Means Yes, No Means No!

The best-known anti-rape slogan is "No means No." As redundant as that statement may seem, for much of history, "no" didn't use to mean "no," but simply "I am female." Male force and female reluctance were an integral part of the construction of "normal" sexuality in the eighteenth and nineteenth centuries. "If she is normally developed mentally, and well-bred, her sexual desire is small," testified the pioneering sexologist Richard von Krafft-Ebing. "If this were not so the whole world would become a brothel and marriage and family impossible. It is certain that the man that avoids women and the woman that seeks men are abnormal."[1] Since women were supposed to have no sexual desires of their own, it fell to gallant men to overpower and ravish them. Women—who didn't desire of their own accord but desired the men to desire them—fanned the men's sexual urges with feigned resistance. Or, as Lord Byron put it:

> A little still she strove, and much repented
> and whispering "I will ne'er consent"—consented.[2]

Byron had tradition on his side. Certainly the idea of the fiery man and the frigid woman goes back as least as far as classical antiquity. The Roman poet Ovid famously stated in his *Ars Amatoria*:

> Though you call it force: it's force that pleases girls: what delights is often to have given what they wanted, against their will. She who is taken in love's sudden onslaught is pleased, and finds wickedness is a tribute. And she who might have been forced, and escapes unscathed, will be saddened, though her face pretends delight.[3]

Aristotle proclaimed that man's inner heat was superior to that of women's—literally. According to him, their lack of inner fire left women in a state of arrested development, physically, intellectually, and above all, sexually. After all, they couldn't even boil their menstrual fluids to produce sperm![4]

Once medicine showed that no measurable difference in temperature existed, a different model had to be created to explain the imaginary difference in temperament between the sexes. The Darwinist nineteenth century found this in prehistory, which they viewed as a sort of *Flintstones* version of Victorian society. That the Neanderthal "caveman"—of whom we have very little historical knowledge, apart from the fact that there are no clues that he ever dragged a Neanderthal woman by the hair into his cave—is still an archetype for gender relations shows how deeply these images—"Me hunter of mammoth, you, Jane!"—are rooted in the general consciousness. And the flintstone lens was used to view every consequent period as well. When the University of Oslo discovered in 2014 that the Viking warriors had by no means all been male, the *Daily Mail* ran the headline: "Raping and Pillaging? Viking Conquests Were More Like 'Romantic Breaks': DNA Reveals Warriors Brought Their Women When Raiding British Isles."[5] What else could a woman do on a raiding excursion? Likewise, three years later, the great male warrior BJ 581, from the medieval Viking town of Birka, was proved by DNA testing to have been a woman. Physical anthropologists had been arguing this since the 1970s, but since "he" had been buried with two horses, shield, axe, spear, sword, and bow—obviously "he" had to be a man.[6]

The only reason a woman would fight, the Victorians held, was to preserve her modesty. Sexologist Havelock Ellis declared in 1910:

> The modesty of women—in its primordial form consisting in physical resistance, active or passive, to the assaults of the male—aided selection by putting to the test man's most important quality, force. Thus it is that when choosing among rivals for her favours a woman attributes value to violence.[7]

Sexual selection was Charles Darwin's major innovation, and, in a way, it accorded women a larger role in reproduction. Having previously been completely passive, she was now allowed to choose which man was to overwhelm her. Darwin wrote: "She is coy, and may often be seen endeavouring for a long time to escape from the male . . . The exertion of some choice on the part of the female seems a law almost as general as the eagerness of the male."[8] This choice, however, did not include to go looking for a sexual partner herself; such behavior was deemed alien to woman's inner nature and would render her unattractive to the virile man. What was survival of the fittest for men seemed to be survival of the weakest and most passive for women.

As Susan Sontag noticed, "Everything pertaining to sex has been a 'special case' in our culture, evoking peculiarly inconsistent attitudes."[9]

Until the twentieth century, the conviction that women were frigid while men were fueled by phallic fire permeated everything: social roles, gender norms, communication, lived and imagined sexuality. That meant that a woman who didn't want a man because she *did not want him* had to fight him physically—and hard—otherwise, he could assume that she was simply a "real woman."

The idea that violence was welcome—the Roman concept of *vis haud ingrata*—was still ingrained in law until the 1970s. In a rape case, the woman had to prove not only that she'd physically resisted her assailant, but that she had kept up her resistance constantly throughout. After all, she could have been inexplicably and mysteriously aroused after her "natural coyness" had been overcome.[10]

To this day bestselling self-help books—like Ellen Fein's and Sherrie Schneider's *The Rules: How to Capture the Heart of Mr. Right* and its many sequels—still initiate their millions of readers into the mysteries of passivity and explain to them that, in order to get a man they must first reject him, because men are repulsed by women who know what they want. Everybody knows the three-day-rule that stipulates that a woman has to wait three days before calling a man after their first meeting (and preferably only after he has called her first.) A job-application manual that told its readers not to send an application, to be late for the interview, and to show no interest in the job would hardly sell, but *The Rules* became so popular that Oprah Winfrey asserted, "*The Rules* isn't just a book, it's a movement, honey."[11] Women's magazines are no different. Feminist author Laurie Penny summarizes their position:

> "No" is one of the most erotic things a woman can say . . . if she wants to "catch" a man she must give every appearance of not wanting him, dropping his calls, not returning texts, playing "hard to get." Real men don't want women to want what they want.[12]

This lead to the paradoxical view that the less desire a woman felt, the more desirable she herself was, whereas a lusty woman was seen as degenerate and therefore desexualized (that is, defeminized). For femininity was by no means equally distributed to all women in Victorian times. In the nineteenth century, femininity was measured at the genitals: the smaller the labia, especially the labia minora, the more civilized the woman and the smaller her sexual desire. Anthropologists developed a veritable obsession with the labia of "uncivilized"—that is, colonized—women, which they measured, described, photographed, and cataloged. Happily disregarding the contradiction of having argued that women were sexually passive in prehistory, now their passivity was the result of civilization.

To have any sexual contact at all in such a repressed atmosphere made it a prerequisite that the man was always "up for it." "Following the mighty impulse of nature, he is aggressive and stormy in his love-making," rejoiced Krafft-Ebing.[13] The other side of this coin was that the men who didn't have a partner for "love-making" suffered from constant sexual pressure in this logic. But even marriage involved sexual frustration for half of the married couple.

Andrew Jackson Davis—to whom we owe the term "law of attraction"—expounded, in accordance with Aristotle, "Woman obtains infallible and periodic relief through the menstrual discharge. The enlarged centers of conjugal vital essences, in the ovarian organization, overflow and are soothed into tranquility with every moon." The man, on the other hand: "how much more superabundant and terribly urgent are his procreative resources." Being physically close to a woman without having sex with her left him "charged to repletion, even to the verge of uncontrollable violence."[14] Jackson entreated men to pull themselves together, regardless of the pressure of their sperm coiled for discharge. This came to be known as the "psycho-hydraulic model of sexuality"—or put more simply: the steam-boiler model—and was the preferred explanation and justification for rape in eighteenth- and nineteenth-century legal discourse. Many physicians considered rape immoral but unavoidable and, if there were no prostitutes available, "infinitely preferable to the perils of masturbation," since regular sexual discharge was indispensable to men's health.[15] As late as 1961 author Norman Mailer took the steam-boiler view, famously telling an interviewer, "It's better to commit rape than masturbate" because "masturbating is bombing. It's bombing oneself."[16]

When the steam-boiler model first emerged, it contradicted the received wisdom that men were the rational sex. How could their sex drives then be so irrational? As a consequence, the areas of sexuality and intimacy disappeared, bit by bit, from the concept of rationality, advancing the separation between body and mind even further.[17] Driven to genius or crime by his overwhelming phallic energy, man was no longer suited for his accustomed role as representative of the moral order. Who better to fill this vacancy than woman, who, due to her lack of passion, was rarely tempted anyway? As guardian of the divine order (according to Hegel) or the moral order (Rousseau), she also carried the responsibility of controlling male sexuality by modifying her clothes and behavior so as not to ignite men's highly inflammable libidos.

Warning women not to drink too much alcohol and "send the wrong signals" to men is a remnant of the steam-boiler model, and is widely and rightly criticized. The first Slutwalk, held in 2011 in Toronto, was organized in reaction to Canadian police officer Michael Sanguinetti advising female students not to dress "like sluts" to avoid being raped. Slogans like "My Dress is not a Yes" were a vociferous critique of the steam-boiler model—but only in regards to female sexuality. Demands on men to "pull themselves together" or "master the Neanderthal within"[18] are still part of the rhetoric to explain the unexplainable phenomenon of rape.

But how was it possible that such a sexual scenario ever managed to become so widely accepted in the face of actual sexual relationships? By defining everything that didn't fit into this narrative as illness or, to use the jargon of the time, "perversion." Paradoxically, perversion was simultaneously declared a normal part of the female psyche: woman, the perverse sex.

Krafft-Ebing, having established the asexuality of women, wrote: "[N]evertheless the sexual sphere occupies a much larger sphere in the consciousness of women than that of men, and it is continual rather than intermittent."[19] So men only thought of sex when they saw a woman, while women were up for it all the time except when they actually had sex with a man?

In the 1940s and 1950s, psychoanalyst Helene Deutsch explained this paradox with female masochism in her highly influential book *The Psychology of Women*. Masochism in women was, for Deutsch, not a variant but the prerequisite for sexual satisfaction. The vagina, according to Deutsch, was completely passive and could only be awakened by the penis. From this originated the deep female urge to be overpowered.

> The "undiscovered" vagina is—in normal, favourable instances—eroticized by an act of rape ... That fantasy is only a psychological preparation for a real, milder, but dynamically identical process. This process manifests itself in man's aggressive penetration on the one hand and in the "overpowering" of the vagina and its transformation into an erogenous zone on the other.[20]

With this, Deutsch referred to Sigmund Freud's theory that the psychosexual development of women was not complete until they had managed to transfer their erogenous zone from the clitoris (which, according to Freud, was a retarded male sexual organ and thus active) to the vagina (the actual female sexual organ, and thus passive). In his *Three Contributions to the Theory of Sex*, Freud had declared, "If the transference of the erogenous excitability from the clitoris to the vagina has succeeded, the woman has thus changed her leading zone for the future sexual activity; the man on the other hand retains his from childhood."[21] It goes without saying that women's sexuality encountered manifold dangers and opportunities for getting lost on the way. Thus the prerequisite for "becoming a woman" was at the same time a prerequisite for "woman's preference for the neuroses, especially for hysteria, [which] lie in this change of the leading zone as well as in the repression of puberty. These determinants are therefore most intimately connected with the nature of femininity."[22]

But even without developing neurosis or hysteria, the prognosis for female sexuality was pessimistic; the psychiatrist Leopold Loewenberg explained that, at least the first time, penetrative sex *was* "nothing more or less than rape" for women because of the loss of virginity.[23] Deutsch went even further, asserting that penetration would remain rape at its core: "Woman's frequent fear of coitus originates in the fact that it implies an injury to her physical integrity."[24] Sexuality—and that meant exclusively coitus; any other form of sexuality was considered a regression—was therefore not natural for women, however masochistic.

Yes Means No

Reading all these psychoanalytical texts that never mean sexuality when they say *sexuality* but something a lot darker and deeper, one can't help feeling that rape and masochism stand in for something else as well—that sexual power and impotency might just mean power and impotency in general.

True enough, Freud, Deutsch, and Ellis wrote about masochism not as a sexual fantasy but as a (neurotic) character trait, which makes their texts less studies in sexual psychology than psychological studies of their society on the basis of sexual symptoms. And that was how they were read. Apart from a small group of experts, most people would have been hard pressed to get excited about the problems of Rat Man or Anna O., but everybody wanted to know what men and women really thought and felt and wanted. Freud and Ellis informed their spellbound audiences—in a surprisingly frank way—that the sexual drive wasn't just male in its active and female in its passive form, but that masculinity itself was defined by being dominant, and femininity by being dominated. This definition was so influential that masochism is still a loaded subject. Only recently the soft-porn bestseller and film adaptation *Fifty Shades of Grey* sparked a debate about whether women were, deep down, yearning to be dominated by men—as if women confused their sexual preferences with their social life, work, and politics. Newsweek dedicated a cover story to the male dominant and female submissive of the novel and asked, "Why, for women especially, would free will be a burden?"[25]

Laurie Penny answered:

> Things that Jean-Jacques Rousseau really liked included the philosophy of universal liberty, and having young ladies spank him into a frenzy ... Nobody has ever suggested that this meant that the great enlightenment philosopher secretly wished men didn't run the world ... For women, though, the mainstreaming of kink—and particularly sadomasochism—is supposed to prove that we're not as into all this liberation shtick as we might think.[26]

Even our ideas about the distribution of sexual preferences along gender lines—that men are mainly dominant and women mainly submissive—owe a lot more to Deutsch, Freud, and Ellis than to lived sexualities. A 2015 study in Germany found that men and woman as a group don't differ in their sexual predilections: there are equally as many men and women on either side of the dom/sub spectrum, and sexual preferences can change during a person's lifetime.

The outrage about *Fifty Shades*, a harmless Cinderella story with (not even very) masochistic bedroom scenes, shows the extent of the damage done by the psychoanalytical discourse on masochism, not to mention Freud's famous assertion in his *Psychopathology of Everyday Life* that a woman may have difficulty defending herself against sexual assault because a part of her really wants to be raped. Freud exemplified this theory not with a case from his practice but with an extract from *Don Quixote*. In the story, a woman reports having been raped to Judge Sancho Panza, whereupon Panza takes the accused's purse and gives it to the woman as compensation. But as soon as she is gone, Panza sends the accused after her to regain his purse. It doesn't take long before the two arrive back at the court, fighting and cursing. Sancho Panza says to the woman: "Had you shown yourself so stout and valiant to defend your body (nay, but half so much) as you have done to defend your purse, the strength of Hercules could not have forced you."[27] Freud came to the conclusion that "under a demure demeanour the raging fires of desire still lurked in the female breast, giving her an overactive sexual imagination that sometimes led to false accusations of rape."[28]

His American colleague, the eminent neurologist Bernard Sachs, elaborated the link between "hysteria" and false accusations of rape even further. He asserted that "hysterical women were liable to make these accusations when in a state of great excitement, such as during menstruation."[29] Accordingly, doctors believed at the beginning of the twentieth century that "one of the proofs of hysteria in a woman was a propensity to throw about accusations of sexual immodesty."[30] On this basis, jurist John Henry Wigmore penned his immensely influential *Treatise on the System of Evidence in Trials at Common Law*—better known as Wigmore's Code—in which he advised judges to guard against hysterics and pathological liars by obliging all rape complainants to undergo psychiatric examination.[31]

But even if they weren't suspected of lying, victims had become the focus of research by the 1940s, with the emergence of a new academic discipline called *victimology*. "If there are criminals, it is evident that there are (also) born victims, self-harming and self-destroying,"[32] Hans von Hentig explained in a founding text of the discipline, *The Criminal and His Victim*. Rape in particular was understood as a victim-precipitated crime. In 1960 the psychoanalyst (and former director of research at New York's Sing Sing prison) David Abrahamsen stated, in his influential study *The Psychology of Crime*:

> The victim herself unconsciously also may tempt her offender. The conscious or unconscious biological and psychological attraction between man and woman does not exist only on the part of the offender toward the woman but also on her part toward him, which in many instances may to some extent be the impetus for his sexual attack. Often a woman unconsciously wished to be taken by force.[33]

These almost telekinetic powers by which women caused men to become criminals are even more surprising given that, at the same time, women's supposed lack of sexual energy was translated into a lack of criminal energy. Indeed, early criminologists seemed to talk about women as perpetrators only when they wanted to explain why women *didn't* commit violent crimes. Cesare Lombroso, the father of criminology, compared women to children, arguing that their "moral sense is deficient" but their "defects are neutralised by piety, maternity, want of passion, by sexual coldness, weakness and undeveloped intelligence."[34]

As hard as it was to imagine women as perpetrators of crimes, it was even harder to imagine them as perpetrators of *sexual* crimes—with the obvious exception of prostitution. Willem Adriaan Bonger, who would go on to become the first professor of sociology and criminology in the Netherlands, wrote in 1916 that "the role of women in sexual life (and thus in the criminal sexual life) is rather passive than active."[35] In the unlikely event that a woman felt a sexual urge, everybody assumed she wouldn't have to rape a man, because no man would say no to sex. "While excesses of passion in man, not directed into proper channels, lead to assaults and sexual perversion," social reformer Frances Alice Kellor explained in 1898, "in woman its existence more frequently culminates in mental degeneracy or physical disease."[36] "Men rape; women rave," sums up Joanna Bourke.[37]

It's easy to sneer at out-of-date gender norms, but as soon as rape comes into play, all these outdated norms still reverberate through our present discourse. The bulk of our "rape knowledge" is based on ideas about masculinity and femininity that most of us would dismiss as plucked out of thin air if we knew what we were referring to. But, being invisible, these ideas take on the mantle of natural laws. As Penny notes, "Stories shape us, even the shit ones. Even the ones that are simplistic and obviate a great deal of real-life experience by design. Stories are how we organize our lives, how we streamline our desires . . . our cravings and identities."[38] It starts with language. Sex is depicted as something that men *give* to women—or take from them. Words like *coitus*, *penetration*, and *fucking* center on the penis and convey what it and its substitutes—dildos or digits—do and feel, as if the orifices penetrated aren't involved in the act at all.

There are, of course, lots of sexual acts that merit closer inspection, but penetration is undoubtedly the biggest linguistic blinker. For this reason, author Bini Adamczak proposes *circlusion* as an antonym to *penetration*: "Both words signify the same physical process but from opposite perspectives. *Penetration* means to insert something or to put something in. *Circlusion* means to surround or to clasp. That's it. But it allocates activity and passivity inversely."[39] Adamczak argues that it should be easy to introduce this neologism, as "circlusion is already part of our everyday experiences. Just think of the net that catches the fish, the mouth that chews the food, the nutcracker that crashes the nut ... Circlusion enables us to express sensations that we've always been experiencing," thereby changing not only language but the concept of sexuality.[40] What would classics like Donald Symons's *The Evolution of Human Sexuality*—which Thornhill and Palmer cite as the inspiration for their *Natural History of Rape*—sound like if a term like *circlusion* had been in general use? "Among all peoples it is primarily men who court, woo, proposition, seduce ... give gifts in exchange for sex and use the service of prostitutes," states Symons. He understands rape as the result of the "male's greater visual arousal, greater autonomous "sex drive,' a lesser ability to abstain from sexual activity, much greater desire for sexual activity *per se*, a greater willingness to engage in impersonal sex, and a less discriminatory criteria of sexual partners."[41] In other words, as the result of a sexual scenario that only knows penetration. No wonder so many laws have held that one needs a penis to be able to commit rape.

His views on rape aside, Symons's sexual worldview is still mainstream. If you feed the words *men*, *women*, and *sex* into any search engine, you'll get aphorisms like this one, attributed to Jay McInerney: "Men talk to women so they can sleep with them and women sleep with men so they can talk to them."[42] And in 2010, the popular British author and broadcaster Stephen Fry hit the headlines when he stated in an interview, "Women don't really like sex ... Sex is the price they are willing to pay for a relationship."[43] The fact that he'd probably never said it in this precise way didn't damp the enthusiasm with which his sentence was debated. "The Science of Women and Sex: Is Stephen Fry Right After All?" The *Independent* asked in the headline of an article that fell back on Darwin to explain why men want sex and women want babies: "As a species, human males fall somewhere between gorillas and chimpanzees in terms of their propensity to promiscuity. We can say this from looking at the relative size of a man's testicles compared to those of the gorilla (slightly promiscuous, small testes) and chimps (highly promiscuous, very large testes)."[44] If that sounds suspiciously like "big nose, big hose," that's because it is just as scientific.

Popular primatology tells us to look at female monkeys to see that our human forebears were already sexually shy and reticent. The catch is that there is no proof for this. Anthropologist Meredith Small lists various classes of primates where the female initiates sex with the male or other females by rubbing her genitals on their face and in various other ways.[45] Female baboons seem to enjoy jumping on and copulating with male after male. And female bonobos are not only sexually active during their whole cycle but are the leaders of the male bonobos—prompting ethnologist Frans B.M. de Waal to speculate that if scientists "had known bonobos first . . . We would at present most likely believe that early hominids lived in female-centred societies, in which sex served important social functions."[46]

As it is, the fact that women are not primarily aroused by chocolate, proposals, and babies is still so surprising that it has to be proved by science again and again and again. Until recently, such data was collected by asking people to fill in questionnaires. Test subjects were shown images or films and checked off the ones that aroused them or rated them on a scale from one to ten. The results were as expected: men reacted mainly to visual stimuli like breasts or genitalia, while women weren't aroused by sexual images at all but by emotional content. The results varied slightly if the surveys were anonymous, but when it comes to sex, there is one thing people seem to do first and foremost: they lie.

Or they lie to themselves. Or they don't notice the signs their bodies send them.

For that reason, psychologist J. Michael Bailey measured the physical reactions of test subjects' genitals to explicit images.[47] The study showed that heterosexual men were most stimulated by looking at images depicting heterosexual intercourse, followed by lesbian sex and in the last place gay male sex—or, for gay men, the other way around. So far, so predictable. The female test group had the same self-assessment—only their bodies told a different story: their circulation and moisture suggested that they reacted the most to any kind of homosexual act, while heterosexual intercourse scored slightly lower—but even copulating bonobos got a reaction. The study presented a couple of problems—it was only constructed along the binaries of men/women and heterosexual/homosexual and located sex solely in the genitals—but it put paid to the myth that, when it comes to sex, men are turned on by visual stimulants and always up for it—and women aren't.[48]

The biggest surprise about these insights is that they are considered groundbreaking and not simple common sense. So yet they have to be proved over and over. Dr. Heather Rupp from the Kinsey Institute and Kim Wallen, professor for psychology and neuroendocrinology at Emory University, measured the amount of time people looked at erotic images without averting their gaze.[49] Even down to a hundredth of a second, they found no differences between male and female test subjects. Whereupon they showed them pictures of sunsets to find out whether they generated more brain activity when looking at sexy pictures than when looking at the scenery. They did. But when Rupp and Wallen evaluated *which* parts of the pictures their subjects had looked at the longest, it got interesting: eye movement tracking disclosed that men spent more time looking at faces; women who were not on hormonal contraception preferred genitals; and women on hormonal contraception looked at the clothes of the people in the pictures and at the background. So much for: Men always look at tits.

The female libido is not an invention of the sexual revolution or the feminist revolution or the sexual feminist revolution. It has been the elephant in the room for centuries. When the Vatican opened the archive of the Apostolic Penitentiary, the highest internal court in the

Catholic Church, to academics in 2011, researchers found thousands of letters written by women in the fifteenth century, demanding sexual satisfaction.[50]

That's why it's so indicative that Laurie Penny told me in 2015:

> When I was writing *Unspeakable Things,* one of my ideas was that I was going to talk about my own sexual experiences and the positive experiences that I had. And in the end I thought: Well, if I put too much of that in, that will be what everyone will focus on. But actually that's the one thing about the book that I regret. In my political writing, I found out, it was easier to talk about being raped, than to talk about all the positive sexual experiences that I have had.[51]

No Means No!

When the women's movement coined the slogan "no means no" in the 1970s, they set it against centuries of arguments that "the female of the species just wants to be overpowered by a real man." It was an ingenious feat: smashing an old narrative with a newer, snappier one. But it only broke with part of the narrative—it didn't question the concept that men are sexually overactive while women's activity is limited to saying no; that male sexuality is monstrous and dangerous versus "good" female sexuality, and so on. I have carried "No means no!" on banners on countless demonstrations, even written it with eyeliner on my belly, though I felt slightly uneasy with it. "Which part of no do you not understand?" was at least funny, and contained a touch of communication. But "no means no" was the equivalent of "Another word and you go straight to bed without dinner." Still, if it would rid the world of rape, it seemed a small price to pay that our rhetoric hardly differed from the rhetoric of those we were fighting.

"No means no" appeared around the same time, and from the same movement, as the book that changed the way we talk about rape more radically than any other work of the twentieth century, the book that is lauded for breaking the "conspiracy of silence,"[52] and making it possible to talk about rape at all: Susan Brownmiller's 1975 bestseller *Against Our Will.* It was one of the first feminist books to be celebrated by the mainstream. *TIME* magazine named Brownmiller one of its "women of the year." She was seen as a trail-blazer, "uncovering the existence of rape as an important element in world history, one which historians have ignored or trivialized."[53] Her book triggered a debate that changed the rape laws in the United States and many other countries.

The immense impact of the book was due to the fact that *Against Our Will* didn't just tell the history of a crime: it provided a political analysis, using rape as a lens to look at society. Brownmiller argues that rape is the cause and origin of patriarchy. Like Krafft-Ebing—and Ellis and Darwin—she harks back to primeval times and the assault of weak women by strong men, though with a very different interpretation:

> In the violent landscape inhabited by primitive woman and man, some woman somewhere had a prescient vision of her right to her own physical integrity, and in my mind's eye I can picture her fighting like hell to preserve it. After a thunderbolt of recognition that this particular incarnation of hairy, two-legged hominid was not the *Homo sapiens* with whom she would like to freely join parts, it might have been she, and not some man, who picked up the first stone and hurled it. How surprised must he have been, and what an unexpected battle must have taken place.[54]

Despite her progressive views on sexual self-determination, Brownmiller's "primitive woman" couldn't win that fight, because she had something that made her inherently vulnerable: her genitals. "Had it not been for this accident in biology, an accommodation requiring the locking together of two separate parts, penis into vagina, there would be neither copulation nor rape as we know it.[55] Brownmiller argued.

Critics pointed out that Brownmiller started her cultural history with a fictional story,[56] her book was widely (and rightly) criticized by black feminists for reproducing racist stereotypes of black rapists. Yet nobody seemed to take umbrage with the biologistic assumption at the core of its argument: "By anatomical fiat—the inescapable construction of their genital organs—the human male was a natural predator and the human female served as his natural prey."[57]

It is important to read these lines in the context of their time. American women could be fired from their jobs for being pregnant until 1978, couldn't get credit with a bank (unless their husband co-signed the card) until 1974, and had only recently been allowed to serve on juries. Little wonder that women felt gaslighted by men. And given that we are all made up of the same genes, the reason for the difference in power—and the resulting opportunity to misuse this power—had to lie elsewhere. What could be more obvious than to look for it in the only parts of the body that were evidently different?

Political theory of the 1970s had two major explanations concerning the development of human behavior: *nature* and *nurture*. Nature being fixed, it was up to society to change nurture. And on close reading, *Against Our Will* refers to rape as being determined both by the shape and function of human genitalia *and* by cultural imprint. Brownmiller describes the original sin, "the first rape," as a key moment for the fleeing woman—as well as for her male pursuer. who "indubitably" starts planning "the second rape."[58]

> Indeed, one of the earliest forms of male bonding must have been the gang rape of one woman by a band of marauding men. This accomplished, rape became not only a male prerogative but man's basic weapon of force against woman, the principal agent of his will and her fear. His forcible entry into her body, despite her physical protestations and struggle, became the vehicle of his victorious conquest over her being, the ultimate test of his superior strength, the triumph of his manhood.[59]

The idea of sexual assault as "the triumph of [the rapist's] manhood" still constitutes an unquestioned part of the rape narrative, together with "man's discovery that his genitalia could serve as a weapon to generate fear."[60] Which is interesting, considering that there are few parts of the human body less suited as a weapon than the penis—but we'll come to that later. Brownmiller reasons: "It seems eminently sensible to hypothesize that man's violent capture and rape of the female led first to the establishment of a rudimentary mate-protectorate and then sometime later to the full-blown male solidification of power, the patriarchy."[61]

As a movement book, the express purpose of *Against Our Will* was to change society. It provided the analysis and leverage to do so: rape could be understood as *the* prerequisite for patriarchy, just as patriarchy was a system to rape women—so changing rape would destabilize patriarchy. The book's most famous sentence argues that rape "is nothing more or less than a conscious process of intimidation by which *all* men keep *all* women in a state of fear."[62] Brownmiller's definition carried such weight because it answered the crucial question of feminism: "How did it all start?"[63] That made rape the origin story not only of patriarchy but of second-wave feminism.

After all, for nineteenth-century feminists, the question of sexual violence had played a marginal role, if any. "It is remarkable, in fact, how little emphasis nineteenth-century feminists placed on rape," note historians Ellen DuBois and Linda Gordon.[64] They accorded the role of "quintessential female terror" instead to prostitution.[65] Anti-vice organizations debated "how to stop male lust and keep women pure."[66]

"Woman's redemption from sex-slavers can only be achieved through man's redemption from sex-obsession," asserted British suffragist Frances Swiney, echoing, not incidentally, the frigid women/fiery men model of human sexuality.[67] These views on what makes us men and women—and by extension human—are so ubiquitous that they transcend the political spectrum, becoming largely invisible in the process.

When second-wave feminists started out, their predecessors had left a whole set of arguments and mindsets ready and waiting for them. The difference was that the fear of and fight against prostitution and venereal disease had been superseded by the fear of and fight against rape. To say that second-wave feminism in America centered around anti-rape activism wouldn't do justice to this incredibly important social movement. But in the United States, the question of rape played a similar role as did the fight for legal abortion in Europe: it provided a unifying experience and became the reference point for everything that was wrong with gender relations. In the words of author and New York Radical Women founding member Robin Morgan, "It is the ultimate metaphor for domination, violence, subjugation, and possession."[68]

Before cecond-wave feminism there had been a fixed set of perceptions about rape. Some will be familiar by now: rape is sex, and women say no when they mean yes. Victims are beautiful young women whose attractiveness arouses men so much that they can't help themselves—or loose women who provoke men willfully and get their just deserts. Either way, the victim is at least partly responsible for getting herself raped, because she asked for it by wearing a miniskirt. Deep down, women want to be taken against their will—especially women who invite a man home on a first date. No woman can be entered against her will if she puts up a real fight (but, paradoxically, no woman can really defend herself against a male attacker, so it is better not to try at all and thus avoid getting hurt). Real rape is incredibly rare, while false accusations of rape are epidemic because the complainants are hysterical, want to get back at a man who rejected them, or want to account for an illegitimate pregnancy. Rapists are foreigners, outsiders, psychopaths, and/or sex fiends. Rape occurs outside, not in the home; victim and perpetrator are unknown to each other. Perpetrators are the stranger behind the bush. And so on.

When the anti-rape movement arrived on the scene, they offered a "new rape story"[69] by taking all these convictions and revealing them across the board as *rape myths* whose existence was proof of the fact that we lived in a *rape culture*. Each revision became, simply and brilliantly, the opposite of the old script. Sociologist Ken Plummer, whose work highlights the role of the stories we tell ourselves and others, describes this as a rhetorical move that

> takes all the elements of the old narrative and in one sweep undoes them. It provides in effect the tightest, most minimal account of the old narrative structure, and by placing them in a frame of "myths"

> immediately discredits then. Indeed, by simply inverting each myth the key elements of the new story are provided ... [This] is a classical rhetorical ploy: to see that every position is constructed out of a sense of opposition. Stories are not formulated in isolation but through antagonism. "Myth debunking" makes this very explicit.[70]

In the case of rape, that meant that where before only beautiful young women could be raped, all women were now perceived as potential victims; rape was a *common* crime that happened *frequently*, while false rape accusations were incredibly *rare*, etc.

This is not to suggest that the old discourse was right after all, but that the old discourse determined the new one—albeit as a negative foil. For instance, victims of rape were still understood to be exclusively female and perpetrators exclusively male, because of woman's vulnerability and man's wish to dominate her.

The myth debunking centered around two assumptions: "No means yes!" became "No means no!" And Brownmiller redefined rape as a crime of *violence* as opposed to a crime of passion—*real* sex was based on consent and was free from force, so rape couldn't be sex at all. Brownmiller did this to rebut all attempts to blame the victim. If rape was violence and not sex, the victim's looks, dress, and behavior became irrelevant. In other words, if it wasn't about sex, it didn't matter how sexy she was.[71] This was particularly pertinent to court cases, and eventually changed procedure in the United States and Europe. Victims are no longer supposed to be interrogated about their previous sex life—as was routine up until at least the 1980s, since a woman who had had sex voluntarily (or, worse, enjoyed it) didn't fit the image of the "real"—meaning virginal—rape victim. After all, if she'd agreed to sex with one man, what would stop her from agreeing to sex with another?

Still, the definition that rape was violence and not sex never went unchallenged. The feminist lawyer and law professor Catharine MacKinnon, who mostly agreed with Brownmiller, posed the famous question: "If it's violence, not sex, why didn't he just hit her?"[72]

When philosopher Michel Foucault was asked about the problem of rape at a roundtable in 1977, his assessment sounded like a belated answer to MacKinnon's question. "There is no difference, in principle, between sticking one's fist into someone's face or one's penis into their sex," he determined. "Sexuality can in no circumstances be the object of punishment. And when one punishes rape one should be punishing physical violence and nothing but that."[73] He went further to suggest that it would be problematic even to distinguish between rape and any other kind of violence,

> because what we're saying amounts to this: Sexuality as such, in the body, has a preponderant place, the sexual organ isn't like a hand, hair or nose. It therefore has to be protected, surrounded, invested in any case with legislation that isn't that pertaining to the rest of the body.[74]

Surprisingly, there were no cheers, even though Foucault's statement that rape was "nothing more than an act of aggression"[75] was—not intentionally, but in effect—a paraphrase of Brownmiller's famous dictum. On the contrary, Foucault, who was at the height of his fame and could have said nearly anything, was accused—by the women on the roundtable, and subsequently by numerous feminist academics—of relativizing rape.[76] This was because Foucault and Brownmiller had talked about entirely different aspects of the complex tangle that is rape. While he—from the point of view of the (presumed male) perpetrator—tried to minimize the power of the discourse about sexuality as an instrument of social and political control, she—and with her the second wave of feminism—wanted to exculpate (presumed female) victims from any guilt for the crime against them.

Moreover, the aim of Brownmiller's redefinition was to make it easier for women to talk about having been raped without being sexualized in the process. That didn't mean, though, that the damage done by sexual violence decreased in any way. Where *the rapist's motivation* was violence and nothing but violence, *the impact on the victim* was radically different from any other form of violence, because the target wasn't her body but her right of self-determination regarding that body—which doesn't sound like much of a difference until one considers that physical, emotional, and legal self-determination is the definition of the emancipation of women. That makes rape, as author Susan Griffin expounds, "an act of aggression in which the victim is denied her self-determination. It is an act of violence which, if not followed by beatings or murder, nevertheless always carries with it the threat of death."[77]

In the wake of *Against Our Will* followed a deluge of books about rape, most notably Marilyn French's novel *The Women's Room*. French adapts Virginia Woolf's famous parable of Shakespeare's sister. But whereas, in Woolf's imagination, the playwright's sister "called Judith, let us say" is doomed because she cannot get an education, nor work, nor the opportunity to look for inspiration outside the home, in French's scenario Judith Shakespeare is raped, becomes pregnant, and marries a man she doesn't love in order to feed her child. French concludes, "Shakespeare's Sister had learned the lesson all women learn: men are the ultimate enemy."[78] Few feminists agreed with this deduction—and even fewer with the sentence that went on to become synonymous with French and her novel: "All men are rapists, and that's all they are."[79]

Nevertheless, the theory of rape as the mainstay of patriarchy was generally accepted, and rape played an essential role in countless feminist novels of the 1970s and 1980s. Literature professor Maria Lauret calls these texts "feminists' fictions of subjectivity," or more explicitly, stories about "how I became a feminist."[80]

Given all this, it's no coincidence that the first criminal trial ever to be broadcast live on American TV—daily and for months on end—was a rape case, the most famous trial of the 1980s: the Big Dan's rape case. Big Dan's wasn't an ill-chosen euphemism for the perpetrator but a pub in New Bedford, Massachusetts, where, on March 6, 1983, a woman was gang-raped on the pool table while the rest of the customers watched and cheered.[81] This remarkable lack of compassion shocked America and public feeling was strongly on the side of the victim. It was the first rape case that explicitly drew upon the arguments of the women's movement. The jury was disgusted by the defense's attempts to discredit the victim by using her sexual past against her.[82] And when the culprits received the maximum penalty, the press exulted: at last, even judges seemed to understand that it wasn't only virgins who had a right not to be raped.[87] The verdict was seen as a triumph of feminism.

Reality told a different story, though, one that was far less heroic and a lot messier. Publicist Helen Benedict criticized the one-sided assessment of the case and argued that the victim "should go down in history as one of the worst-treated rape victims of the decade."[84] She pointed out that even though four of the six rapists were being sent to jail, the law had no power to convict the cheering spectators, who seemed—to the people watching the case unfold on television—even more culpable than the culprits. This led to an increase in racist reporting. While in the early news coverage, victim, perpetrators, and spectators had been identified by name, soon the men turned into "working-class immigrants from Portugal" while the woman was described as "a mother of two," though she had the same so-called roots.[85]

The message was clear: the *others* had perpetrated the crime and—even worse—authorized it by the act of watching. "Putting deep racial-sexual anxieties into the mouth of the criminal or the discredited serves white America well, for it allows it simultaneously to speak them and disavow them," media scholar John Fiske commented.[86] Buzzwords like "clash of cultures" made the rounds—as if only people from Portugal would rape—and it wasn't long until the telephone lines started ringing in local radio stations, with outraged callers demanding that "all Portuguese be sent back to Europe." The Portuguese community of New Bedford began to feel as if *it* and not the woman had been raped.[87] The erstwhile whaling metropolis was a town in decline, and the rape became a metaphor for its economic and social demise.[88] Headlines like "A City and its Agony" and "The Crime That Tarnished a Town" transformed the body of the raped woman into the body of the town. John Bullard, who would become New Bedford's mayor, recounted: "It hurts us more than it would a lot of other cities. It's one more nail. It's, 'Oh, my God, we really are a terrible place.' Then we just have to try that much harder to get back up to zero."[89] With every new article the mood shifted more and more against the rape victim, along the lines of: if she was capable of wreaking such havoc by reporting the rape, she must, in some way, have been the aggressor during the act as well.

Such reactions are so common that there are psychological terms for them: *just world hypothesis* and *defensive attribution hypothesis*. Law professor Ulrike Lembke explains, "The motivation behind these victim-blaming behaviours are that no unfathomable evil may happen in the world—thus the victim simply must have done something wrong. This is a self-shield mechanism to ensure that no danger will befall oneself. As a result the victim is depreciated and rejected."[90]

But the denigration of the twenty-two-year-old New Bedford victim went a lot further than that. Eyewitnesses remembered, "People would go to her house . . . They would throw things at the house and damage it . . . There was real bloodletting in this community. It was the closest I've come to seeing mob hysteria."[91] After the trial, she fled town, but she never escaped the fear that her ex-neighbors would track her down. A friend reported: "She was so scared they would come and kill her, she thought they were following her. When she drove she didn't just look at the rear-view mirror, she stared at it."[92] Less than three years later, she died in a car crash.

That the case and its tragic conclusion are widely misremembered is because they were restaged—with a very different ending—in the 1988 blockbuster *The Accused*, starring Jodie Foster as the victim and Kelly McGillis as her attorney. The infamous rape scene—which takes place on a pinball machine instead of a pool table—caused controversy even before the film was released, and viewers flocked in droves to the cinemas to form their own opinion. Within twenty-four hours it earned $18 million. Jodie Foster won an Oscar and a Golden Globe. *The Accused* is often called the first feature-length film about rape, which is only partly correct. Media historian Tanya Horek points out that "rape is arguably bound up with the very origins of cinema and plays a prominent role in founding films such as D. W. Griffith's *Birth of a Nation* (1915). But *The Accused* remains unique as the culminating product of over two decades of feminist consciousness-raising on rape."[93]

Ergo the story told in *The Accused*, then, is not the story of the Big Dan's case but a kind of feminist best-case scenario of how to negotiate a rape case in a court of law—and, by extension, the court of public opinion. Its central conflict is how the victim can speak her truth and by doing so inscribe it into the law. To heighten the drama, her attorney, Kathryn, first accepts the defense's plea bargain to downgrade the charge of rape to reckless endangerment (which was the film's original title). Foster's character (renamed Sarah Tobias, which the screenwriters deemed to be more neutral than a Portuguese name) accuses Kathryn of depriving her of her chance to make her story heard. Kathryn explains that, as a single mother with a prior conviction for drug possession, Sarah doesn't fit the stereotype of a "good victim" and would not receive a fair trial. By shifting the focus from racism to questions of class, the filmmakers wanted to speak for *all rape victims*. (They must have concluded that a nonwhite rape victim wouldn't have been universal enough or victim enough—another problem to which we will return). The project "to provide popular culture with an authoritative depiction of the 'reality' of rape"[94] (as if just one story existed about rape that would now be told) gained an air of incontrovertibility by using quasi-documentary elements, like including statistics about rape in the credits. "This asserts the historical truth of the story that has just been depicted but more than that, it presents the film as a kind of memorial to all rape victims," Horek observes.[95]

The filmmakers' ambition was for *The Accused* to function as a kind of public therapy, giving female viewers the opportunity to mourn their collective trauma and to vanquish—together with Sarah—the obstacles to their vindication. These are—as Sarah shouts at Kathryn: The perpetrators hadn't been convicted of their real crime; therefore, in the eyes of the law, she hadn't been raped. Only convicting the rapists of rape would pronounce *her* innocent, because—as a rape victim—she was as much on trial as the rapists, if not more so. And finally: A woman who is not acknowledged immediately as a victim becomes fair game for predatory men.

Sarah Tobias is the woman in the street who speaks the truth—and the truth sounds as if it comes straight from the pages of *Against Our Will*. The situation can only be solved through a symbolic act in court. Kathryn decides to sue the spectators for incitement to commit a crime, to give Sarah a second chance to make her voice heard.

Susan Brownmiller proclaimed that she became a feminist when she "learned that, in ways I preferred to deny, the threat of rape had profoundly affected my life."[96] Accordingly, Sarah's testimony in court is to be read as her awakening as a feminist: "I said no. Is no not enough?"[97]

Still, the film's cathartic climax is not Sarah's account of her own story but that of a male witness who finally comes forward to testify against his fellow males. This is all the more surprising since the "real" case didn't require male authority before the victim was believed. But the desire to be unambiguous was so immense in *The Accused* that the makers failed to see the paternalism of the courtroom scene. "Seldom has a set of male eyes been more privileged; without their witness, there would be no case—there would in fact, as the defense attorney notes, be no rape," writes film studies professor Carol Clover.[98] Only when the male witness describes it, is the rape scene, that has up until now been omitted, shown. In the logic of cinema, he speaks it into existence. The truth is seen and therefore believed.

The Accused marked the high point of a debate that changed the representation of rape in mainstream media. Scenes in which a woman relishes being raped became increasingly unacceptable after the 1980s, and the focus of empathy shifted in favor of the victim, whose disgust and repulsion are now mostly at the heart of the portrayal. Yet the famous scene on the pinball machine was neither described in Sarah's words nor shown from her point of view. By contrast, in Shekhar Kapur's 1994 film *Bandit Queen*, about the Indian bandit Phoolan Devi, the camera literally takes up Devi's position and shows the rapists' naked legs entering her intimate space, one after another. In *The Accused*, the feeling of being so close to Sarah Tobias as to be practically inside her psyche is achieved exclusively by the use of flashbacks. Film historian Janet Walker calls this technique "trauma cinema,": the retelling of past experiences by equating filmic flashbacks to the flashbacks we associate with trauma.[99]

It was a popular belief in the 1980s that traumatic experiences were effectively recorded by the subconscious as if by a film camera and would later be "released" in flashbacks *exactly as they had happened*—a perfect memory time capsule, so to speak—not as they would have been perceived at the time. The "objective" flashback in *The Accused* is informed by this belief. When it is finally shown, Sarah relives her trauma—only this time she is not alone but supported by the assembled court, which exonerates her from the stigma of being a lewd woman roaming the pubs on her own at night and now identifies her correctly as a victim. Having thus successfully externalized her torment, the therapy is completed and the accused—representing the majority of the male population—are pronounced guilty.

Reactions to the Big Dan's case were characteristic of the tense relationship between the sexes at the time. In *Ms* magazine, Mary Kay Blakely wrestled with the prospect that her own sons might one day cheer a rape and addressed her essay to one of the "34 percent of men who are repulsed by the sexual violence of men against women."[100] The question of where Blakely got her statistics from aside, the article is remarkable for its pervasive sense of menace—"I want you to feel fear . . . I want you to imagine that you have only 20 seconds to react"—which in hindsight sounds like a scenario from a totalitarian regime where parents can't even trust their own children—if these children are male. *The Accused* was the cinematic manifesto of this stance. Critic Penny Ashbrook praised the film, because it came "remarkably close to a conceptualisation of Susan Brownmiller's famous assertion that 'rape is a conscious process of intimidation by which *all men* keep *all women* in a state of fear.' "[101]

"Female fear"[102] effectively became a synonym for rape. As Griffin wrote, "I have never been free of the fear of rape. From a very early age I, like most women, have thought of rape as part of my natural environment—something to be feared and prayed against like fire and lightning."[103] Rape was understood as a "condition of women's existence which is all-pervasive and continuous."[104] Anti-rape activists thus paradoxically achieved exactly what Brownmiller had assumed "all men" wanted to achieve: for a significant part of the female population to live in constant fear. This fear had obviously existed before anti-rape activism as well, but it became ubiquitous afterwards. For fear functions as a social virus: it isn't created by media coverage, but is multiplied and heightened by it. "Once we make it through the workshops and pamphlets on date rape, safe sex, and sexual harassment, no matter how bold and adolescent, how rebellious and reckless, we are left with an impression of imminent danger," comments Katie Roiphe.[105]

2

A Fate Worse Than Death: Honor and Honesty

The idea that rape was a special crime because it targeted the soul or essence of a woman—evident in talk of victims being defiled, ruined, or marked—didn't arise in the 1970s though, it goes back as far as the opposing conviction (that women yearned to be ravished). But how did the axiom that a woman's essence is her sexuality emerge in the first place? After all, the right to sexual self-determination is important for all human beings—indeed, so important that it is considered a Sexual Human Right.[1] Moreover, self-determination doesn't stop at the bedroom door but extends to all aspects of life. Why, therefore, was a woman's sexuality isolated from the rest of her personality and not only put on a pedestal but put in place of everything that made her herself? To understand this, one has to understand the concept of honor.

Honor

The Western concept of honor has been shaped to a great extent by classical antiquity, mainly by Aristotle's *Nicomachean Ethics* (though nowadays hardly anybody has read this ten-book tome). Better known—though not necessarily under this name—are two stories that epitomize these ideas: the Battle of Thermopylae, dealing with men's honor, and the rape of Lucretia with women's.

In the Battle of Thermopylae, in 480 BCE, the Spartans were so immensely ashamed of having avoided the battle of Marathon ten years earlier that they sacrificed their lives. They knew they wouldn't change the outcome—the battle was already lost and the legendary "three hundred" could only provide cover for the retreat of the Greek army. This was not about winning a war but about winning back their honor. What seems strange to us now was understood then: Consequently, they were honored after their death with a monument bearing the famous couplet by Simonides of Ceos: "Stranger! To Sparta say, her faithful band / Here lie in death, remembering her command."[2] This inspired Friedrich Schiller's beloved poem "The Walk" and Heinrich Böll's most famous short story, "Stranger, Bear Word to the Spartans We . . ."

For a man's honor was negotiated in the public sphere: on the battlefield or on the job. Accordingly, in the Middle Ages there were "honorable" and "dishonorable" professions, which had nothing to do with ethical considerations but with the three estates—peers, commoners, and clerics—and who belonged and who didn't. Being a blacksmith was an honorable job; being a tinker wasn't. Titles like *The Honourable* or *The Right Honourable* are remnants of this.

A woman's honor, on the other hand, was located in her body: in her virginity or in her state as an honorable wife or widow. Thus a woman—and only a woman—possessed something that could be stolen or destroyed by rape. This was all the more precarious as her place in society was determined by her honor: if she lost the one she lost the other, which often meant her livelihood as well. Women's bodies didn't belong to them but were public property. But men's bodies weren't private property either; they were no less exploited—for example, in war. The difference was that *their* honor was only in danger if they refuted the system, say by deserting, which led to them losing their place in society as well (mostly by execution).

Consequently the tale that epitomizes female honor takes place not on the battlefield but in the bedchamber. Roman historian Livy introduced the chaste Lucretia in his *Ab Urbe Condita*. Her story is set in the sixth century BCE, when despotic King Lucius Tarquinius Superbus ruled over Rome. Lucretia's husband, Lucius Tarquinius Collatinus—there didn't seem to have been enough names to go around in ancient Rome—agreed to a bet with a group of patricians, among them Sextus Tarquinius, nephew of the hated king. The object of the bet was to establish whose wife was the most virtuous. When they arrived at their various homes, they found all their wives making merry with their friends; Lucretia alone was sitting at her spinning wheel, spinning. The following night, angry to have lost his bet, Sextus Tarquinius crept into Lucretia's bedchamber and, pressing his dagger to her heart, demanded sex. She denied him, famously vowing she would rather die than be unfaithful (that is, dishonorable). So he threatened to kill her and also a male slave and drape the slave's naked body next to hers, upon which Sextus would go to her husband and tell him he had caught them *in flagrante delicto*. So she would lose her honor anyway. Seeing no way out, Lucretia gave up, and Sextus raped her. Of course, neither the term *rape* nor the related concepts existed in this time. Instead, there was a whole cluster of words to describe sexual violence—*stuprum*, *raptus*,[3] *violentia*, *sontaminatio*—that covered a whole spectrum of meanings: "dishonor, defilement, derision ... violation, ruin, fornication, compulsion, robbery," even simply "sexual intercourse."[4] For example, *stuprum* means disgrace, dishonor, unchastity, *and* adultery.

After the rape, Lucretia called for her husband and father. She told them what Sextus had done and said that she had made up her mind to take her own life. The men implored her to stop, but she declared she wanted to make sure that "no unfaithful wives would invoke her to escape punishment." Then she thrust a dagger through her heart. The lines attributed to Lucretia make it clear that this is less documented history than didactic story. The point was to show that Lucretia had lost her honor by being raped and could only get it back by getting rid of her defiled body. Lucretia's suicide was seen as a heroic deed, on the same scale as the Spartans' heroic deaths.

The famous paintings by Botticelli, Cranach, Dürer, and Rembrandt show the rapist with his dagger or sword at Lucretia's breast, or Lucretia holding a dagger to her own breast. George Frideric Handel wrote a cantata in six movements for her. Shakespeare's epic poem "The Rape of Lucrece" made him famous. The Wikipedia entry for *rape*—just as the German Wikipedia entry for *Vergewaltigung*—illustrates its subject with Titian's painting *Tarquin and Lucretia*, with Tarquin in red trousers threatening a naked Lucretia separated from him by a thin white veil in front of her pudendum. The virtuous Roman is so omnipresent in art and literature that she has become a point of reference for rape.[5] As a matter of course, she has found numerous successors in novels and films, most infamously in the Nazi propaganda film *Jud Süß* (1940), in which the innocent German Dorothea is raped by Jewish Joseph Süß Oppenheimer and then drowns herself. Tanya Horek sums up this merciless narrative logic: "Rape, if it does not result in biological death, is nonetheless coded as a form of symbolic death."[6]

This isn't an inevitable lesson from history though, but a very selective lesson, because classical antiquity offers enough counterfigures to chaste Lucretia. In *Ab Urbe Condita,* Livy also recounts the story of the Celtic queen Chiomara, who in 189 BCE was abducted during a raid led by the Roman consul Gnaeus Manlius Vulso and raped by one of his centurions.[7] When he realized that he had captured a queen, he demanded she get her husband Ortiagon, chieftain of the Tolistobogii tribe, to pay a ransom. Chiomara agreed. A slave was sent to the Tolistobogii and a secret meeting place appointed—and while the centurion sat counting the gold, Chiomara gave her people the order to cut his throat.[8] It is hardly surprising that Chiomara wasn't seen fit to act as a role model, though she did have the advantage of being a real person who had actually lived.

Another Celtic queen fared slightly better: Boudicca, for whom the crime—done in this case not to her but to her daughters—didn't mean the loss of honor but *dial*, the Welsh word for vengeance. Boudicca was lucky because her name was more or less identical with Queen Victoria's—both mean "the victorious"—and Victoria urgently needed to put herself into a tradition of female rulers, just as Elisabeth I had.[9] So she made Boudicca the role model and symbolic justification for her reign. After Victoria ascended to the throne, Henry Courtney Selous painted Boudicca bare-breasted, leading her people exactly as Delacroix had painted Liberty (Marianne) leading the French people. Alfred Lord Tennyson immortalized her in a poem; and in 1905 a statue of Boudicca and her daughters riding a chariot was erected opposite Big Ben. But for all her chariot-riding and sword-wielding, when she opened her mouth, Boudicca sounded like a British version of Lucretia—not surprising, since all we know about her comes from Roman sources, mainly Tacitus and Cassius

Dio. Before the final battle, Tacitus gives Boudicca her famous speech: "I am avenging lost freedom, my scourged body, the outraged chastity of my daughters. Roman lust has gone so far that not our very persons, nor even age or virginity, are left unpolluted."[10]

From Lucretia it was only a short step to the statement that "rape is a fate worse than death." A phrase that incidentally also goes back to Roman antiquity, though not to any real Roman source but to *The History of the Decline and Fall of the Roman Empire* (1788), Edward Gibbon's six-book history of the trajectory of Western civilization. Gibbon depicts the rape of Roman wives and virgins by the Goths as "injuries more dreadful, in the apprehension of chastity, than death itself."[11] Victorians took the idiom up so enthusiastically that it became a synonym for rape. But the credit for transporting it into the twentieth century belongs to Edgar Rice Burroughs and his megabestseller *Tarzan of the Apes,* in which Jane Porter is snatched by an ape and carried away to a "fate a thousand times worse than death."[12] Just like the virgins in the hands of the looting Goths, the white body of Jane over the ape's dark shoulders was the perfect illustration of the barbarian black rapist violating white innocence. Tarzan, though raised in the jungle, was white enough, being a British lord's son, to save Jane and Jane's honor and finally make her his wife and the mother of his son.

The idea that rape is the theft of a woman's honor is not a tendentious interpretation cherry picking stories from history and mythology, it *is* literally the meaning of the English word *rape*, which comes from the Middle English *rapen*, *rappen*—"to abduct, ravish, snatch, carry off"—which in turn comes from the Latin root *rapere*—"robbing." Even the oldest law known to us, the Code of Hammurabi, treated rape as the theft of virginity.[13] *Rape* was originally used for any kind of elevated theft, like its German derivative *Raub*. But its meaning was narrowed down more and more, until in the fifteenth century it denoted "the abduction of a woman, for sexual purposes or to marry her against her will" (as in Shakespeare's *Titus Andronicus*) and "carnal knowledge of a woman forcibly and against her will" (as in Milton's *Paradise Lost*). In Britain rape carried the death penalty until 1841, and in the US until the 1970s.

But this happened only if the woman had "owned" an honor that could have been stolen from her, as opposed to a "slut" who had lost it on her own accord or any of the various classes of women—black, colonized, prostitutes, the poor—who were not considered to have any honor in the first place. The reputations of married women and widows were examined, as were the bodies of unmarried women. In the eighteenth and nineteenth centuries, in most European countries, an unmarried woman who reported a rape was subjected to a "two-finger test" to find out, based on the elasticity of her vagina, whether she could "endure" sexual intercourse.[14] Virginity dominated the discourse about honor to such an extent that any postmortem examination of a female corpse started with the hymen, to make sure the dead woman hadn't taken her own life out of shame because she had lost her honor.[15] The terms *virginity* and *honor* became nearly interchangeable—which is why, even though we don't talk about honor anymore when we talk about rape, virginity still plays a massive role.

In 1977 Filmmaker Roman Polanski had fled the United States, wanted for the rape of thirteen-year-old Samantha Gailey. So when Polanski was nominated for seven Academy Awards in 2003, Larry King, host of CNN's most prominent talk show, invited Samantha (now Geimer) to the show instead and asked her as par for the course, "You were a virgin?"[16]

She answered kindly, "I just figured I wasn't—no, I wasn't."

King was baffled: "You were not a virgin?"

"No, I had a boyfriend for quite some months before."

But still King insisted: "So you had sex before?"

The question seemed to have preyed on his mind so much that he repeated it nearly verbatim when she came back on the show in 2010: "You'd had sex before that?"

Again Geimer answered, "I had a boyfriend for a long time. And we had become sexually active, yes."

"Before age thirteen?"

"Very—well, I was almost fourteen. But within weeks, but, yes."

This just didn't fit into King's worldview. He tried a compromise: "Was there a lot of pain involved or no?"

But Geimer sank that boat before it had even sailed: "No, no. It was nothing like that."

The surprisingly voyeuristic idea that what makes a rape "really" unbearable is the forcible rupturing of the hymen is a modernized version of the belief that the truly detrimental aspect of rape is the loss of honor (virginity).

This is all the more fascinating as to this day, nobody has actually *seen* the famed hymen. Nevertheless, everybody believes in the existence of a thin membrane stretched tightly across the vaginal opening, like the cling-film that seals fresh meat in the supermarket to show it is still pristine. *Hymen* is Greek for "membrane." In fact, there is no tight membrane at all but a ring-shaped row of folds of mucous tissue, a *corona*—Greek again, for "garland" or "crown." In 2009, the Swedish Language Council, on the advice of the Swedish Association for Sexual Education, decided to replace the ideologically charged term *mödomshinna* (Swedish for *hymen*, literally "virgin's membrane") with *vaginal corona*.

The corona is situated one to two centimeters inside the vagina and in no way forms a hermetic seal; indeed, in the exceptional case that it does, this is a medical problem that must be treated by a gynecologist so as not to block the flow of menstrual blood and other vaginal fluids. It is not ruptured by an intruding penis or finger, nor torn during sports or other physical activities. On the contrary, the intimate mucous tissue is remarkably elastic and doesn't disappear miraculously after "the first time" either (whatever that means). After all, most of us are our own first sexual partners. Ultrasounds have shown that embryos masturbate in the womb. Pleasuring ourselves comes as naturally to us as breathing—well, technically, *before* breathing—and there are more ways to have sex than heterosexual penetration. But penetration is all we think of when we speak about "losing one's virginity." Even if a person has had heterosexual genital intercourse, this can't be ascertained by looking at their vaginal corona, which is why "virginity tests" are usually just glorified versions of the "finger test." The same goes for blood on the sheets, which isn't proof of a woman's virginity but means what blood—except for menstrual blood—usually means: that there has been an injury.

The hymen is the "here be dragons" of anatomy, the only difference being that dragons on maps are a quaint anachronism, while the mythological hymen is still very much present in anatomy books. At the same time, something as real and important as the erectile tissue of the clitoris is overlooked more often than not.

Since bodies couldn't determine a woman's honor conclusively, it had to be done another way. Again, Lucretia was the role model. Her suicide—the ultimate proof of her innocence—restored her honor in death. Her father and husband paraded her body through the streets. And the Romans, who had founded their city on the abduction and mass -rape of the Sabine women, were now so appalled by the same deed that they killed Sextus Tarquinius and chased his uncle, the bad king Tarquinius Superbus, out of town. This was how Rome became a republic.[17] Making The Rape of the Sabine Women *and the ostracism of* the Rape of Lucretia icons of Roman ideals.[18]

However, all this became a big problem with the advancement of Christianity. The concept of female honor wasn't questioned, but suicide was now considered a sin. In the fifth century CE, Augustine of Hippo determined—with far-reaching consequences—that either Lucretia had killed an innocent woman after the rape—and thus couldn't be revered as virtuous,

> Or perhaps . . . she slew herself conscious of guilt, not of innocence? She herself alone knows her reason; but what if she was betrayed by the pleasure of the act, and gave some consent to Sextus, though so violently abusing her, and then was so affected with remorse, that she thought death alone could expiate her sin? . . . Then she did not kill an innocent woman; . . . this case of Lucretia is in such a dilemma, that if you extenuate the homicide, you confirm the adultery: if you acquit her of adultery, you make the charge of homicide heavier; and there is no way out of the dilemma, when one asks, If she was adulterous, why praise her? If chaste, why slay her?[19]

Why indeed? Well, she was a woman who had had sex with a man other than her husband, and extramarital carnal knowledge was considered a sin. Though there were certain exceptions for rape victims, Augustine agreed that "when a woman is violated while her soul admits no consent to the iniquity, but remains inviolably chaste, the sin is not hers, but his who violates her."[20] Which sounds reasonable, until we remember that in this worldview, all women secretly wanted to be ravished. How then could a woman prove that she had remained chaste? After all, it wasn't the woman's deeds that were on trial but her sentiments, which were measured by her sensuality. Even a woman who had fought back with all her strength could have been "betrayed by the pleasure of the act" later (albeit a lot later).[21] And even if she *had* remained chaste, the rape could still indicate a flaw in her moral character.[22] Augustine "reckoned that the rape could have been a way to humble her, conceivably as a result of her vain conceitedness," writes Gesa Dane.

> Even if women hadn't been guilty of having been "unduly puffed up," they could still have been raped for a reason that was rooted in their own character: in a "lurking infirmity which might have betrayed them into a proud and contemptuous bearing, had they not been subjected to the humiliation."[23]

Still, Christianity has its rape martyrs, like Saint Agnes of Rome (291–304 CE), who avoided being raped with the help of miracles—the most famous of which was when hair grew over her whole body so she couldn't be touched—so she had the consolation of being beheaded as a *virgo intacta*. Likewise, Saint Maria Goretti (born 1890 in Corinaldo, Italy, and murdered in 1902 in Nettuno) was canonized because she died rather than lose her virginity. The perpetrator, Alessandro Serenelli, later stated in court (and in front of a Vatican commission) that he had given twelve-year-old Maria every opportunity to yield to his will and he would not have killed her. But she had only said: "It is sin, Alessandro."

Of course, Augustine considered it appropriate that a woman would long to die after a rape—in fact, the quality of her stolen honor was measured by the vehemence of her death wish: the bigger her desperation, the bigger her erstwhile honor. She just was no longer allowed to put that wish into practice. At best, she would waste away and die through no fault of her own. If not, she would have to prove *for the rest of her life* that she hadn't subsequently lost her chastity, preferably by becoming a nun. To stop mourning would be to admit that her honor hadn't been so great after all. There was no going back to the status quo; if a woman was raped, her life was irretrievably interrupted.[24]

Honesty

Against Our Will hasn't had a new English edition since 1993. At the forty-year anniversary of its publication, feminists like Jessica Valenti and Kate Harding speculated whether it was "Time to let go of a Hero,"[25] the hero being Susan Brownmiller.[26]

This disenchantment is due in equal parts to the book's strengths and weaknesses. On the one hand it changed the perception and handling of rape so radically that the worldview of the 1970s is so alien to us now as to be nearly incomprehensible; on the other the strong gender antagonism at its core—*all* men against *all* women—is as useful for current analysis as watching *The Kardashians* to find out about home life in America. The concept of what gender is and can be has expanded massively. Gender identities such as transgender, nonbinary, agender, genderfluid, hijra, two-spirit, and many more destabilize what it means to be "typically male" and "typically female."

Strangely, this doesn't seem to be the case when it comes to rape. With uncanny regularity, TV reports and articles about rape cases sound like quotes from *Against Our Will*. In 2011 Patricia Riekel, then editor-in-chief of Germany's *Bunte* magazine, wrote that "in the prehistoric part of the brain there still lurks the expectation that man has a right to woman."[27] She was reacting to Germany's most prolific rape case of the last decade: the trial of weatherman Jörg Kachelmann for the rape of his ex-girlfriend Claudia D.

The facts were as follows: on February 9, 2010, Kachelmann and his then-girlfriend Claudia D. had sex; on the nineteenth she went to the police and reported that he had raped her at knifepoint. The following day, Kachelmann was arrested at the Frankfurt airport. But that was all anybody could agree on.

Word stood against word and journalist argued against journalist. But as much as they differed as to whether it had been rape, the gender images in the German media resembled each other spookily: Kachelmann mutated into a Neanderthal dragging a primeval woman by the hair to his lair, while Claudia D. became more and more passive with each article until all she did was sit at home and wait for him "on standby for eleven years, clinging to promises, hoping for better times."[28] He, on the other hand, "raced through the republic like a storm," sowing his wild oats into other women.[29]

US lawyer Susan Estrich makes it clear that rape is only coded as such when it corresponds to our preconceived ideas of what constitutes a "real rape"; thus the law can only be as effective as the cultural narrative upon which it is built.[30] So it is up to us to change the narrative as well as the law. The problem is that there is not one single narrative but many conflicting narratives that stretch across a vast expanse of expectations, with the knife-wielding stranger behind the bush at one end of the spectrum and on the opposite end Joanna Bourke's conviction that "sexual abuse is any act called such by a participant or third party."[31]

Of course we have to differentiate between interpersonal interpretations (such as legal definitions) and personal ones ("To *me* it was rape"), and between different communicative settings, as well: if a friend tells me they have been raped, I wouldn't dream of asking for proof. But even "objective" legal definitions are controversial. According to the German law applied in Kachelmann's trial, for the act to constitute rape the perpetrator had to use "force" or the "threat of imminent force for life or limb."[32] This was widely criticized as disregarding the majority of rapes and finally changed in 2016 (more about that later). Catharine MacKinnon, on the other hand, argues that "whenever a woman has sex and feels violated" it is rape, and that she would love to see this enshrined in law.[33] Her definition was criticized just as widely for being dangerous and one-sided.

Everybody is against rape, but hardly anybody is against the same thing when they are against rape. Rape is an "essentially contested concept."[34]

Luckily the rape that Jörg Kachelmann was accused of didn't fall into any of the grey areas, or so it seemed at first. When Claudia D. went to the police, she had skin scraped off her throat by a knife and a hematoma on her thigh. The only ambiguity was whether Kachelmann had caused her injuries. While the experts that were consulted on the case pointed out: "It's impossible to determine with certainty, whether the witness or the accused are telling the truth. We aren't lie detectors"[35]—defense lawyer (though not Jörg Kachelmann's defense lawyer) Steffen Ufer was convinced that Claudia D. had inflicted the injuries on herself. He told *Focus* magazine, "It wouldn't be the first time. You'd be surprised how many divorce cases end with the wife getting the car or the house or custody of the children by threatening to accuse the husband of rape." It soon became clear that what Ufer was really interested in was criticizing the 1997 change outlawing marital rape. "The Kachelmann trial is virtually a textbook example of how the new law can be taken advantage of and abused," he complained.[36] Women's fear of the "rapist in her own bed" seemed—at least in certain circles—to have turned into men's fear of their own wives crying rape. Forensic scientist Klaus Püschel testified, "In recent years we've had to record a rise in so-called fake-rape-cases. We used to estimate that 5 to 10 percent of all reported rapes were wrongful accusations; now there are institutes that calculate it's nearer to 50 percent."[37]

But even statistics meant to bolster the cases of victims revealed a lot more about the writers' agenda than the facts. Riekel wrote, "According to a study every fourth woman experiences sex against her will in a relationship at least once in her life. Official figures estimate that the number of unrecorded cases is a hundred times higher."[38] That would make it 2,500 percent which didn't mean that every victim was raped multiple times but that Riekel had mixed up percent and times.

"Women are always crying rape" is one of the classic rape myths, so it has become taboo (at least in feminist circles) even to suggest that a reported rape is anything but the truth—to avoid going back to the bad old times when the police didn't take any reports seriously and judges were prejudiced against all complainants from the start.

But of course there are wrongful accusations of rape; it would be weird if there weren't. That would separate rape from the realm of human interactions and make it something universal, like a natural law that couldn't be changed. By the very nature of things, the numbers can only be guessed at, and ideas about what constitutes a wrongful accusation are even more diverse than about what constitutes rape.[39] The only thing that seems to be certain is that the reasons are a lot more complicated than vengeful ex-wives.

The estimated numbers of false reports that are repeatedly cited range from 2 percent to 41 percent.[40] The latter only pertaining to one city in America (and not claiming to apply to any other control sample)[41] and the former going back to Susan Brownmiller who provided "a rather obscure source for the figure,"[42] so the real numbers must fall somewhere between—as with any other crime.

And it is worth bearing in mind that wrongful accusations are a crime. In Germany, that crime carries a prison sentence of three months to five years; in Britain, people who make false accusations can be charged with "perverting the course of justice and wasting police time," which carries a maximum sentence of life imprisonment.[43] In practice, the conviction rate for false accusations is as low as the conviction rate for rape.[44] But once a person is falsely convicted of having perpetrated a rape they are treated just as cavalierly as rape victims used to be before the feminist movement. There is the example of teacher Horst Arnold, who was sent to prison in Germany in 2001 for raping his collegue Heidi K. Insisting on his innocence constantly, he refused to undergo therapy and therefore had to serve his full sentence. Only after his release it became clear that Heidi K. had lied to get his job at the school they'd both worked for. At the retrial Horst Arnold was acquitted of all charges. Still that didn't mean that he could go back to his old job that he had only lost because of the wrongful accusation. The school refused to take him. A couple of months later he died of a heart attack, attributed to the stress of having been wrongfully sentenced and his failed rehabilitation.[45]

This is a tragic example, but it is also incredibly rare. Hardly any false rape accusations end with a conviction and prison sentence.[46] The most detailed study on the subject, commissioned by the UK's

Home Office in 2005, showed that out of 216 accusations deemed false, in only 126 cases did the accuser log a formal complaint. Only thirty-nine complainants named a perpetrator at all. Only two led to charges that were later dropped as false.[47] That seems hardly believable in view of the legal scandals that hit the headlines regularly. Is rape special after all? Of course not. A closer look at the wrongful accusations shows that a substantial percentage consists of young girls from very strict families who stayed out past their curfew or, worse, got pregnant and were afraid to tell their parents the truth. In these cases, it is often the parents who go to the police; nearly half of all false rape claims are lodged by a person other than the alleged victim.[48]

The situation looks different on social media, which has become *the* platform to talk about these themes even before #metoo made it impossible to ignore the flood of personal stories about rape, sexual abuse of power, and sexism. The problem is that social media follows its own rules and patterns, escalating a lot quicker and shriller into victim-blaming and dehumanizing of the accused respectively. With even less information on the veracity or even the context of the accusation—plus the fact that the internet openes up a space to talk about so-called gray area cases—people should be even more careful when reacting to them. Sadly, the opposite is the case.

In 2013, Joanie Faircloth published a statement on the website *xoJane* accusing US musician Conor Oberst of raping her when she was a teenager. After some back and forth, Oberst threatened to sue Faircloth for slander. She retracted her statement, explaining she'd only done it because "I was going through a difficult period in my life and trying to cope with my son's illness." That should have been it. Instead, pop-culture critic Chris Ostendorf decried the lawsuit, arguing that it could intimidate real victims of rape and that it promoted the idea of men as victims of false accusations[49]—even though that's exactly what Oberst was. After Oberst dropped his suit, *Bustle*'s Caroline Pate praised his decision and referred to the saga as "a roller-coaster for both parties." Cultural critic Cathy Young commented that Pate was "treating the false accuser and the wrongly accused as morally equivalent."[50]

But just as it is important to take victims of rape seriously, it is important to take victims of false accusations of crimes, including rape, seriously. "We are still far from the day when every woman who makes a rape accusation gets a proper police investigation and a fair hearing. But seeking justice for female victims should make us more sensitive, not less, to justice for unfairly accused men,"[51] Young argues. "In practical terms, that means finding ways to show support for victims of sexual violence without equating accusation and guilt, and recognizing that the wrongly accused are real victims too."[52] This proves to be such a challenge because honesty and honor still play such a crucial role in rape cases.

The Kachelmann trial revealed something about the impossible expectations often placed on criminal trials. Alice Schwarzer, editor-in-chief of Germany's biggest feminist magazine, *EMMA,* wrote that in "this distressing trial it is to be hoped—not just for the presumed victim or the presumed perpetrator—that the court will arrive at the truth"—as if it were possible for the court to arrive at *a* truth, let alone *the* truth.[53] This faith in courts to determine "truth" can lead to alarming conclusions, like that reached by Gisela Friedrichsen in *Der Spiegel*: "A victim who tells the truth will get justice in court."[54] As a journalist who covers many court cases, she should know better than most that this just isn't realistic.[55] TV legal expert Karl-Dieter Möller called on "all rape victims to 'stick with the truth,' it would all come out in the end."[56] The truth, evoked in these messages in a quasi-religious manner, amounted to a wish for an all-explaining flashback that would make the invisible visible, so that it could be understood by everyone *in the same way*. It is important to keep in mind that even when interviewing eyewitnesses, it is rare for two people to have the same memory and interpretation of an incident. And nearly everyone lies in court, where the messy reality has to be squeezed into a linear narrative that is intelligible within the narrow parameters of the law. That is not to say that rape is relative and can't be judged, but simply that the expressed desire for truth—shared by journalists, lawyers, the public, and even the accuser and the accused alike—was not a cry for judgment but, as in *The Accused*, for catharsis.

The interested public gained a lot of useful information from countless newspaper pages and in numerous TV and radio reports: how many relationships Jörg Kachelmann maintained simultaneously, which pet names he used for his lovers, and how to give oneself particularly impressive bruises. Detailed theories about how Claudia D. had got her bruises by taking aspirin first were spread over many newspaper columns. The case was consumed like a crime drama with lots of episodes—the only difference being that it didn't culminate in a denouement but instead ended where it had begun: with insinuations. "We discharge the accused and the accuser with a potentially everlasting suspicion—him as a potential rapist, her as a potential vengeful liar," pronounced presiding judge Michael Seidling, adding, "It is simply absurd to insinuate that the court didn't strive for the truth with all our might."[57]

Rights

Rape laws are a maze of different discourses fighting for predominance, defining and redefining who is included into the category of rapeable subject, the role of honor, the severity of the crime, and the possibility of retribution. The earliest known legal system in the British Isles that we know of, Celtic law (approximately 1000 to 55 BCE), comes close to modern understandings of rape, in that it didn't expect a woman to die for her lost honor, granted her compensation (usually as high as her "dos" or bride-price), and recognized two types of rape: forcible rape and rape of a woman who couldn't consent (due to intoxication or mental illness). But Celtic law *did* expect women to be chaste, to cry out for help during the act, and to report the crime immediately afterwards.

During the Anglo-Saxon period, prostitutes were seen as subjects worthy of protection from rape by the law as well. The downside was that the punishments for rapists shot through the roof, which would have made convictions a lot more difficult to obtain: in the most severe cases, it was death, plus castration, *plus* castration of the rapist's male animals, whereupon his possessions would be given to the victim.

William the Conqueror reduced the penalty to merely castration and loss of both eyes. In the eleventh and twelfth centuries, it was reduced again, to two years' imprisonment, though the death penalty was reintroduced for a while. Prostitutes were exempt from the law, and then included again. But most importantly, victims were required to run through the streets immediately afterwards and to make a "hue and cry," showing their injuries and torn dress to "men of good repute."[58]

At the end of the sixteenth century, English common law finally codified rape as "the carnal knowledge of a woman forcibly and against her will." Early colonial American rape statutes, known as carnal-knowledge statutes, incorporated this common-law definition of rape. Just as the most important German penal code of the early modern period, the 1532 *Peinliche Halsgerichtsordnung Kaiser Karls V. Constitutio Criminalis Carolina*—or *Carolina*—from 1532, corresponded to English common law when it defined a rapist as an "evildoer who stole the honor of respected wives, widows, and virgins forcibly and against their will."[59]

"Forcibly" was important. To be more precise, it was the victim's use of force that interested the law the most, because her honor was measured by that resistance. The more a woman fought back, the greater her erstwhile honor. Moreover, it needed her "utmost resistance" to prove that the perpetrator's force had been violence, as opposed to welcome force, i.e. that he had raped and not ravished her. "Simple resistance doesn't turn force into violence," lawyer Friedrich Oskar von Schwarze warned victims in 1873 explicitly.[60] Last but not least, the victim had to uphold her massive physical resistance *throughout*. "If a woman gave up fighting back eventually, the man had to assume that she'd consented after all."[61]

However, to win a rape trial, the victim not only had to prove that the perpetrator had attacked her honor,[62] but mainly that she'd *had* an honor in the first place—a dishonorable woman had nothing to lose, after all.[63] She did so by displaying the appropriate pain—physically and psychologically—for her stolen honor.

So it wasn't just a penchant for purple prose that led Alice Schwarzer to describe Claudia D. during the trial as "a delicate, blonde young woman, her face pale but collected . . . One thing is certain already, the man in the dock has severely humiliated and hurt her."[64] Claudia herself emphasized her fragile femininity in every interview: "The past 16 months have hurt and intimidated her deeply but she fights to regain her life."[65] Thus presenting not her body as the crime scene but her soul—or, even more old-fashioned, her honor.

Rape trials are so crucial because they are the social spaces where honor and the possibility of its reconstitution are negotiated. Even laws that seem callous to us today deal at least in part with the reparation of honor.

Biblical laws demanded that the rapist marry his victim (see, for example, Exodus 22:16–17 and Deuteronomy 22:28–29). Read in the context of their time they appear less hard-hearted and more pragmatic, securing the social position of the victim, i.e. her honor, and providing for her financially. Her father—though not she herself—could then decide whether to "give her to him," or not, but she would still get the full bride-price. Such laws were based on Middle Assyrian laws from 1000 BCE which obliged the rapist to pay triple the normal bride-price; while the victim's father still retained the right to reject the match. There was one addition in Assyrian Law though that went further than looking after the victim financially: If the rapist was already married, his wife was to be given to the victim's father to be raped.

The idea that honor could be regained—at least gradually—if the court accepted a rape as rape, and therefore recognized the woman's honor albeit as stolen, is a constant subtext in rape trials. Eighteenth-century literature was quite enamored with it, as Friedrich Schiller's *Fiesco's Conspiracy at Genoa* demonstrates. In the full-length drama, republican Bertha is raped by the feudal tyrant Giannettino Doria, nephew of the Doge of Genoa. Her shocked father, Verrina, draws his sword to kill her, in the tradition of Lucretia. But unlike the legendary Roman, Bertha doesn't want to die. With a broken heart, Verrina laments: "Honor was our sole capital."[66] In the next scene, he refuses young Bourgognino her hand in marriage because she is now no more than a "mud puddle,"[67] fair game for everyone: Like Sarah

Tobias two centuries later in *The Accused* and two decades later still, Claudia D. in the trial against Kachelmann.[68]

This shows how social states of mind can contain older understandings of justice. The Statutes of Westminster had changed the English definition of rape in the thirteenth thirteenth century so that it became a crime against the state, and not against an individual or against a family. In the same way, the German Reichsstrafgesetzbuch from 1871 treated rape as an "offense against the community" and subsumed it under the chapter "crimes and offences against morality and public decency." That meant that rape didn't infringe upon the victim any more but upon "objective decency"—in short, upon the state. Accordingly, rape was specified as "any intercourse that doesn't occur inside a state-sanctioned monogamous relationship, i.e., marriage, between husband and wife and therefore does not serve the purpose of reproduction."[69] This included male homosexuality,[70] masturbation, sex before marriage, and adultery.

The Sexual Offences Act of 1967 legalized homosexuality in the UK. France followed in 1971 and, Germany in 1973.[71] Italy had already abandoned its homosexuality law in 1887. Most of the other "indecent" acts had either been legalized by then or ceased to be indecent.[72] That opened the doors for a change in perception as well as in law—so that rape is no longer a crime against common decency but a crime against sexual self-determination. "The matter-of-fact way in which all legal commentators declare the right to sexual self-determination to be the central objective of the law, is impressive and belies the fact that, only ten years ago, that central objective was the protection of marriage and family," Lembke reminds us.[73] Legal rights and general feelings of right and wrong don't always agree, but their reciprocal relationship means that one will likely follow the other in a democratic state—eventually.

In most other crimes, it is a given that some people lie in court, but to claim the classification "rape victim" requires the immediate affirmation of the simultaneous classifications "honesty" and "innocence," otherwise the social status of the women is endangered. This intricate mesh of meanings and references goes beyond the wording of the law, it also pertains to its place in the body of law. Though honor is no longer mentioned explicitly, it still haunts court cases and reports of rape, especially where a victim's honesty is concerned. If a woman's account isn't believed, she is dishonest – a pattern that closely relates to "honor." This is precisely why it was so painful to large parts of the public when Claudia D.'s statements were called into question. NGOs like *Terre des Femmes*, the *Weißer Ring*, the *Bundesverband Deutscher Frauenberatungsstellen* (the German rape crisis centers), and many more warned that women might now think twice before reporting a rape.[74] The subtext was that by calling Claudia D. "an alleged victim of rape" instead of "a victim" she wasn't just potentially dishonest but potentially dishonorable.

It is these half-conscious concepts that fueled a debate in 2010, when Swedish activists and lawyers called for changing rape laws so that the accused should have to prove his innocence instead of being considered innocent until proven guilty, as in any other court case.[75] Their aim was to turn our social scripts on their heads and examine and attack the accused's (man's) honor instead of the accuser's (woman's)—to invert Matthew Hale's famous assertion, "In a rape case it is the victim, not the defendant, who is on trial."

That (some) human-rights activists were prepared to cede hard-won civil rights for which they would ordinarily fight determinedly says a lot about our understanding not just of victims but also of perpetrators. "What was initially seen as an *act* involving sexual violation became eventually conceived as part of an *identity* ('the rapist'). The designation 'rapist' is modern, first used as late as 1883," explains Joanna Bourke, comparing the discourse around rape to Michel Foucault's analysis of homosexuality.[76] Foucault dates the "birth" of the "homosexual" to 1870, thirteen years before the "birth" of the "rapist." Men who had until then done and loved lots of different things—painting, riding, playing an instrument, reading books, *and* the "crime of sodomy"—suddenly became "homosexuals," people whose whole being was defined by having sexual intercourse with people of the same gender. The rapist "became a personage, a past, a case history, and a childhood in addition to being a type of life, a life-form, and a morphology . . . Nothing that went into his total composition was unaffected by his sexuality."[77] Applied to rape, this meant that a rapist wasn't someone who had committed a crime but someone who *became* his crime.

As a result, the description "fair game" doesn't exclusively apply to victims any more but also to a lot of alleged or actual perpetrators. Roman Polanski sued the editor of *Vanity Fair*, Craydon Carter, for printing an article stating that Polanski had molested an actress on the way to his wife's funeral. The article was a pure fabrication; Polanski had been nowhere near the place where the assault was supposed to have taken place. Carter defended the article on the grounds that Polanski's reputation had already been ruined by the 1977 rape case against him and could not be damaged any more.[78] The same sentiment prompted Hans-Hermann Tiedje, the erstwhile editor-in-chief of magazines *Bild* and *Bunte*, to say to Jörg Kachelmann live on television: "You have lied nonstop. But that was your private life and you can't be punished for that. You're just a rotten egg."[79]

Tiedje was referring to a line of argument that had opened a chasm of ambivalence in Kachelmann's case: did Claudia D. perhaps have a reason to feel misused but no other legal handle on him? After all, she had believed for more than a decade—from age twenty-six to age thirty-seven—that they were living in a monogamous relationship with a future. Only a few weeks before the alleged rape they had looked at a house together, and debated which room to put her piano in, though he had never intended to move in with her. Psychologist Luise Greuel, interpreted: "For Kachelmann, Claudia D. had never been more than an affair, someone to project his hubris on and therefore: replaceable. When she recognized her real place in Kachelmann's emotional ranking, it amounted to a collapse of her identity, an existential destruction."[80] It is remarkable how much Greuel's diagnosis ("collapse of her identity, an existential destruction") resembles the description of rape trauma.[81]

Of course, sex by deception *was* legally rape for a long time, to make sure that a man didn't promise marriage in order to get his evil way with a maiden (what other reason could she have to engage in sex, after all?). Behind this was the idea of sex as an exchange—virginity for matrimony—so that consent pertained to the whole transaction, which if not completed amounted to a theft of virginity/honor. In fact, rape by deception is still an integral part of the UK's Sexual Offences Act, though quite vague and rarely applied nowadays, as author Jane Fae summarizes: "deceiving an individual as to age, marital status, wealth or even HIV status doesn't invalidate consent."[82] Lying about sex or gender, however, does. In 2012, Justine McNally, then seventeen, was found guilty of rape by deception for having consensual sex with a girl one year younger than herself. The case is complicted because at the time of the trial she identified as female though during the relationship McNally had identified as male and the girlfried knew her as Scott. The whole thing blew up because the girl's mother had kept questioning McNally. Whereupon McNally offered to undergo gender-reassignment surgery. But the mother went to the police instead, with drastic consequences. *Huffington Post* ran the headline "Justine McNally, Who Pretended to Be a Boy to Take 16-Year-Old Schoolgirl's Virginity, Jailed."[83] The judge set great store by the deceived girl's virginity as well. "She had her first sexual experience with you, and you abused her trust so badly she finds it difficult to trust other people,"[84] he said and upheld the draconic sentence of three years. The trans community was shocked and there was a storm of protest. Finally McNally was released on parole after eighty-two days but will be a registered rapist to the end of her life, which means that she has to report to the police any time she changes her address or goes on vacation outside the UK. She can't go near places frequented by children, like playgrounds or schools—and if she doesn't comply, she'll be sent back to jail.

McNally is far from the only one. In 2015, Gayle Newland was christened "fake penis woman" by the press and sentenced to eight years in prison for pretending to be a man to have sex with her unsuspecting girlfriend.[85] The situation was so tragic that it could only be topped by the girlfriend's statement in court that she "would have preferred to have been raped by a man."[86]

In other countries, the borders are drawn along other lines. In 2010, the case of Sabbar Kashur made international headlines. He was a Palestinian convicted by an Israeli court for "rape by deception" after having consensual sex with an Israeli woman because he had introduced himself as "David" and the woman had presumed he was Jewish. Even though Judge Tzvi Segal agreed the sex had been consensual, she sentenced him to eighteen months in jail for the law had "a duty to protect women from smooth-tongued criminals who can deceive innocent victims at an unbearable price."[87]

These cases show the blind spots in our laws and sexual mores. When we talk about rape, we don't just talk about sexual consent—there was no question of the bodies not consenting—the idea that rape is an "offense against morality" still lingers. It is about which bodies are allowed to engage in sexual acts together, and which sexualities are regarded as socially adequate.

On the other hand, those cases also show that consent extends to more than just physical consent.

3

The Aftermath: Trauma and Healing

Just as honor is always present and at the same time invisible in the discourses surrounding rape, the concept that results from honor—or from its loss—is also omnipresent: shame. It used to be the case that when a woman's honor was stolen, she was disgraced and had to react with shame.[1] Now, we don't use the words honor and disgrace, but we do still talk about shame, which incorporates the whole process. Hardly any article about the aftermath of rape fails to mention "fear, guilt and shame"[2] or "pain, anger and shame."[3] Julia Schellong, chairwoman of the German Society for Psychotraumatology, confirms: "Predominantly there are feelings of shame."[4] And anti-rape activist Amber Amour described her feelings on Instagram immediately after being raped: "I have all those fucked-up feelings that we get after rape ... shame. "[5] This discourse risks presenting shame as a kind of automatic body reflex, like an itch or a sneeze, rather than a culturally learned and highly complex emotion.

While in the past a woman's life was shattered by rape because it destroyed her position in society, it's as if now the conflict has moved inside her. Rape has become an attack upon a woman's sexual identity, creating a "psychic wound," a "violation of the self." Joanna Bourke traces the change from social to psychological discourse, noting that "this intense focus on the body as marker of identity and as a locus of truth is a profoundly modern conception"[6]—and at the same time profoundly *pre*modern, honor having always been located in the physical as well as the spiritual female body.

But whatever the cause, the woman's life is shattered; that goes without saying. "While each woman is unique, we seem to accept only one response from a rape or abuse victim: total collapse," objects author Vanessa Veselka. "Every major media piece on the subject of rape or abuse presents us with the same version of this collapsible woman."[7]

Since it was coined in 1978, the term *post-traumatic stress disorder* (PTSD) has been predominantly associated with war veterans and victims of rape or sexual abuse. TV dramas and documentaries are full of rape victims who are afraid to leave the house, develop an obsession with washing, put on lots of weight, self-harm, etc. This creates a very narrow image of what a *real* victim looks like. "My very survival incriminates me," confirms author Virginie Despentes:

> You're supposed to be traumatized by a rape—it brings with it a whole range of obligatory, visible scars: fear of men, of the night, of independence, disgust for sex, and all kinds of other delights.[8]

Vanessa Veselka writes:

> As a culture, we teach girls from a young age that rape is the worst thing that could ever happen to them. We paint it as something that will destroy their lives and that will steal their sense of purity. We tell those who were sexually abused that it is normal and natural to feel dirty. We do this because we're trying to prepare them so that they don't feel alone when it happens. But aren't we also setting them up to be destroyed, to feel dirty and impure? How much are we training ourselves to crumble?[9]

Her article appeared in 1999 in *Bitch* magazine and has been cited as an important inspiration by numerous feminists (including German cultural critic Katja Peglow), so it's surprising that her point wasn't picked up more widely. The main reason is that it's been such a long, hard struggle to get recognition for rape victims. And even though that fight hasn't been won completely—as anyone who has ever opened a newspaper can confirm—public awareness has undergone a fundamental change.

On March 6, 1986, three masked men broke into the vicarage of St. Mary's Church in the London borough of Ealing, demanding money and "jewels." Finding none, they beat Reverend Michael

Saward and his daughter's boyfriend, David Kerr, with cricket bats until they were unconscious, then raped Jill Saward brutally. The case made the front pages, because twenty-one-year-old Jill had been a vicar's daughter and a virgin, but also because the only burglar who *didn't* take part in the rape got the longest sentence of the three (he had planned the burglary). Judge John Leonard justified his decision with the statement that Jill Saward's trauma "had not been so great."[10] The ensuing protests led to a change in rape law in Britain, so that victims now have the right to appeal against lenient convictions and the media aren't allowed to report in any way that might lead to the victim being identified (even though this still happens). In 1993, Leonard apologized publicly to Saward and called his decision a "blemish" on his career that would haunt him till the end of his life.[11]

In 1990, Jill Saward published her book *Rape: My Story*, to document the immense impact of rape on victims. "There are definite stages, though nobody really explained that to me at first. That's one of the reasons I want to share my experience. So nobody need feel that she is cracking up, or going mad, when she is sitting there feeling the greyness, the nothingness."[12] After hearing her pain denied by the court, Saward felt she had a responsibility to speak for *all* rape victims. All the same, it was a terrifying message to all victims and potential victims: that the crime would suck the soul out of your body and leave you an empty shell.

These sentiments eventually gave birth to the terms *soul murder* or *spiritual murder*[13] for rape, to emphasize the severity of the crime and especially its long-term consequences, which also got a name: *rape trauma syndrome*, suggesting that there is "an acute phase of disorganization immediately after the act, but also a long-term impact affecting the sufferer's lifestyle physically (e.g., genito-urinary difficulties), psychologically (nightmares, phobias), socially (minimal social functioning) and sexually (a fear of sex, an avoidance of men)."[14]

One can't help noticing that these symptoms strangely resemble the historic "symptoms" of being a woman—similar to the passive, frigid femininity described by authorities from Aristotle to Krafft-Ebing. "She is fragile, humorless, and diluted, bearing an uncanny resemblance to the sickly Victorian angel of the house"[15] Vanessa Veselka remarks:

> The single model of recovery from sexual abuse and rape that requires a woman to live in a cocoon of self-obsession and call it a safe environment has the same potential for social isolation as 50s middle-class suburbs. It also bears an eerie resemblance to the "separate sphere" mentality that early feminists fought so hard to destroy. In the Victorian age, for example, it was popular to be sick. There were even fainting couches, furniture designed to collapse on. The idea was to wane visibly because it was better to be honored for a tragic demise than not honored at all.[16]

Jill Saward's book is shocking and moving and gives voice to feelings otherwise kept hidden—like her disappointment that she *didn't* get pregnant after the rape—but the international attention focused solely on her panic attacks and suicidal thoughts. These were read by the US women's movement as a public confession, with subsequent public absolution: "I have found my voice. Amen to that."[17] True, *Rape: My Story*, like other survivors' stories, gave victims a narrative structure and thereby a voice.[18] However, this was only *one* voice and only *one* story for a whole spectrum of experiences.

It is crucial that trauma be taken very seriously. At the same time, this specific survivor story pressed a very heterogenous group—people who had experienced rape—collectively into *one* incredibly narrow position of pain. But people who have different resources and live in different environments will also react differently to violence and will need to find their own ways to heal. Veselka is uncomfortable with the fact that "survivor," like "rapist," has become an identity. Nobody in their right mind would treat a person who has been in a car crash as if the accident had changed their personality, but that is exactly what happens to rape victims. They become "the collapsible woman—one model of mental health for an unaccountable number of individuals."[19]

In the 1990s, anti-rape activists began holding demonstrations on campuses, called Take Back the Night. After the marches came speak-outs, with students stepping up and telling *their* rape stories.

> The strange thing is that as all these different girls—tall and short, fat and thin, nervous and confident—get up to give intensely personal

> accounts, all of their stories begin to sound the same. Listening to a string of them, I hear patterns begin to emerge. The same phrases float through different voices. Almost all of them begin "I wasn't planning to speak out tonight but . . ." even the ones who had spoken the previous years. They talk about feeling helpless, and feeling guilty. Some talk about hating their bodies.[20]

In short, they talk about shame. Jagoda Marinic demands that we get "the shame out of women's heads: that would do more to strengthen the victims than anything else."[21] But is shame really, or only, "in women's heads"? Or in other words: What *is* shame? Classicist Edith Hall explains:

> Shame is crucial to everything in ancient Greek literature and society. It's not actually an internal state of mind, as in: I feel ashamed. It's: I feel shame being directed at me by other people! The etymological root in ancient Greek for both words for shame—and there are two and they do mean slightly different things—comes from words to do with how you are visually seen by other people. How you appear in the world. Not how you are inside.[22]

Classically, then, shame isn't inside the head to begin with, but is externally imposed if someone doesn't conform to social norms and expectations. For society to function smoothly, that person must then make it their own and internalize it. "It's very effective in maintaining an orderly, hierarchical society. Confucius, the Chinese philosopher, wrote about government: "Without any shame you have to use force to run a people. With shame you can rule them. Because they have internalized various rules about how they behave vis-à-vis other people."[23]This means that respect for victims' shame is at the same time respect for the very social norms that cause that shame in the first place. "With the best motives we still say to her: 'I'm sorry for your loss.' We will ask her to 'reclaim' her experience, rather than realize its effects," Vanessa Veselka clarifies:

> As long as we cling to the concept of rape or abuse as theft, we are ultimately led back to the belief that a woman's worth and sense of self lies in her sexual purity, and we speak of her condition only in terms of ownership and loss. To imply that deep within every woman is something essential that can be seen or touched, a vessel containing the "real her" that can be stolen by someone else, is a form of objectification of women.[24]

Language plays a pivotal role in the way we assess rape, but also in the way we process it. We need narratives to understand and remember the things that happen to us. Any event without a narrative is a nonevent, inaudible to our inner ear and hence twice as dangerous. It is only through narratives that we communicate our inner world to the outer world. The alchemistic way we turn experiences into memories is necessarily a creative and complex process. We tell most stories again and again, looking at them each time from a slightly different perspective. As soon as the story is one about rape, however, all these different perspectives become condensed into one hard truth about the victim's life.

This becomes especially conspicuous when victims don't behave according to the script. Natascha Kampusch, an Austrian girl who was abducted by a man named Wolfgang Přiklopil when she was ten years old and held captive in the cellar of his house for eight years, is a prescient example. When she managed to escape in 2006, she was hailed as the "girl who had come back from the dead." But very soon the public grew vexed. They couldn't fathom Kampusch, who against all expectations did not seem to be broken. On the contrary, when she was interviewed on TV she appeared so self-reliant—she said, for example that she didn't want any medication but would "deal with it on my own"—that speculation immediately arose about whether she had really been the victim of such a horrific crime. "People hit her in the streets and called her a liar; the media debated at length her financial gain from the whole affair."[25] After all, hadn't she sold the broadcasting rights for a six-figure sum? And weren't her interviews watched by millions?

In fact, the public's hunger for her pain was so blatant journalists threatened the eighteen-year-old that if she wouldn't talk to them, they would simply invent stories. Only by talking could she could do it on her own terms—not that this stopped the media from fabricating fictions, of course: that she'd given birth to a child in the cellar where she was held captive, or that she had abetted a pedophile ring, or that she hadn't been abducted at all but had eloped with the perpetrator and had had an affair with him (at the age of ten!). "It is preposterous, really." she commented. But why had she left so much out of her memoir? "Everybody has a right to privacy and I don't have to tell everything. Certain things are very personal and are not really pertinent to the crime. Why should I have to talk about humiliating experiences?"[26]

The entitlement with which the caring public invaded Natascha Kampusch's privacy, exhibits a striking resemblance to the perpetrator's transgressions. Take the 2016 book on her case, written by ex–police officer Peter Reichard, formerly of the British Criminal Investigation Department (CID), who quotes video recordings the captor had made of Kampusch over the years—and, just like him, the author didn't ask Kampusch for her consent to use the material. She filed a suit asking for certain passages to be removed from the book, but, incredibly, didn't succeed. As Linda Martin Alcoff and Laura Gray-Rosendale warn, "When breaking the silence is taken up as the necessary route to recovery or as a privileged political tactic, it becomes a coercive imperative on survivors to confess, to recount our assaults, to give details, and even to do so publicly."[27]

The helpline Stop Rape concludes: "Most of the time a woman talking about her rape will start off calling it something else."[28] Despentes, writing of her own experience, says she was skeptical:

> What a load of nonsense. This sounds damn improbable, why wouldn't they say a word, and anyway what does this chick know? Does she think we're all the same, or what? . . . Suddenly, I see the light. What have I, myself done up till now? The few times—mostly very drunk—when I have wanted to tell this story, have I used the word? Never. The few times I have attempted to talk about it, I'd skirted around the word "rape": "assaulted," "mixed up," "in a tight corner," "hustled" . . . whatever. As long as the aggression is not

> called "rape," the attack loses its specificity, can be compared with other attacks like getting mugged, picked up by the cops, held for questioning, beaten.[29]

This refusal to say the word is usually read as a sign of shame, the power of patriarchy over its victims, the rapist's ultimate victory. But when we consider the incredible restrictiveness of our rape narratives, it could also be seen as a survival strategy. If you don't accept the identity of "victim," you don't have to live that identity. Kampusch explained famously, "I said, 'I'm not a victim', because I knew if I accepted being a victim, nobody would ever again accept me as a normal person."[30] Samantha Geimer adds, "It is wrong to ask people to feel like victims, because once they do, they feel like victims in every area of their lives."[31]

This is not to say that talking about rape, or even shame itself, is a problem. On the contrary, language is crucial for all our cognitive processes, because if we can't communicate things to the outside world, we usually can't communicate them to ourselves either. But how we speak and listen is double-edged. "Speech is no mere verbalization of conflicts and systems of domination," Michel Foucault argues, "it is the very object of man's conflicts."[32]

"One of the many reactions to my story has been, 'And you carried on hitchhiking, after that?'" Despentes, who had been raped while hitchhiking, recounts. "I hadn't told my parents, for fear of being put under lock and key for my own good."[33] Rape reduced her in the eyes of the world to the stereotype of the little woman who should stay put and look after home and hearth and her genitals. (Strictly speaking, the *threat* of rape can be enough to keep women in the home, since—to speak with Despentes—"rape is something you catch and can never get rid of."[34])

The heart of Despentes's book *King Kong Theory* is a call for self-determination, sexual and otherwise, a demand not to be "saved" from life, because

> although I wasn't raped again, I risked it a hundred times . . . What I experienced during that time, at that age, was unique, so much more

> intense than shutting myself up in school learning to be docile, or sitting at home reading magazines. Those were the best years of my life, the richest, the noisiest, and I managed to find the strength to deal with all the shit that came with them.[35]

Of course, this doesn't mean that victims should just pull themselves together and everything will be puppies and kittens—rather, that the price for recognition, for empathy, and perhaps even redress can't be that every victim's life has to become proof of the wrong done to them, that they have to preserve their psyche as a crime scene that can be inspected at any time. "With all the media coverage and attention paid to rape victims in recent years, we still lack models that praise women for getting on with their lives rather than just getting through them," observes Veselka.[36]

In Sarah Dunant's 1997 novel *Transgressions*, protagonist Elizabeth Skvorecky (Lizzie) is a translator and starts—first discreetly, but soon very significantly—to change the thriller she is translating in order to enable the female victim in the story to take her fate into her own hands. In various postmodern scenes that mirror the thriller intricately, Lizzie becomes a victim herself. She is pursued by a stalker who gains entrance to her flat and changes it deftly, just as she changes the book she is translating. In response, she deposits her freshly renarrated pages as messages for him, to communicate that he can't intimidate her. The novel culminates in a highly controversial scene in which he breaks into the house and tries to rape her. Convinced he will kill her if she shows fear, Lizzie does the only thing left to her: she approaches him sexually. The critics couldn't fathom what was going on, mainly because Dunant was a prominent feminist. "At the center of the debate over the feminist status of *Transgressions* lies a question about the contract between the feminist writer and her female readers," Tanya Horek notes.

> After considering Dunant's arguments that her novel challenges fictional stereotypes of women as passive victims, [*Guardian* journalist Angela] Neustatter asked: This is all very well, but couldn't it be deeply upsetting to a woman who has been raped and felt

> paralyzed with fear, unable to do anything but exist, to see fiction suggesting she could have done better if she had been up to a quick seduction?[37]

That Dunant had never suggested anything remotely like that didn't matter. Because it was a novel about—among other things—rape, it wasn't read as literature but as a precedent that could influence all further dealings with rape victims—not in literature, but in life. By invoking the figure of "a woman who has been raped and felt paralyzed with fear,"—i.e., a *real* rape victim, Neustatter doesn't have to speak for herself but can "protect" an imagined victim.

Why don't we apply this same logic to other well-documented causes of trauma and PTSD? We have yet to see criticisms of James Bond on behalf of traumatized veterans. It would seem absurd to do so. Why? Because we don't treat any other experience that might result in PTSD the way we treat rape. Rape is a special case, always. While we can only understand the things that happen to us in our lives—even life itself—as a process, rape is supposed to be the only essentialist story, the last elemental truth, a kind of secular god.

That's why it's so hard to think about and think up other stories—including this book. Not to present a new truth but to create diverse narratives, diverse opportunities of being in the world—to get on with life as well as collapse, and everything in between and beyond. This lack of narratives entails other lacks, particularly in the transfer of knowledge. Stories about healing are rare and hard to come by. After her rape, Despentes discovered to her amazement:

> Books could do nothing for me. This had never happened before. When I was hospitalized for a few months in 1984, the first thing I did when they let me out was read . . . Books were there to keep me company, to make things bearable, sayable, shareable. Prison, illness, abuse, drugs, abandonment, deportation: all traumas have their literature.[38]

But in this case: "No guide, no companionship. [No] knowledge, or survival instructions or simple practical advice. Nothing."

Those were the 1980s, before Riot Grrrl and long before #metoo. The ensuing years have brought more resources, including the book *Yes Means Yes!* by Jessica Valenti and Jaclyn Friedman. But even in that impressive book, the only practical survival tip is to try drinking nettle tea.

Healing

As if these weren't enough contradictions, rape seems to be simultaneously the worst thing to happen to a woman *and* the yardstick for her attractiveness. "Rape is the curse of beauty," Alain Corbin writes in his book about sexual violence in history.[39] Likewise, *A Natural History of Rape* warns that young women "should be made aware of the cost associated with attractiveness."[40] In fact, a woman's beauty has long been constructed along the lines of her "rapeability," even if she has not actually been raped. "Female honor was part of her physique: that meant the more female her form, the more endangered her honor was by weak-willed men."[41] Gesa Dane describes the feminine *trio infernale*: being passive, being dominated, being rapeable. "There is even evidence that women perceived as being 'plain' or 'obese' are less likely to be believed, and are therefore less likely to report a rape."[42] The implied question is: who would want to rape her anyway?

It is common knowledge that advertising highlights female fragility by showcasing women with exposed throats, weirdly crossed legs, and eyes wide open. Women learn they are more attractive to men the more vulnerable and helpless they are. "You can't tell women anymore that they can't achieve (except in maths). Who'd believe you? But you can tell women that, if they do achieve, they'll be miserable," observes author and journalism professor Caryl Rivers:

> What were among the most e-mailed stories about women that appeared in the *New York Times* between 2003 and 2006? Stories claiming that men won't marry smart women, that young Ivy League women are creating an "Opt-Out Revolution" returning to home and hearth. All of those stories proved to be untrue, based on bad science, but they live on forever in cyberspace, getting repeated over

> and over again . . . The news media today sells anxiety to women the way that advertising sells insecurity about their faces, bodies, and sex appeal.[43]

These stories tell women that insecurity and vulnerability don't just make them more attractive; these are the traits that make them female in the first place. The language we use for trauma is the language of the walking wounded. No wonder, as *trauma* is Greek for "wound." But what does trauma actually mean?

Trauma was first included in 1980 in the *Diagnostic and Statistical Manual of Mental Disorders* (DSM) by the American Psychiatric Association, the classification system that is the basis for defining psychiatric disorders internationally.[44] With a diagnosis of trauma, patients would now be entitled to receive therapy. But it also meant that they had a diagnosis that something was *wrong with them* as opposed to a wrong having been *done to them*.[45] So the definition turned a trauma caused by outside influences (i.e., the attacker) into a psychological wound rooted in the soul of the attacked. Martina Hävernick, one of the founders of Wildwasser, the first crisis and information center for victims of sexual abuse in Germany, writes:

> People who have experienced sexual violence . . . are all seen as traumatized. But trauma, or more precisely "post-traumatic stress disorder," is a psychiatric diagnosis. That means they are no longer seen as victims of a crime but as psychologically ill. Of course, this diagnosis acknowledges that sexual violence has repercussions.[46]

But this acknowledgement comes at a cost; the repercussions of the experience become inextricable from the person who has been raped.

This rings true to my experience of publishing this book in Germany. Whenever I read from my book people come—or write—to me afterwards to tell me their stories, and rape as diagnosis rather than crime is a recurring motif. One mail read:

> Whenever my partner and I fight, there comes a point when we ask ourselves whether this is all due to the fact that I had been raped as

> a teenager. Reading your book has given me the permission to look at my relationship problems as relationship problems and not as rape problems.[47]

A participant in one of my workshops confessed: "For a long time I didn't think I had really been raped because I didn't show the appropriate symptoms." Another added, "Oh, I do think I am traumatized, but I am not just traumatized by the rape—and I'm not allowed to talk about anything else." Blogger Hannah C. Rosenblatt summarizes: "I want to talk about my experiences with sexual violence without being read as woman/victim/everything that is the opposite of self-determination."[48] All of these testimonies were deeply moving. But perhaps the most moving was the young woman who had been raped only a few days before. She came to my talk and said that my book had been important to her because "I don't want to give the perpetrator the right to change who I am."

I couldn't help being reminded of the victimology discourse of the 1940s—now back in a neurological guise. We may no longer expect victims to make a hue and cry and spend the rest of their lives in convents, but they still have to prove with their very being that what has happened to them was rape and no lesser crime. And to make things worse this implies that not all traumas are equal, as Naomi Wolf puts it:

> I learned again and again that the young women who presented this constellation of "symptoms" had suffered childhood or adolescent sexual assault, or had been raped. I noticed that this cluster of symptoms was very different from the presentation of the many other young women we had in the program who had suffered just as severe, but other, nonsexual forms of trauma.[49]

It strikes me as odd that the cause for this "constellation of 'symptoms'" is found at the very site that used to be the location of female honor. Wolf too was surprised, so she described what she had seen to therapist Nancy Fish: "I spelled out to her my theory that . . . the vagina mediates a woman's sense of her core self. 'Does this make sense, in your experience? Or is this crazy?' I asked."[50]

Fish, who specializes in vulvovaginal pain, agreed emphatically: "A lot of women *feel* crazy for feeling that their whole sense of self is involved with the vagina, but I tell them they are not."[51] Wolf "wondered if that core sense of self in relation to the vagina's well-being could be evolutionary or neurobiological. I heard so many women from so many different cultures and economic backgrounds say that they felt like 'damaged goods' when there had been an insult or trauma to the vagina." She questioned Fish further: "How often do you hear the expression—'I feel like damaged goods'—from your patients?" The response was: "Almost with every person I see . . . It's almost impossible not to say that, it seems, at a certain point."[52]

The question remains: if these feelings are evolutionary or hard-wired into the brain, why would evolution make women say they feel like damaged goods before the notion of "goods" was even around, damaged or otherwise?[53] But be that as it may, the outcome was that Wolf and Fish incorporated shame securely back into the body, as a natural reaction of the pudendum, which coincidentally translates as the shameful body part: *pudere* is Latin for "shame." Worse still, Wolf claims, "We should understand that while healing is possible, one never fully 'recovers' from rape; one is never just the same as before."[54]

Needless to say, Wolf's *Vagina* book has been highly controversial because it transformed the vagina into a mysterious organ that could mess with the brain—just like its neighboring organ the womb (or *hystera* in Greek), that for more than two millennia was thought to roam the female body freely and play havoc with its rationality, making it the basis for the psychological diagnosis "hysteria."[55] That didn't stop the book from becoming a bestseller in numerous languages. Now it was obviously never Wolf's intention to reduce women to the function of their genitals, but rather to extend the space of the soul to include the sexual organs. Nevertheless, it's hard to read her assertions without thinking of a female essence to be protected and guarded, that could be destroyed by outside influences at any time. These might take on the most trivial forms. In one scene, Wolf attends a dinner party where vulva-shaped pasta with the descriptive name "cuntini" is served: it gives Wolf writer's block for half a year. She declares:

> Understood in this way, and with this significant evidence, rape and sexual assault, with their attendant trauma, should be understood not just as a form of forced sex; they should also be understood as a form of injury to the brain and body, and even as a variant of castration.[56]

Because sex was over as well—at least for an indefinite period (no pun intended). She extrapolates that "the trauma of rape or childhood sexual abuse can lead to dysregulation of the sympathetic nervous system, a dysregulation that leads in turn to the vagina's *physical inability* . . . to engorge with blood."[57]

"If you have been raped or abused, you're scarred for life," comments Vanessa Veselka drily, adding,

> You will never be as you were before the experience. This is also true for falling in love, getting your heart broken, going to war, having a child, or reading a great book. Everything that cuts deeply marks us. We're all scarred for life the moment we intimately relate to the outside world.[58]

To get away from the idea of the victim as being ultimately destroyed, the term *survivor* was adopted in the 1990s. The aim was to turn the person who'd experienced sexual violence from a passive victim into an active survivour: She survives (active). Versus: She is being victimised (passive). The term did achieve that, but it didn't break with the narrative of rape as an attack on the vital essence of womanhood, as Katie Roiphe points out: "To call . . . rape victims 'survivors,' like survivors of a fire, a plane crash, or the Holocaust, is to compare rape to death."[59]

Whereas rape has long been seen as the crime that affects all women (though certain women are certainly emphasized) with an attendant trauma that "occurs across cultural boundaries and is experienced regardless of ethnicity, religion, class, or other qualifying factors," psychologist Ariane Brenssell shows that, on the contrary, *any* trauma is intrinsically bound up with outside parameters. While the event might be objective, the way we process and integrate it depends on a whole range of personal factors (like resources and resilience) and social conditions (environment, culture, social norms). "Because sexual violence is individual and social, it is personal and political at the same time."[60] Rape reports from different historical periods seem to confirm that. Author Jenny Diski describes her state of mind after having been raped:

> I didn't think that it was the most terrible thing that had ever happened to me. It was a very unpleasant experience, it hurt and I was trapped. But I had no sense that I was especially violated by the rape itself, not more than I would have been by any attack on my person and freedom. In 1961, it didn't go without saying that to be penetrated against one's will was a kind of spiritual murder. I was more disgusted by him than I was shamed or diminished. A different zeitgeist, luckily for me.[61]

At that time the most dreaded consequence of rape was not spiritual but social death: What would the neighbors think? How would the boss/church/parents react, if they found out?

Nearly four decades later, when sociologists Cheryl Benard and Edit Schlaffer interviewed teenagers who wanted to get on with their lives after the crime, the zeitgeist had changed for the better *and* worse. Victims could expect a lot more empathy, but mainly for psychological problems resulting from the rape; if they didn't display these problems, that was seen as problematic itself. Benard and Schlaffer were impressed by Nora, who—after having locked herself up in her room for two weeks—showed definite signs of recovery. "Nora's composure confused and worried her family and friends. The official line was that she had to work through her experience, and that meant longer than two weeks. She shouldn't be in denial about it. That would inevitably backfire."[62] Etta Hallenga from the rape crisis center in Düsseldorf told me a similar story:

> A young woman came to me who had been raped two years previously. After she'd told her best friend and her mother, they did some research and sent her to us to undergo therapy, because the rape "could come up at any time." I asked her whether it *had* come up already. No, and actually she was feeling quite all right. And I thought: What an awful thing to say to a young woman, as if she is a ticking timebomb. And I told her she could come back at any time and start therapy if anything did come up—but it might never happen.[63]

It shouldn't be necessary to spell this out, but neither of these young women is presented as better than others in any way. Each person's response to rape is personal, and I firmly believe that there should be no right or wrong way to be a victim. What is representative in these cases, however, is the way their environment has *dealt* with them—very much as if there *is* a wrong way to be a victim. "I have watched as women blamed themselves for their inability to fall apart,"[64] says Veselka. Brenssell confirms, "That shows that the way 'we,' the society, treat people who have experienced violence plays a crucial part in processing trauma."[65]

The women's movement fought for the recognition that "the first thing in working with women who have experienced sexual violence, is the acknowledgment that what happened to them *did* happen . . . and that it was wrong."[66] That remains a crucial first step. But it has to go further.

This is where Veselka's critique comes in: "It's as if we see moving beyond the trauma as denying its impact."[67] Brenssel's approach, on the other hand, widens the perspective from the initial event to the social environment and the person's situation, asking us to "not see trauma as a singular, isolated 'clinically separated' experience, but as a process."[68] She draws from the work of author and psychoanalyst Hans Keilson, a Shoah survivor who did a revolutionary long-term study on Jewish children who survived the German occupation in the Netherlands while their whole families were killed. Brennssel turned to Keilson not because she thought sexual violence and the Holocaust are similar events, but simply because he was the first to recognize that trauma isn't just caused by an originating event but has different stages. He calls this *sequential traumatization*. He pointed out that the period after the war—when the persecution had stopped and the trauma should have been processed but couldn't be, for various reasons—was a crucial part of the traumatic experience. "Many described this [not the war] as the most distressing and painful period of their life."[69] He also noticed that "children who grew up under relatively good conditions in the postwar years" dealt with their trauma better "than children who suffered (comparatively) less during the persecution of the Jews but had a hard time after the war." He concluded it was not just the gravity of the trauma itself that was responsible for psychological problems, but further life conditions, especially how life went on after the event. This approach bridges the psychosocial and political dimensions of trauma.

What has all this got to do with rape? A lot.

One example: In 1977, filmmaker Roman Polanski was commissioned by *Vogue* to do a photo shoot with young models. He auditioned thirteen-year-old Samantha Gailey (Samantha Geimer) and persuaded her to pose naked. She was impressed and awed by the famous director with the tragic past: as a child Polanski had survived the Holocaust in hiding in Poland; his mother had been murdered in Auschwitz; he was assaulted and nearly murdered himself after the war; and in 1969 his pregnant wife, Sharon Tate, had been murdered by the Manson Family. After the photo shoot Polanski gave Samantha champagne and a third of a of methaqualone pill and proceeded to have sex with the unwilling teenager, who pretended to have an asthma attack to get home. In short: her raped her.

When Samantha's mother found out what had happened, she called the police. From that moment on, everything got worse. Polanski was arrested for rape. Polanski was famous. The assault had taken place in Jack Nicholson's house (albeit in his absence). Nicholson was famous. From the first minute, the case was a cause célèbre; even while the trial was still going on, Judge Laurence J. Rittenband was already talking to celebrity magazines like *People*.

To keep Samantha's identity from the public and to prevent her from being eaten alive by the press, the prosecution and the defense agreed: Polanski would plead guilty to having had unlawful sexual intercourse with a minor. He would be sentenced to time served—forty-two days—and probation, and that would be it. "At that time, my lawyer Lawrence Silver, wrote to the judge that the plea agreement should be accepted and that that guilty plea would be sufficent contribution to satisfy us,"[70] confirms Geimer. The public disagreed. But Geimer was not interested in the length of the sentence, for her it was—just as Brennssel had established—all about the recognition of the fact that what had happened to her had happened and that it was wrong: "My family and I simply wanted him to admit to what he'd done, and then vanish from our lives."[71]

But at the last minute, Judge Rittenband announced he wouldn't honor the agreement and would demand fifty years in prison for Polanski instead. In his biography, Polanski recorded that on that day there was one seat left on a British Airways flight to Heathrow Airport in London: Polanski bought it. Samantha Geimer says she was relieved: "All I could think was FREEEEEDOMMMMMMM. No more telling my story. No more seeing myself called 'sex victim girl' in the paper."[72] She was so naive to think that that would be the end of it all. Nothing could have been further from the truth, as she later wrote:

> Looking back, there can be no question that he did something awful. It was a terrible thing to do to a young girl. But it was also 25 years ago—26 next month. And honestly, the publicity surrounding it was so traumatic that what he did to me seemed to pale in comparison.[73]

Polanski was nominated for an Academy Award in 2003—and whenever he was in the media, so was she. Reporters were camping in front of Geimer's house again. Only this time they were ambushing her sons as well, asking them what they thought about their mother's rape. "Never mind the absurdity of asking me whether Polanski should win an Oscar for a movie I've never seen . . . there was a great deal of upset for my children: *Oh, something bad happened to Mom. Oh, now we're all part of it. Mom is damaged.*" Geimer made it clear:

> The analogy that always comes to mind when I think of the way I was treated is this: What if, instead of being raped, I were injured in a different way? Say I have a really bad cut on my arm that is covered by a bandage and that is just barely starting to heal. Would it be appropriate for anyone to say to me: *Wow, will you tell me all about how it happened? Can you take the bandage off so I can look at it? It's stopped bleeding, can you squeeze it a little so it starts to bleed again? Did it hurt worse now?*[74]

Since 1977, reporters, psychologists, and self-proclaimed experts have dissected her case mercilessly. On one side sits the anti-Geimer brigade, like Gore Vidal, who said in 2009, "I really don't give a fuck. Look, am I going to sit and weep every time a young hooker feels as though she's been taken advantage of?"[75] On the other side are those Geimer calls the "victim-advocacy business," among them American legal commentator and television host Nancy Grace. Talking on her show with gynecologist and talk-show-personality Evelyn Minaya, Grace observed: "This is a child, a thirteen-year-old girl. It affects them forever." Minaya confirmed: "Forever. And not only that, the physical aspects of it also. Remember, she had anal sodomy. Do you know that that puts her at an increased risk for anal cancer in her future?" Geimer comments drily: "I was used to having my character maligned because of the rape. But now I was being told that because of the rape I was more likely to get cancer. Great. What next?"[76]

On September 26, 2009, Polanski, who never went back to America, was to be honored for his lifetime achievement at the Zurich Film Festival. Instead he was arrested at Zurich airport; the United States had made an extradition request to Switzerland. That was the last normal day for Samantha Geimer as well. The press hunted her, hunted her family and even distant cousins because Geimer is such a rare name in the US that any Geimer was presumably related to her by marriage.

> Probably in the minds of these media folks, I was having horrible flashbacks from decades ago. I was—but it was horrible flashbacks of *them* . . . Over the years, I have had bad dreams about the legal

> morass, the publicity, the questioning in the courtroom. But I don't think I ever dreamed about Roman or that night at Jack Nicholson's house. That doesn't mean it wasn't terrible. It was. But the terribleness didn't haunt me. Other aspects of that time did. When Roman was arrested in Switzerland, it wasn't exactly déjà vu, but it reminded me of the sense of powerlessness I had experienced as a thirteen-year-old-girl.[77]

Rape crisis centers like Wildwasser keep pointing out that healing is all about having power over one's own life. Apart from practical help, like accompanying victims to the police if they want to report the rape, Wildwasser's job is simply to listen and support survivors in their own journey to recovery. Anything else would be detrimental and perpetuate the feeling of powerlessness.

Blogger Hannah C. Rosenblatt couldn't agree more. "I need and want support, but much too often I got help whether I wanted it or not," she writes, in a startling blog post with the title "Rejecting Help." The "help" she is referring to is the numerous attempts to rescue her, if only she'd agree to the perfect "treatment" or learn to see herself in the right way.

> The problem is not that nobody has ever helped me—but that this help came with conditions that I couldn't meet without harming myself or allowing the helpers to harm me . . . Usually people know very well what helps them, precisely because it helps them. Not because somebody tells them it will help, really, if only they would believe in it . . . But why should I trust someone who doesn't trust me to know best what I want and need and believe?[78]

Rosenblatt, now an expert on mental health who advises others on how to get support, understands rape, trauma, and therapy as questions of agency.

"Agency is the ability to obtain—in conjunction with others—control over one's own individually relevant living conditions,"[79] explains Ariane Brenssell. Where rape takes agency away from victims, healing is about regaining agency.

This is the complete opposite of the way the press and the American legal system have been treating Samantha Geimer for the last forty years. When Polanski was arrested in Zurich she filed a "Victim's Statement" with the Appeals Court pleading to dismiss the case so that she could finally be free from it—as well as free from reporters hounding her and her children. The court rejected her appeal with a twelve-page dismissal, informing her that she "has no right or authority to dictate the outcome of a criminal case, nor is she entitled to examine evidence possessed either by the prosecution or the defense."[80] The *Los Angeles Times* ran the headline: "Polanski's victim is not judge and jury"[81] and declared bluntly: "the case against Polanski was not brought to satisfy her desire for justice or her need for closure. It was brought by the state of California on behalf of the people of California."

Geimer remembers: "The months of Polanski's incarceration in Switzerland, the legal wrangling—it was awful. The panic attacks and insomnia I'd suffered from on and off for my entire life returned in full force. I was finding it harder and harder to concentrate at work, and my boss, while understanding, was also concerned. I was afraid I'd lose my job—which added to the insomnia and panic."[82]

In the end she didn't lose her job, because after nearly nine months the Swiss authorities decided to reject the extradition request and released Polanski, who had spent part of that time in prison and the rest of the nine months under electronically tagged house arrest. But the case is still hanging over both of them, causing a renewed flurry of attention whenever Polanski makes a film or has to appear in court again, as in 2015 when Poland finally decided not to extradite him. In her book Geimer explained that her testimony in court in 1977 was the worst experience of her life, worse than the rape itself, still to put an end to this attention, Samantha Geimer appeared in court again in person in 2017.[83] She described eloquently that she couldn't take the media spectacle any longer, nor the neverending court drama and asked the judge to drop the case. Judge Scott Gordon not only denied her request but used her own words to do so, ruling: "Her statement is dramatic evidence of the long-lasting and traumatic effect these crimes, and [Polanski's] refusal to obey court orders and appear for sentencing is having on her life." Adding, somewhat cynically, that the court wasn't obliged to dismiss the case "merely because it would be in the victims' best interest."[84]

There was no outcry that his decision could be a massive deterrent for victims to report a rape in the future. On the contrary, at the press conference it was Geimer who was asked how she could face other rape survivors after having spoken out for her rapist in court. She described what she would say to them. "Do the best you can to recover, don't let people tell you you can't recover, don't let people tell you you must be injured to prove that the crime was wrong," she answered, echoing Vanessa Veselka. "You don't have to fall apart to show that what happened to you was wrong."[85]

Samantha Geimer's case is a textbook example of the fact that trauma doesn't just have a personal dimension, but a social and political one as well. And also a very practical one. When Hannah C. Rosenblatt ran away from her abusive home at fifteen she asked the social worker at her school for help: "I described to her what I now call 'trauma burnout': being massively exhausted by lack of sleep and the strain of permanent fear, exacerbated by my distress about suffering from these very symptoms." The social worker didn't notice that the teenage girl with the backpack in front of her needed something to eat and a place to sleep, instead she referred her to a therapist. Rosenblatt declined.

> I hear all the time that traumatized people just don't take the help offered to them. But it isn't just traumatized people that don't accept help or (more often) don't go looking for help . . . Because—news flash—traumatized people often don't just need help that is related to their trauma. Sometimes they need help . . . dealing with Microsoft Office.[86]

Or, in Rosenblatt's case, a hot meal and a friendly ear.

"Critical psychology is based on the understanding that the psychological is not just an individual and inner matter, but the subjective part of the way in which a person has control over their objective living conditions," Brenssell writes, which is why she won't talk about trauma without also talking about social conditions and power relations.[87] If, for example, a person is living in a situation where their boundaries are transgressed regularly, healing will be harder. That applies not only to violent personal relationships but to exploitative working conditions. Healing begins with the most basic things:

> To have stable relationships with friends or a job that pays for food or a secure place to live is also central when it comes to dealing with trauma, as we have learned from studies in war or crisis-stricken countries. A program to repair fishing boats after a tsunami can be better therapy than flying in trauma trainers.[88]

Of course rape can cause trauma, but it does not in itself explain trauma. The way it affects people—or doesn't—is more complex. It has a lot to do with their circumstances, the rest of their lives—but also with social expectations.

4

Black-and-White Thinking

Racism

The so-called Sex Wars of the 1980s saw the US women's movement grapple with the hazardous topic of sexualities and mostly split into two camps, which were given the unfortunate—and ultimately incorrect—labels "sex-positive" and "sex-negative" feminists. The dividing line, although the differences and alliances were a lot more complex, is commonly drawn using two famous quotes of the time: Robin Morgan's "Pornography is the theory, rape is the practice"[1] and Annie Sprinkle's "The answer to bad porn isn't no porn, it's to try and make better porn."[2]

This chapter is about a different "sex war" that split the movement just as effectively—and that was also ignited by the question of rape. This time the divide was race. Angela Davis writes, "If Black women have been conspicuously absent from the ranks of the contemporary anti-rape movement, it may be due, in part, to that movement's indifferent posture toward the frame-up rape charge as an incitement to racist aggression."[3] Indeed, the anti-rape movement of the '70s had often neglected to challenge—and sometimes outright endorsed—racist portrayals of black rapists lusting after the flesh of white women. Much of the anti-rape movement assumed that most rapes were committed by black men, because it was black men who were mostly being convicted for rape. Tragically the (predominantly white) women's movement wasn't able to look at their own position in the tangled web of power relations, and certainly not at their own entitlement. If the men and heroes of the traditionally left-wing student and civil rights movement treated discrimination on gender grounds as a "distraction," so too did the women's movement treat class and race as distractions, and gender as the root and cause of all discrimination.

This became blatantly evident with Susan Brownmiller's treatment of Emmett Till in *Against Our Will*. Till, a black fourteen-year-old from Chicago visiting relatives in Mississippi in 1955, had either flirted with a white woman, Carolyn Bryant; or whistled at her; or done nothing of the kind. The facts are blurry, since witnesses contradicted each other and Bryant later confessed that she had made up most of her testimony. In any case, it is clear that this was the extent of his presumed crime, which prompted Bryant's husband, Roy, and his half-brother, J.W. Milam, to abduct and torture Till before throwing his mutilated body into the Tallahatchie River. His murderers were acquitted by an all-white jury and went free and sold their story with all its gory details for $4,000 to *Look* magazine.[4] "We are rightly aghast that a whistle should be cause for murder," Brownmiller concluded, "but we must also accept that Emmett Till and J. W. Millam [*sic*] shared something in common, they both understood that the whistle ... was a deliberate insult just short of a physical assault, a last reminder to Carolyn Bryant that this black boy, Till, had in mind to possess her."[5] Davis points out, "While Brownmiller deplores the sadistic punishment inflicted on Emmett Till, the black youth emerges, nonetheless, as a guilty sexist—almost as guilty as his white racist murderers. After all, she argues, both Till and his murderers were exclusively concerned about their rights of possession over women."[6]

Brownmiller had included the case in the book to show how, after years of smiling serenely in memory of Emmett Till when black men had wolf-whistled her on the streets, she had now freed herself from her concerns about racism and realized that all that mattered was sexism: Brownmiller was oppressed because she was a woman. End of story. That was bold, to say the least, because the term *sexism* had been coined by the women's movement as an analogy to racism, to show gender/sex as a discriminatory category. But Brownmiller wasn't the first. Shulamith Firestone, five years before, described sexism as the *cause* of racism (as well as imperialism, classism, etc.) in her influential work *The Dialectic of Sex*. According to Firestone, all "races" were part of the family of (wo)man, with the white man as father, the white woman as mother, and their black and brown children. Let's call them Oedipus and Electra. In a theory loosely based on Freud's Oedipus complex, Firestone concluded that the black man was consumed by the wish to kill his father and have sex with his mother, the white woman. But, true to Greek tragedy, his enterprise was doomed, because

> due to his virulent hatred and jealousy of her possessor, the white man, [the black man] may lust after her as a thing to be conquered in order to revenge himself on white man . . . but however he may choose to express this ambivalence, he is unable to control its intensity.[7]

The only alternative to his overwhelming desire for the white woman were: "1. He can give in to the white man on the white man's terms, and be paid off by the white man (Uncle Tom–ism). 2. He can refuse such an identification altogether, at which he often surrenders to homosexuality."[8]

The black woman didn't fare any better. Firestone diagnosed her with the corresponding Electra complex, which meant that she identified with the father and began "to reject the female in herself. (This may be the cause of the greater aggressiveness of the black woman compared with the docility of her white sisters.)"[9] That this sounds outrageous today shows how far we have come. Firestone wasn't a raving racist personally: she simply voiced her society's innate racist projections of the hypersexualized black women and the brutish black devouring white women without questioning them. No wonder a lot of black women didn't feel represented by this feminism, which they perceived as a white middle-class phenomenon.

This conflict really exploded when Eldridge Cleaver, a founding member of the Black Panther Party, claimed in his 1969 book *Soul on Ice* that he had raped white women as a revolutionary act, having first "rehearsed" by raping black women: "Rape was an insurrectionary act. It delighted me that I was defying and trampling on the white man's law, upon his system of values, and that I was defiling his women."[10] Later in the book, he comes to the realization that this had been a tragic misdiagnosis on his part which wasn't just destructive for the victims but also ate up the perpetrators from the inside out. Cleaver ended the book with love letters to his white lawyer and a hymn to reconciliation between black men and women—but no part of his book, or indeed of any book by any contemporary black writer, was quoted as relentlessly as his rape rant, which was read as proof of black men's insatiable and brutal hunger for white womanhood.

The lines had by no means always been drawn between (white) feminists and black civil rights activists. The white author and suffragette Harriet Beecher Stowe was one of the most prominent abolitionists, with her 1852 novel *Uncle Tom's Cabin*, just as the black activist Sojourner Truth became known for her 1851 "Ain't I a Woman" speech, which explicitly made the connection between racism and sexism. In the middle of the nineteenth century, white women saw a lot of parallels between the oppression of slaves and their own situation as their husbands' property, without legal or economic independence or the right to vote. Radical social reformer Abby Kelley wrote, "We have good cause to be grateful to the slave . . . in striving to strike his irons off, we found most surely that we were manacled ourselves."[11] But with the calculated propaganda about black men raping white women en masse, the two were effectively split up.

As Angela Davis notes, the timing of the arrival of this trope after the Civil War tells us all we need to know about what it was used for.

> Throughout the entire Civil War, in fact, not a single black man was publicly accused of raping a white woman. If black men possessed an animalistic urge to rape . . . this alleged rape instinct would have certainly been activated when white women were left unprotected by their men who were fighting in the Confederate Army.[12]

Actually, the first wave of lynching's after the war wasn't justified as retaliation for rape, but simply "as a preventive measure to deter the Black masses from rising up in revolt. At that time, the political function of mob murders was uncamouflaged. Lynching was undisguised counterinsurgency, a guarantee that Black people would not be able to achieve their goals of citizenship and economic equality."[13] But much to the lynchers' surprise, these murders were met with horror and outrage by their white neighbors. There was only one way to make them socially acceptable: by calling them punishment for the ultimate crime. More insidious still, this turned a horrendous crime into a heroic deed and its victims (more than 10,000 in the three-decades after the Civil War alone) into criminals who had only themselves to blame.[14] Diplomat and author Thomas Nelson Page wrote at the time that "the crime of lynching is not likely to cease until the crime of ravishing and murdering women and children is less frequent than it has been of late."[15] The word *rapist* was used for the first time in 1883 in the *National Police Gazette*, in conjunction with the n-word.[16]

As a consequence, fewer and fewer white women spoke out against lynchings. Who would want to defend a rapist? Chattel slavery having been abolished, they redirected their energy into preserving white women's purity: that is, the abolition of prostitution.[17] By the end of the nineteenth century the term "white slavery"—which had hitherto referred to slaves in ancient Rome or indentured servitude—was appropriated and illustrated with images of blonde girls being carried away by black or brown men to work in harems as sex slaves. And because the victims were white, it was the inevitable conclusion that "white slavery" was much worse than real slavery. Victoria Woodhull, who in 1872 had been the first woman to run for the US presidency, declared that she "would rather be the labor slave of a master, with his whip cracking continually about my ears, than the forced sex slave of any man a single hour."[18]

At the beginning of the twentieth century, international treaties were signed against "white slavery" with the expressed aim of discouraging single women from emigrating to America—targeting them with warnings of the sexual hazards that would undoubtedly befall them if they chose to leave their home countries. The fear for the 600,000 girls sold to the sex industry each year—a completely fictitious number—led to the establishment of a new government agency in the United States to control brothels and find white slaves: the Federal Bureau of Investigation, or FBI. By now, it is well documented that white slavery was not nearly as prevalent as it was made out to be—historians call it a "moral panic"—but the idea still lingers.[19]

Thank god that is all over and done with.

Well, let us go back to a night in the not-so-distant past: On January 9, 2016, the cover of the German news magazine *Focus* was a photo of a naked blonde woman, her body covered in smudgy black handprints. The text bar, strategically placed in front of her bare white breasts, read: "Women accuse us, after the sex attacks by migrants: Are we tolerant or already blind?"[20] The same day, the cover of one of the biggest daily newspapers showed an image of a black arm pushing its way up between white legs, with the quote: "Many young Muslims can't deal comfortably with the opposite sex. These are always hypersexualized situations."[21] Of course, those covers were nothing compared to a right-wing Polish weekly that led with an illustration of a blonde woman crying for help as dark arms ripped the only cover off her naked body: the blue and gold European flag. The headline: "The Islamic Rape of Europe."[22]

What happended? 2016 began with reports that, during the New Year's festivities, numerous women had been raped and assaulted in front of the famous Cologne cathedral and in the main train station next door. On January 1, the police received more than a hundred reports, but the figure grew tenfold after the media urged victims to come forward and contact the police. Local, national, and international media reported the incidents intensely and would keep doing so for weeks and months on end. The general feeling at the beginning of 2016 was that hundreds of rapes had been perpetrated on the historic site where, as legend has it, the devil once made a pact with the cathedral's architect. But it soon transpired that the mass rapes had never happened. So again: What happened?

Few crimes have been investigated more thoroughly than the Cologne incidents. More than a hundred police officers formed a special task force for a year, amassing an incredible amount of data. Investigative journalist Walter von Rossum imparted their findings to the public:

> There were around 1,200 reported crimes, most of these petty crimes like stolen mobile phones. Around 500 reports were of a sexual nature, but that doesn't mean rapes. There was no single case of forced intercourse—two such cases were construed, but fell through. Twenty-one reports were sexual assaults, where the attackers tried to or managed to insert fingers into the vaginas of their victims. But the lion's share of the reports cover cases of harassment, usually called groping or kissing without consent.[23]

The information that there were 1,179 fewer rapes than expected wasn't met with relief. On the contrary, Rossum was accused of trivializing sexual violence. Of course, there is no threshold for when rape should be taken seriously. Twenty-one is itself a shocking number. Furthermore situations can be very intimidating even when they are not punishable by law, and it's important to deal with what has happened. But the difference—that it was twenty-one and not hundreds—means that Cologne can no longer be seen as a singular turning point after which nothing would be the same ever again.

An aggravating factor was that most of the assaults—like touching breasts or buttocks—weren't classified as sexual assaults according to German law, but "insults." This led to the strange situation that a whole nation was shocked by a crime that it didn't recognize as a crime by law. Of course, this is only strange if one disregards another factor that every media outlet reported around the clock: namely that the assaults hadn't been perpetrated by someone, but by someone *else*, someone *foreign*. More precisely—although not much more precisely—by men of "Arabic and North African appearance™," as blogger Nadia Shehadeh christened this newly constructed identity.[24] But even though initiatives like *Syrians against Sexism* and *Muslims against Sexism* sprang up immediately and demonstrated in front of the cathedral,[25] since New Year's Eve, people of "Arabic appearance™" have been inseparably linked in the Western mind with sexual threats to (white) women.

After the German Federal Criminal Police Office announced to the press they had "information about a modus operandi in Arabic countries known as *taharrush gamea*," or group sexual harassment in crowds, the term entered German (and, by extension, British and American English).[26] The newspaper *Die Welt* described it as a "phenomenon" that had "long been known in Arabic countries" and now "had arrived in Germany."[27] Iranian-American journalist Alex Shams warned in *Huffington Post*, "Unsurprisingly, the use of an Arabic phrase to describe what was now being thought of as a supposedly Arabic cultural phenomenon spurred commentators across the political spectrum to begin speculating how Arabs had brought it there."[28]

But newspapers just couldn't resist headlines like "The Arab Rape Game," especially since *gamea* looked so similar to *game* (it was pronounced differently, but who knew how to pronounce it anyway?).

In fact *Taharrush gamea* had become internationally known in 2005—though not as a sexual custom, but as police repression against demonstrators occupying Tahrir Square in Cairo. Egyptian feminists like Mariam Kirollos and Noora Flinkman pointed out that the sexual violence there had been a political weapon calculated to demonstrate the power of the state and intimidate protesters, and couldn't be compared to the drunken assaults in Cologne.[29] But hardly anybody took notice, because they were too busy painting a whole region—including many different countries with different laws and different cultural codes—with the same brush. This is what Edward Said described as "orientalism": the denial of differences and the affirmation of an "oriental"—now Islamic—"essence." The stranger behind the bush is back, only now he is the stranger of Arabic appearance™ in front of Cologne Cathedral.

While vigilante groups roamed the streets of Cologne (and other cities in Germany) to "revenge our women," feminists mobilized: "Against sexual violence and racism. Always. #ausnahmslos" (without exception).[30] Within hours, thousands had taken part in the hashtag campaign. Quite a few feminists have learned from the mistakes and blind spots of the 1970s and 1980s, and have taken those lessons to heart:

> Sexual violence shouldn't just be talked about when the perpetrators are the Other, or what we presume to be the Other: Muslim, Arabic,

black or North African men—in short, all those that right-wing populists see as "non-German." And it shouldn't just get attention when the victims are (presumably) white cis women.[31]

Is Multiculturalism Bad for Women?

If femininity has long been coded as being vulnerable and lacking in libido, this is by no means the case for all women. Though fragile femininity was defined as having been "natural" from the beginning of evolution, at the same time it was posited as a result of *civilization,* thus excluding women of color and poor white women. Philosopher Ann Cahill emphasizes that "It is precisely the dominance of a white femininity that has often served to define women of certain ethnicities or classes out of their femininity (and thus, importantly, out of their humanity)."[32]

This becomes glaringly obvious when we look at the contemporary situation of refugees. The danger of encountering sexual violence rises drastically when a person has to flee from war, persecution, or natural or social catastrophes. Teresa Rodriguez of the UN Development Fund for Women declared in 2006: "Rape has become so prevalent that many women take birth control pills or shots before setting out to ensure they won't get pregnant. Some consider rape the 'price you pay for crossing the border.' "[33] The German government's commissioner for the prevention of sexual abuse, Johannes-Wilhelm Rörig, attests that "sexual assaults happen in all refugee shelters" (perpetrated by other refugees, security guards and staff, and even volunteers).[34] Yet those victims don't get nearly as much public empathy as the "victims of New Year's Eve."[35]

This empathy hierarchy doesn't stop there. As philosopher Hilal Sezgin wrote in the immediate aftermath of "Cologne," when the cry went up to send all refugees home:

> Regarding deportation, I'd like to ask all the spontaneous or even long-term feminists who are now clamoring for harder deterrence: do you really want to send men who have committed sexual violence—even under the auspices of a Western democracy—home

> to "their own" women? If there really have been Syrians among the assaulters and rapists, is that your understanding of solidarity with women, to send men like that back to civil-war-torn areas knowing full well that any form of war, civil war, and insurgency increases the occurrence of sexual violence massively?[36]

Jan Phillipp Reemtsma, founder and director of the Hamburger Institut für Sozialforschung, outlines three forms of violence. In a nutshell: "*locating violence* doesn't target the body as body but as moveable mass. The body is in the way and has to be shifted to somewhere else ... *Raptive violence* uses the body to perform some (usually sexual) action upon it. *Autotelic violence* wants to hurt or destroy the body."[37] And just as only violence against certain groups of people is recognized as violence, only certain forms of violence seem to be apprehensible. Thus, locating violence—used to deport refugees or bar them from entering Europe in the first place, which leads to three to four thousand deaths on the Mediterranean each year[38]—can best be enforced and justified by the threat of raptive violence.

Even before "New Year's Eve" there were rumours of refugees that didn't just cross geographical but sexual borders as well. In autumn 2015, Uwe Wappler, then the leading member of far-right party Alternative für Deutschland (AfD), told journalists that a twelve-year-old girl had been raped by refugees in Unterweser but the police had refused to intervene because of "political correctness." Asked by journalists for proof, or even evidence that the crime had occurred, Wappler conceded that "the case somehow doesn't exist."[39] Then came "New Year's Eve." Wappler called for Germans to shoot at groups of foreigners to prevent rapes, a position too far right even for the AfD. But the sentiment if not the demand was shared by crowds of people who took to the streets. Two weeks later, on January 16, 2016, the cousin of thirteen-year-old Lisa, who had presumably been abducted and raped for thirty hours by "a group of Mediterranean-looking men,"[40] spoke at a demonstration of Germany's other far-right party, Nationaldemokratische Partei Deutschlands (NPD, National Democratic Party of Germany), in Berlin-Marzahn. Her tearful voice gave credence to the placards behind her with slogans like "STOP foreign infiltration! Secure borders" and "Rapefugees not welcome."[41] By then, however, it was clear that there had been no rape and no foreigners either. Lisa had run away from home because of problems at school and had hidden in the flat of a (white German) friend.

Of course, it is statistically likely that some refugees commit crimes, some of which may even be rapes. But when white people do the same, only the perpetrator has to answer for the crime and stand trial (if that)—not everybody who looks like them or has the same sized shoes, not even their family. Kin liability was abolished in Germany after fascism because it didn't conform to the principles of constitutional rights. But it seems to be a characteristic of stories about rape that they are read as narratives signifying and creating meaning far beyond the story. As Tanya Horek puts it, "The question of who is represented by, and excluded from, the terms of the body politic, is made plain through images and stories of rape."[42] In the context of the refugee crisis, it's as if the "defiled" body of the rape victim was the body of the country, penetrated by a dark threat. The difference between before and after "New Year's Eve" is that it became normal in mainstream Germany—not just in AfD and other right-wing circles—to discuss whether people from "the Muslim world" pose a threat to equal rights for men and women (though, of course, not all refugees are Muslims and not all Muslims refugees). Such sentiments are not restricted to Germany: a 2016 poll in Britain showed that two-thirds of respondents thought that Islam was not compatible with British values.[43] Not that the UK was able to define British values—as opposed to universal values like democracy, tolerance, and freedom of speech. The most anyone could agree on was that the British have a tendency to be self-deprecating and like to get very drunk.

And similar dynamic played out in the UK in reference to pedophile rings like the Rotherham gang: groups of men found to be grooming and raping vulnerable children and young adults. The news broke in 2012 shortly after the scandal that Jimmy Savile, a well-known white BBC presenter, had been doing precisely the same thing. But that didn't deter groups like the far-right English Defence League (EDL), trying to construct the issue as a clash of civilizations and a problem with "Islam." It was true that the five main perpetrators in the Rotherham case were British-Pakistani men, but it was just as true that a senior EDL member was sent to prison for sexually abusing a ten-year old girl in 2018.[44]

Still, the notion that multiculturalism is bad for women is by no means a new one. In 1997, political philosopher Susan Moller Okin wrote an influential essay titled, "Is multiculturalism bad for women?" Her answer: Yes, definitely. "Western cultures, of course, still practice many forms of sex discrimination," Okin admits, but "while, virtually all of the world's cultures have distinctly patriarchal pasts, some—mostly, though by no means exclusively, Western liberal cultures—have departed far further from these pasts than others."[45]

We often hear that Islam is "backward" or "stuck in the Middle Ages—this does not refer to the actual Middle Ages, though, during which Islamic cultures were much more developed and innovative than Christian ones, but to a fictional Middle Ages halfway back along a fictional arrow of history. This linear model of the development of cultures—with a patriarchal primordial horde at the beginning that develops into women's-rights-loving modern men and women the further they advance—has its roots in colonialism. Colonial nations could best justify themselves by claiming that they brought the colonized not just culture but women's rights. Economist James Mill wrote in 1840 that a culture's level of development could be gauged by the way it treated its women: the more traditional, the more oppressed; the more modern, the more emancipated. This was tricky as the legal and economical position of women would have placed nineteenth-century England into the category of a traditional culture, had the evaluation of this question not been left to the colonial power, who came to the indisputable conclusion: modern.

"Modernity was constructed as a corrective to tradition,"[46] law professor Leti Volpp writes: "Improving the position of women was a component of the civilizing process, along with the rule of law, education, and Christianity. For example, British colonial officials in Egypt specifically invoked the veil and treatment of women under Islam as a justification for colonialism."[47] To this day, non-Muslim Westerners treat the headscarf as a symbol for the subjugation of women in Islam.[48] Sociologist Ali Rattansi calls this the "strong incompatibility thesis"[49] that turns the "migrant victim woman"[50] into the antithesis of the liberated Westerner.

Death by Culture

It is curious that anachronistic concepts like honor are invariably located in "other" cultures, as in "honor killings." Obviously these are very serious crimes, but Rattansi warns:

> If "honor crimes" are treated as separate from other forms of domestic violence, there is a danger of stereotyping minority communities as more accepting of domestic violence, and an unhelpful distinction can become entrenched between crimes of "honor" characteristic of the East and crimes of passion associated with the West, with the added overlay of regarding minority individuals as more determined by "culture" and those from the majority as subjects to individual aberrations.[51]

Accordingly, terms like "honor" and "culture" didn't crop up once in the media coverage of George Bush's 2001 decision to scrap funding for all NGOs that provided abortion counseling or referrals.[52] This "global gag rule" was introduced by Ronald Reagan, repealed by Bill Clinton, reinstated by Bush, re-repealed by Obama, and re-reinstated by Donald Trump. Likewise, after Trump had been voted into office, nobody was afraid that American tourists might import their misogynistic attitude toward women, after all they had a president that boasted he'd "grab them by the pussy" "without waiting for their consent."[53] If we talk about misogyny in the context of Western countries, we do it as a kind of litmus test for general attitudes toward women, and not as a marker for their "specific culture." But after "New Year's Eve" nearly every newspaper reported: "Migration imports archaic views on women."[54]

The conviction that people with Arabic or African appearance™ are more sexist than "we" are is cemented by the assessment of sexual violence in the West or by white Westerners as a crime perpetrated by individuals, but as part of a (sexist) culture if perpetrated by "others." Savile is understood as a lone "bad apple," but the Cologne attackers are understood as "rapefugees." "This is related to the general failure to look at the behavior of white persons as cultural, while always ascribing the label of culture to the behavior of minority groups,"[55] Volpp explains.

Before discussions of the headscarf dominated the media, it was "dowry deaths" in India: the term given to murders of women, usually by pouring kerosene over them and setting them on fire, when their families refuse to pay or cannot pay a higher dowry. Their perpetrators commonly claim such murders are domestic accidents. Dowry deaths are indeed shocking, but they are crimes—not a cultural practice, as they are commonly represented in the Western media. The more appropriate analogy is to understand dowry murders as domestic violence, directly comparable to domestic murders in the United States and the "West," as philosopher Uma Narayan points out. Narayan has calculated that death by domestic violence in the United States is numerically as significant a social problem as dowry murders in India. But only one is used as a signifier of cultural backwardness: "They burn their women there." As opposed to: "We shoot our women here." In Narayan's words, "When 'cultural explanations' are given for fatal forms of violence only in the Third World, the effect is to suggest that Third World women suffer 'death by culture.'"[56]

But cultures aren't cults. They are complex, inconsistent, contradictory, incoherent, heterogenous, and in a constant process of negotiation and change. To suggest otherwise is to use "culture" as a thin cloak for racism. Volpp argues, "Because the Western definition of what makes one human depends on the notion of agency and the ability to make rational choices, to thrust some communities into a world where their actions are determined only by culture is deeply dehumanizing."[57]

Predictably, one of the most controversial facts about my own book when it came out in Germany has been that the statistics simply don't show that migrants commit more crimes, specifically more sexual crimes than other Germans do. Except for breaching migration laws and to some extent theft, a crime that correlates heavily with poverty, people "from somewhere else" are equally likely to break the law than people from "somewhere here." Indeed, criminologist Sandra Bucerius has found that migration actually *lowers* the crime rate of the host country slightly, *but* that "there could be a rise again in the second generation—if there is insufficient integration."[58] This means that exclusionary steps intended to prevent crimes—like banning refugees from New Year's Eve celebrations a year after the events in Cologne—might have the opposite effect. The way forward is not fear on all sides, but more communication.

But instead of facing these challenges head on after "New Year's Eve," the cry for surveillance went up. Even though German police points out that that doesn't prevent assaults, but merely relocates them around the corner. In the meantime not just criminals but everyone else is also being watched, which does something to them too. It makes us watch ourselves, and in the process transform the ordinary gaze into a suspicious one. Surveillance turns us into objects instead of subjects of society. For that reason, sexologist Sophie Roznblatt suggested a different alternative in her southern German hometown. After "New Year's Eve" she started offering consultation hours at a local GP's practice to address the climate of sexual fears on all sides. In a specially designed letterbox people could post their questions and she would answer them once a month—friendly and unagitated but even more importantly without reservations, no matter whether they were about the length of a friend's penis (two meters long! why is mine so small?) or about the perils of masturbation (is that the reason I eat so many gherkins?). Initially started for refugees, Roznblatt is being bombarded by questions and requests from non-refugees as well, because everybody is in dire need for good sexual education. In interviews she says insightful sentences like: "The ones shouting fucky-fucky the loudest, usually feel ashamed soonest and bring flowers as a way of saying sorry."[59] This isn't to say anything so naïve as "education will eliminate rape," rather it is to suggest that creating a healthier sexual climate—one free from shame; one that unpacks questions of honor, trauma, and culture; and one that promotes healthier interactions, sexual and otherwise—is an essential part of demystifying and reducing sexual violence and the harms that surround it.

Rape Culture

Just as education isn't the panacea for all transgressional behaviour, changing a sexual culture doesn't end all rapes but it can change a rape culture. Which leads to the big question: What is "rape culture"? One of #ausnahmslos's most widely criticized statements after the New Year's Eve attacks in Cologne was that "Rape culture wasn't imported to Germany—it has always been here."[60] This does not imply—as it has been misunderstood widely—that rape is worse in Germany than anywhere else, but simply that it doesn't help to condemn rape as something "Muslim men" do or even something "men" do, but that it is necessary to analyze it specifically. While it was hard for some to stomach the idea that it's not just other cultures who are or have a culture, it was even less easy for them to accept that rape doesn't happen in a vacuum. The problem with the words *rape* and *culture* in connection is that they conjure up images of rape as a cultural achievement, like writing books or being good at football. *Rape culture* sounds as if we were proud of rape, which is definitely not the case. No nation would say, "We have the best rapists in the world."

Attitudes toward sexual boundaries are a different matter though. But again: What are these attitudes? Are they sexist song lyrics and rape jokes? Societal messages that advocate traditional gender roles? Are they advertisements with women in miniskirts or advertisements of fully dressed women staying at home with the kids? Are we talking about the fact that many rapes go unpunished or that reproductive rights are still (and again) up for dispute? All of that? None of it? Although the term has entered popular culture with a vengeance in the wake of the Slutwalks and the Indian Besharmi-Morcha movement there is no agreement on what constitutes a "rape culture"—which is not surprising, since "rape" and "culture" are contested concepts as well.[61]

The term *rape culture* first appeared in writing in the 1974 book *Rape: The First Sourcebook for Women* by the New York Radical Feminists.[62] A year later Susan Brownmiller, who was a member of the group, described America in *Against Our Will* as a "rape supportive culture." By that she meant that American culture trivializes, excuses, and glorifies sexual violence. The same year, Margaret Lazarus and Renner Wunderlich released the documentary film *Rape Culture*. In 1978, the term was mentioned in the *Congressional Record*.[63] But even then it was challenged on all sides. Philosopher bell hooks objected to the fact that it treated rape as an isolated phenomenon:

> I believe that violence is inextricably linked to all acts of violence in this society that occur between the powerful and the powerless, the dominant and the dominated ... So far the feminist movement has primarily focused on male violence, and as a consequence lends credibility to sexist stereotypes that suggest men are violent, women are not; men are abusers, women are victims. This type of thinking allows us to ignore the extent to which women (with men) in this society accept and perpetuate the idea that it is acceptable for a dominant party or group to maintain power over the dominated by using coercive force.[64]

Despite her reservations, hooks contributed to the 2004 anthology *Transforming a Rape Culture,* which defined the term in its introduction as a culture that "condones physical and emotional terrorism against women and presents it as the norm."[65]

But that would let Germany—and most countries—off the hook. Certainly nobody condoned what had happened in Cologne. When performance artist Milo Moiré posed naked in front of the cathedral with a placard announcing: "We are not fair game, even when we are naked!!!"[66] the media duly gathered and applauded her efforts: Well done, tell them to stop raping! Nobody apart from Norman Mailer would seriously maintain: "A little bit of rape is good for a man's soul."[67] Therefore blogger FlightScarlet confessed: "I'm not sure that I agree that people simply aren't being told not to rape. It seems like it's everywhere: in the media, in schools, in universities."[68]

Especially in universities. American universities have gone further in their efforts to eradicate rape culture than institutions anywhere else.

Still, in 2014, the oldest anti-rape organization in the United States, Rape, Abuse and Incest National Network (RAINN), urged a White House task force to overhaul colleges' treatment of rape:

> In the last few years, there has been an unfortunate trend toward blaming "rape culture" for the extensive problem of sexual violence on campuses. While it is helpful to point out the systemic barriers to addressing the problem, it is important to not lose sight of a simple fact: rape is caused not by cultural factors but by the conscious decisions, of a small percentage of the community, to commit a violent crime.[69]

This statement stirred up a hornets' nest. "RAINN Denounces, Doesn't Understand the Concept of 'Rape Culture,'" thundered Amanda Marcotte on behalf of "all feminists" in *Slate*.[70] Caroline Kitchens, identifying herself just as much as a feminist as Marcotte, countered in *TIME*: "On college campuses, obsession with eliminating 'rape culture' has led to censorship and hysteria." Activists at Wellesley, she added, had recently demanded that administrators remove a statue of a sleepwalking man because, they said, the image of a nearly naked man "could 'trigger' memories of sexual assault for victims."[71]

These examples aren't plucked out of thin air but represent different approaches to the problem. One camp has a very wide definition of rape culture and sees the task of stamping it out as very large; the opposing camp only looks at rape and assault, dismissing attempts to examine the role of culture as ridiculous. And both accuse each other of "victim-blaming" and "paranoia," respectively. That the fight is being fought at and over universities is no coincidence. American universities have become a microcosm of the way our understanding of rape culture can inform our actions.

Many readers will be familiar with the *New York* magazine cover featuring Emma Sulkowicz, better known as "Mattress Girl" because she carried her mattress wherever she went, with the aim of getting her alleged rapist expelled from Columbia University. Sulkowicz's

Mattress Performance (Carry That Weight) was accepted as her senior thesis at Yale. *Artnet* called it "one of the most important artworks of the year"; New York senator Kirsten Gillibrand invited Sulkowicz to President Obama's 2015 State of the Union address.[72] By that time, the name of the accused student had been written on bathroom walls. He was known all over campus as a rapist and crowds of protesters carried mattresses into one of his classes. While the university admitted that "life at Columbia had become unbearable for him," the administration didn't intervene, even though its investigation had cleared him of all charges.

This is not to say that Sulkowicz's allegations were wrongful. Who am I to judge? I wasn't there, and sexual transgressions are a lot messier than some would have us believe. Sulkowicz definitely had a grievance and I understand that she wanted to act upon it. What I don't understand is the university that established the accused party's innocence and then did not intervene in the aftermath.

Much of this controversy on campuses centers around what is known as Title IX, part of the Civil Rights Act. It is a federal statute to address gender discrimination and funding for women's sports. In 2011, the Department of Education's Office for Civil Rights sent out a quaintly named "Dear Colleague Letter" which expanded the mandate to encompass sexual misconduct.[73] Suddenly, everybody could or couldn't be accused under Title IX. Cases of students charged for sexual assault for kissing their partners as they slept (because there could be no consent if the other party was sleeping) were just as common as rape charges *not* being pursued. But most importantly the charge of sexual harassment and misconduct was not limited to *sexual actions* alone. Hence Laura Kipnis, a media studies professor at Northwestern University, has been investigated under Title IX twice: first for writing an essay, then for writing a book about the first Title IX investigation. She won the first case—a feat in itself because, as she writes,

> The low standard of proof demanded by the Department of Education in Title IX cases ("preponderance of evidence") is inherently unfair to the accused. The preponderance issue may sound

> obscure, but if you're one of the *25 million or so people* working or studying on an American campus—a not insignificant chunk of the population—it's the standard of proof that will apply if or when you're accused of something. In other words, 50.01 percent certainty of guilt ("Fifty-fifty plus a feather" is how our university's Title IX officer put it). Note that being accused doesn't mean you've actually done anything, but given the low bar for a guilty finding and the utter capriciousness of the process, an accusation itself pretty much suffices to constitute preponderance.[74]

Before the "Dear Colleague" letter, US universities were notorious not only for not following up on reports but for actively discouraging claimants from going to the police.[75] Thus the Department of Education and the universities are trying to remedy a real problem here by taking on board the ideas of (part of) the women's movement, like turning the burden of proof around and protecting victims. The problem is that these ideas have never before been put to the test. Title IX is a kind of social experiment on a grand scale and like so many other social experiments, it tends toward the extreme. Kipnis notes that

> typically the accusee doesn't know the precise charges, doesn't know what the evidence is, and can't confront witnesses. Many campuses don't even allow the accusee to present a defense such as introducing text messages from a complainant that contradict his or her statements.[76]

If this sounds Kafkaesque, then this is because it is. The feeling of helplessness, and of being at the mercy of a power that refuses to recognize one as a person worthy of empathy, is not going away, it is just being shifted around.

Given the history of rape on campus, it is important to act, but carefully. This is sensitive territory. But when Secretary of Education Betsy DeVos, announced in September 2017 she would rescind portions of Title IX to ensure a fair process for the accuser and the accused, the hashtag #StopBetsy was trending within hours and the *Washington*

Post ran the headline: "Betsy DeVos's Title IX Interpretation Is an Attack on Sexual Assault Survivors." Though DeVos had explicitly stressed that "every survivor of sexual misconduct must be taken seriously," she also added that "every student accused of sexual misconduct must know that guilt is not predetermined."[77]

To be clear, it is justified to be on your guard when far-right people like DeVos speak up for civil rights—as she proved with her February 2018 announcement that the Department of Education would no longer pursue civil rights complaints filed by trans students, because "Title IX prohibits discrimination on the basis of sex, not gender identity."[78] But why is a fair process for the accused equated to an unfair process for the accuser? And is the opposite necessarily true? Does handling Title IX complaints this way benefit survivors?

The answer is no, no matter which way we look at it. The number of complaints has not gone down, nor is there a greater subjective feeling of security. In fact, as Jennifer Doyle documents, the framework of risk and risk assessment that accompanies Title IX legislation and its implementation has increased a sense of insecurity on campus:

> I was struck by the hardening between the harmful ways in which the system was behaving around my own case in the name of protecting me: an escalation of my fear and sense of threat, an increase of the securitization of my workplace and the presentation of me as a kind of security problem.[79]

But perhaps most importantly, the premise on which most Title IX investigations are conducted doesn't break at all with the gender scripts of women as passive recipients of men's violent desires. As a result, they are paternalistic toward women in the name of "protecting them." One example DeVos recounted in her speech was "a recent case in which the University of Southern California disbelieved a female student's insistence that she had merely 'roughhoused' with her boyfriend, and expelled him for his alleged abuse over her objection."[80] This has become possible because of "third-party complaints"—not only injured parties but literally anybody can file a Title IX complaint, making the whole process even more complicated. When is it right to intervene? When do we have to take a person's word for it that they know best about their (sex) life? Kipnis cites a case of a male student who had consensual sex with a female student. But a friend found a love bite on her neck and reported her lover to the Title IX commission, where she stated repeatedly that the sex had been consensual, but wasn't believed. "The accused student, who was black, by the way, and attending school on an athletic scholarship, received a multi-year suspension, effectively ending his college career."[81] There is also the infamous pepper-spray-cop incident that became an internet meme in 2011. The video shows a group of students peacefully protesting at the University of California at Davis during the Occupy movement. The students had planned on spending the night on the campus quad. When they wouldn't leave Lt. John Pike doused them with pepper spray. The College's defence was that older black men had been seen in the vicinity and they wanted to protect the students. As always when it's about sexual assault, race comes into play sooner or later.

Not being outside the system, administrators' ideas about gender and power mirror social convictions about sex and sex roles (a very simplistic top-down model: Who has power? Only men. Who lacks it? All women). Kipnis traces in Title IX discourse what should by now be familiar tropes: "metaphors veer toward the extractive rather than additive—sex takes something *away* from you, at least if you're a woman: your safety, your choices, your future." She argues that

> shifting the stress from pleasure to danger and vulnerability not only changes the prevailing narrative, it changes the way sex is experienced. We're social creatures, after all, and narrative is how we make sense of the word. If the prevailing story is that sex is dangerous, sex is going to feel threatening more of the time, and anything associated with sex, no matter how innocuous (a risqué remark, a dumb joke) will feel threatening.[82]

She continues with a provocative question:

> Why treat sexual assault as the paradigmatic female experience when there are plenty of other female experiences in which women's embodied, physiological differences from men materially impede gender equality? . . . Instead, all historical inequities between the genders have been relocated to the sexual sphere and displaced onto sexual danger.[83]

The problem is that this makes sexuality the essence of a woman, more essential than any other aspect of her being. The fight against sexual harassment is therefore a fight for women's souls. There is something of the Western frontier spirit in that narrative. This could be one reason why rape activism has been and remains so central for the women's movement in America. While rape activism has been and remains important in Europe, it is generally on par with other agendas, for example reproductive rights and childcare provisions. As Kipnis points out, "While European feminists with a social democratic tradition behind them were demanding and getting subsidized day care, winning resources from the state and employers . . . every American mother still has to figure out for herself what to do with the kids while she's at work."[84]

Trigger Warnings versus Free Speech

I was recently invited to a German university to speak about rape. Halfway through the discussion, I learned that one of the students had gone to her supervisor before my talk, told him she had experienced sexual violence, and asked for permission to leave class if anything triggered her. He not only told her off but also commented to another professor—the one who had invited me—that the student had apparently chosen the wrong subject (social science). The other professor was outraged and assured the student that she could leave any time she chose.

A good part of the discussion that day centered on the question of triggers and safe spaces—are they a danger to free speech or a necessary implement to make people stop and think before they tell students off for looking after themselves? I am happy to report that the student didn't feel it necessary to leave. I'd rather write a hundred trigger warnings that I might find redundant than step on anybody's toes. But sometimes there is no right way to talk about rape. We have to go on doing it in many different wrong ways until we find the right one and deal with all sorts of feelings—other people's and our own. Sometimes a trigger warning is a sign of consideration, and sometimes one of condescension. Roxane Gay, self-proclaimed "bad feminist," writes,

> Many feminist communities use trigger warnings, particularly in online forums when discussing rape, sexual abuse, and violence. By using these warnings, these communities are saying, "This is a safe space. We will protect you from unexpected reminders of your history." Members of these communities are given the illusion they *can* be protected ... I don't believe people can be protected from their histories. I don't believe it is at all possible to anticipate the histories of others. There is no standard for trigger warnings, no universal guidelines. Once you start, where do you stop? Does the mention of the word "rape" require a trigger warning, or is the threshold an account of rape? How graphic does an account of abuse need to be before meriting a warning? ... When I see a trigger warning I think, *How dare you presume what I need to be protected from?*[85]

Because it's not just descriptions of rape that can trigger PTSD symptoms. For Gay, triggers include:

> When I see men who look like him or his friends ... When I smell Polo cologne. When I hear a harsh laugh ... When I go through security at the airport and am pulled aside for extra screening, which seems to happen every single time ... When I see a young girl of a certain age.[86]

What, then, to do? Forbid all young girls to attend Gay's classes at Purdue University? That's obviously nonsense. "Life, apparently, requires a trigger warning," Gay concludes. "This is the uncomfortable truth: everything is a trigger for someone."[87] The good news is that it's not themes that trigger PTSD most of the time, but the way we talk about them and listen (or don't listen). We can't avoid triggering other people or being triggered by them, but we can try to create an environment where we can deal with that respectfully.

Like most tools, trigger warnings can be useful, as can be fair titles (for articles or talks) so that people know in advance what they will be faced with and can make their own decisions. But these are decisions people can only make for themselves. Trying not to trigger anyone by avoiding certain themes isn't just useless—as we can't know what triggers someone—but dangerously patronizing. Having control over our bodies and lives is an acquired skill. We learn by thinking and talking and reading about it. Kipnis fears that with Title IX, "what's being lost, along with job security, is the ability to publish ideas that go against the grain or take unpopular positions." Having been subjected to two Title IX investigations on the basis of her written work, it's hard to argue with her. "Factor in the accusatory mania and the intellectual incursions of the Title IX troops, and self-censorship rules the land."[88]

The higher education regulator in the UK decided in October 2017 to fine universities for "no-platforming" speakers with unpopular opinions, or refusing to allow them to speak. This is a controversial policy, and my citing it here should not be read as a wholesale endorsement. Rather, it is to note that if what has been described so far represents what Kipnis has deemed a kind of censorship, there is pushback. Vice Chancellor Louise Richardson at Oxford University argues, in favor of the new policy,

> We need to expose students to ideas that make them uncomfortable so that they can think about why it is that they feel uncomfortable and what it is about those ideas that they object to. And then to have the practice of framing a response and using reason to counter these objectionable ideas and to try and change the other person's mind and to be open to having their own minds changed.[89]

Empathy versus Hierarchy

In a move that may surprise the disgruntled reader, I now want to make the case for the concept of rape culture. While I don't agree with the approach of looking for it in individual actions, songs, or people and trying to exorcise it by expelling them—ejecting them from the body politic in a move that mirrors calls for deportations for the refugee-criminals of "Cologne"—I think the concept is very valuable when applied to systems.

We can't stamp out rape culture by coming down hard on one side or the other—the alleged perpetrator or the victim. To do so is to leave intact a hierarchical system that has little regard for people's feelings and borders. Rape doesn't happen in a vacuum and isn't predestined genetically, but can be promoted or diminished—like all cultural acts—by cultural messages and norms. Rape culture is at the same time a lot more complex and a lot simpler than we think. There are cultural scripts that promote rape and others that oppose it. However, it is neither necessary nor useful to censor individual expressions or statements expressly because they are part of a structure. Structures have to be addressed structurally. Sociologist Gerlinda Smaus, who did an extensive study of prison rape, writes,

> The most important finding of our study which we didn't expect and definitely didn't try to prove, was that rape is a result of a social space and not of individuals. We didn't use the term *situation*, because we wanted to avoid the conclusion that it was just a question of the right opportunity to commit sexual violence. Rather we were referring to the institutional context that not just allows the practice of rape but actually encourages it.[90]

Psychologist John Pryor came to the same conclusion. In the so-called Pryor test he assessed the tendency of a test subject to harass. Indicators were: a lack of empathy, a belief in traditional gender sex roles, a tendency toward dominance/authoritarianism, but mainly that the environments had a huge effect. These environments were for example prisons but also boarding schools, private security services, and above all the military.

One recruit remembers his first days in the US Marine Corps boot camp: "From the moment one arrives, the drill instructors begin a torrent of misogynistic and anti-individualistic abuse." He was taught that

> good things are manly and collective; the despicable are feminine and individual. Virtually every sentence, every description, every lesson embodies this sexual duality, and the female anatomy provides a rich field of metaphor for every degradation. When you want to create a solidary [*sic*] group of male killers, that is what you do, you kill the woman in them.[91]

That obviously doesn't mean that women are from Venus and men are from Mars, but that character traits and emotions are gendered just as much as bodies are. And one of the most gendered emotions is, after all, empathy. If research on rape has achieved anything, it has shown that a lack of empathy makes it easier for one person to disregard another person's sexual and other boundaries. In its extreme form, being unable to feel empathy is a prerequisite for becoming a psychopath.[92]

But lack of empathy is not men's domain alone. In 2004, US soldier Lynndie England became a household name after photos were leaked from Abu Ghraib prison in Iraq that showed the US military and intelligence service using torture during the Iraq War. The most famous of these photos were of Lynndie England, at that time a specialist in the US Army. In one she is dragging a naked man along on a leash; in another she is shown pointing to the penis of a naked prisoner who was forced to masturbate. The public was appalled and mesmerized at the same time.

> On the internet, civilian men and women posted photographs of themselves "doing a Lynndie." Detailed internet instructions on "doing a Lynndie" start with the phrase: "Find a victim who deserves to be 'Lynndied,'" "Make sure you have a friend nearby with a

camera ready to capture the 'Lynndie,'" "Stick a cigarette (or pen) in your mouth and allow it to hang slightly below the horizontal" ... "point in the direction of the victim and smile." The smile was important: it bestowed individuality and agency, in contrast with the degraded and objectified "victim."[93]

The media—who couldn't deal with the fact that a woman was doing these abarations—called her "a 'phallic female,' 'tomboyish,' a 'leash-girl,' who turned out to be 'something other than a natural lady.'"[94] But England was by no means the only woman implicated. In the dog-leash photo she is accompanied by Private Megan Ambuhl. Specialist Sabrina Harman had her picture taken, laughing and giving a thumbs-up, next to the body of Manadel al-Jamadi, an Iraqi who had been tortured to death, as well as next to a "pyramid" of naked prisoners with plastic bags over their heads.

In fact, there is a military term for torture that entails women performing sexual acts on male prisoners: "invasion of space by a female." American soldier Kayla Williams, also stationed in Iraq, details an incident in which a prisoner was brought into the interrogation room, where a soldier undressed the man and told her to mock his genitals and "remind him that he is being humiliated in the presence of a blonde American female."[95]

As these bizarre humiliations couldn't be accounted for by personal sadism, Cuban-American artist Coco Fusco started to research them for a performance and book project.[96] She writes:

> The most widely circulated theory that has emerged to explain why these tactics have been implemented—that intelligence experts latched on to outdated Orientalist views of Arab men as sexually vulnerable in the scramble to extract actionable intelligence as quickly as possible—is supported by interrogator accounts of how lectures on the so-called "Arab mind" were integrated into their training once the insurgency began.[97]

It might be hard for civilians to imagine using one's body to sexually humiliate another person on orders, but the moment a person enters the military, they surrender the right of self-determination over their bodies. Fusco recounts:

> When I asked a few young women who had served how they felt about being asked to use their sexuality as part of their patriotic duty, they seemed to have difficulty understanding the question, or perhaps they thought it was too sensitive to answer.[98]

Similarly, during the Vietnam War, male soldiers were urged to "search" female prisoners with their penises.[99] During that war the number of female soldiers being raped by their comrades rose tenfold, from 3 percent to 30 percent.[100]

This is not to say that only the military has or is a rape culture, but that it can function as a kind of Milgram-test[101] for social structures or groups: the less empathy, and especially empathy with oneself, a society allows, the less its members can respect other people's boundaries. "Some anthropologists have even suggested that the frequency of rape in a particular society can be predicted by looking at that society's propensity to engage in battle,"[102] adds Bourke. A basic rule of thumb is: If an institution or a community is hierarchical and favors rigid gender roles, its members are more at risk of sexual violence than members of a society that is more equal (in relation to, but by no means restricted to, gender). Gerlinda Smaus concludes:

> Nobody questions that rape is reprehensible. Looking at all the data, though, it doesn't differ fundamentally from the detrimental structure of the hierarchical communication itself, where the will of the dominated (party) doesn't count, only the will of the dominator. Hierarchical command structures are the opposite of consensual communication where decisions are negotiated collectively.[103]

This suggests that social equity, gender equality, balance, consent, respect, and nonviolent communication—outside of the sexual sphere as much as within it—are direct ways to prevent sexual violence.

5

Omissions: Men, Masculinity, and Myths

The Gendered Grammar of Violence

In 1542, geographer and mystic Sebastian Franck wrote that the natives of the island of Hispaniola (today Haiti and the Dominican Republic) "raped everyone."[1] What he meant by this startling claim was that they revolted against Christopher Columbus. Cultural historian Angela Koch comments, "It is interesting that *rape* is used in the context of revolt and not in the preceding chapter where Columbus and his brother oppress and tyrannize the islanders."[2] The reason for this was that their oppression was *legal* force (in Franck's eyes), while the revolt against it was *illegal*. "That implies . . . that rape still denotes an act aimed at one's own community or authority."[3] Like the rape of a country—or the rapes on "New Year's Eve in Cologne."

Language does a lot more than just express the legality or illegality of force. Professor for literature, Sharon Marcus shows how our cultural narratives turn penises into omnipotent weapons with just one aim: to enter the vulnerable inner space of women, who—being defenseless—are at the mercy of this assault.[4] This is quite a linguistic feat, given that penises are by no means raised in attack all the time. On the contrary, they are usually rather fragile and dependent on the ebb and flow of erection. Above all, they are a lot more vulnerable than vulvas, before we even consider testicles.

In her history of rape, Joanna Bourke recalls that "empirical studies consistently show that an extremely large proportion of rapes are 'attempted' not 'completed.' The targeted victim fights or frightens the man off." Moreover, rapists face resistance not just from their victims but from their own bodies.

> For instance, over one-third of men convicted for sexual assault and sent to the Massachusetts Center for the Diagnosis and Treatment of Sexually Dangerous Persons suffered some kind of sexual dysfunction during the attack. Impotence (16 percent of these criminals) and retarded ejaculation (15 percent) were particularly common. This is likely to be a conservative estimate since dysfunction was inapplicable in one-fifth of these cases (because the victim successfully resisted, penetration was not attempted, or the assault was interrupted). Only a quarter of the rapists reported *no* physiological dysfunction during their rape. None of the offenders reported similar dysfunction in their consensual sexual relationships.[5]

Why is it, then, that we never hear these stories? How would it transform the public space if, for every psychopathic super-rapist in news coverage or TV dramas, we also got a story about uncooperative penises and fleeing attackers? No doubt there are dangerous people and situations where resistance leads only to more violence and bigger injuries, but in *no way as often* as we have been told. Virginie Despentes argues that these narratives are not just one-sided but actually teach women how to be raped:

> From the instant I realized what was happening, I was convinced they [the attackers] were the stronger ones. A question of focus. Looking back on it, I am convinced that if they'd been trying to steal our jackets instead, my reaction would have been different. I wasn't rash, but often reckless. But at that precise moment I felt female, disgustingly female, in a way I had never felt, and have never felt since.[6]

And being female means to live with the rape-sword of Damocles over one's head, while men carry their swords between their legs. Susan Brownmiller has called rapists "terrorist guerillas in the longest sustained battle the word has ever known."[7] Sexual violence as the triumph of man's power over woman is a trope in rape narratives. However, Hannah Arendt argued that violence signifies neither triumph nor power but powerlessness. Because power needs *consensus*—even the most despotic system can only continue in the long run if enough people benefit from it—violence arises out of the cracks of power. Violence is capable of destroying power, but unable to create it.[8] Which is why Joanna Bourke concludes: "Rapists are not patriarchy's 'storm troopers', they are its inadequate spawn."[9]

Still, the media stylizes rapists as antiheroes who dominate public attention as hypnotically as they dominate their victims. The archetypal rapist is Jack the Ripper, who—as far as we know—was neither a rapist nor called Jack. Police files from 1888 simply called him the "Whitechapel murderer" or the "Whitechapel fiend"[10]—he got his personal and more lurid moniker only after a letter signed "Jack the Ripper" arrived at the Central News Agency gloating over the most recent murder and the impotence of the police.[11] The letter was soon debunked as a fraud, probably done by a journalist working for said Central News Agency. But the name stuck because it—together with Jack's top hat and Dracula cloak, for which there is no historical evidence either—gave him a unique aura of authority and evil. "Over the past hundred years, the Ripper murders have achieved the status of a modern myth of male violence against women," argues historian Judith R. Walkowitz, "a story whose details have become vague and generalized, but whose 'moral' message is clear: the city is a dangerous place for women, when they transgress the narrow boundaries of home and hearth and dare to enter the public space."[12]

In point of fact there is more uncertain about Jack the Ripper than there is certain: Who was he? Why did he do what he did? Was he a he? Even how many murders he committed is still a matter of debate. Researchers agree that five of the bodies were the victims of the same killer—Mary Ann Nichols, Annie Chapman, Elizabeth Stride, Catherine Eddowes, and Mary Jane Kelly: the "canonical five." More murders were attributed to Jack the Ripper; at least one of those—the murder of Fairy Fay—was pure gothic fantasy. Fay never existed. The "canonical five" were all murdered between August and November 1888 in the East End of London, four of them in the narrow alleys between Flower Street and Dean Street, Victorian London's last slum. Eddowes's body was found just west of those, on

Mitre Square. Because the victims had all worked at least part-time as prostitutes and because the killer used a knife on their vaginas and by the second murder had started to remove the uterus and other organs, "Jack" was seen as a sex fiend and his knife as a surrogate penis. The murders became sex crimes and thus even more captivating for the public, who had been looking at Whitechapel with an explosive mixture of bad conscience and fear long before the Ripper came along.

In the 1880s, huge demonstrations of East End unemployed and day laborers had shaken the West End. In 1886, the windows of a Pall Mall club were stoned and a couple of shops looted. In response, the police banned any demonstrations for the next year and a half, which culminated in "Bloody Sunday" in November 1887, when ten thousand demonstrators—among them writer and feminist Annie Besant, designer William Morris, playwright George Bernard Shaw, and editor of *Freedom* newspaper Charlotte M. Wilson—marched on Trafalgar Square and were brutally attacked by the Metropolitan Police and the British Army. When the Ripper murders started the following summer, they confirmed the West London middle classes' perception of Whitechapel as a pit of evil populated by prostitutes and criminals. Suffragists had begun concentrating on the living conditions in Whitechapel in their fight against the infamous Contagious Diseases Act, which blamed and prosecuted sex workers for the spread of venereal diseases.

A prominent figure of the time was Josephine Butler, who had campaigned for Britain to support the abolition of slavery during the US Civil War, and worked with various charities for sex workers ever since. Like her American colleagues, Butler believed in the "moral panic" of "white slavery," although it has to be said that she tried to help women suffering from venereal disease and tuberculosis in a hands-on way by providing shelter in her own home and nursing them herself. In 1885, Butler met up with the editor of the *Pall Mall Gazette*, W.T. Stead, and convinced him to write a series of articles about "white slavery," which were published that summer under the title "Maiden Tribute of Modern Babylon" and in turn caused a "moral panic."[13] The series

> documented in lurid detail how poor daughters of the people were trapped and drugged in padded cells and sold to upper-class rakes for the sum of five pounds. Stead's revelations forced the passage of the Criminal Law Amendment Act of 1885, which not only raised the age of consent for girls from thirteen to sixteen, but also gave police far greater powers to prosecute streetwalkers and brothel-keepers. It also made "indecent" acts between consenting male adults illegal, forming the basis of legal proceedings against homosexuals until 1967.[14]

All over Britain, vigilance committees sprang up to patrol the red-light districts and attack theaters, music halls, and street walkers. "Thus, in the three years preceeding the Ripper murders, a massive political initiative against non-marital, non-reproductive sexuality had been mobilized, whose initial victims were working-class prostitutes, precisely those women who had been the original objects of feminist pity and concern."[15]

During Jack the Ripper's rise to media antihero, even more "saviors" of innocent maidens roamed the streets and menaced women and Jews (because of the widespread theory that Jack might really be "Jacob the Ripper," which lent a flavor of ritual murders to the crimes).[16] So in turn, the market women of Spitalfields started to chase upper-class gentleman-Ripper-tourists. But as beloved and bemoaned as the victims were at home, outside of Whitechapel the murders were seen as moral lessons about the wages of sin. The *Pall Mall Gazette* described the murdered women as "drunken, vicious, miserable wretches whom it was almost a charity to relieve of the penalty of existence."[17] The *Evening Standard* warned "respectable women" of the dangers of sexuality and public space likewise (after all "public woman" was a synonym for prostitute).[18] But nobody was as ruthless as the social reformer Canon Barnett when he observed that the "'disorderly and depraved lives of the women' . . . were more 'appallin'" than the actual murders."[19] "Men like Barnett finally manipulated public opinion and consolidated it behind razing the common lodging houses of the Flower and Dean street area," showed Walkowitz.[20] "The Rothschild Buildings (1892), for respectable

Jewish artisans and their families, appeared over the site of the lodging houses where Catherine Eddowes and Elizabeth Stride once lived." Even though social researcher Charles Booth's survey of 1889 had proven that the criminal element of the population of Whitechapel was actually quite small and much less representative than the sensational press claimed.

The term for this kind of media coverage is *fear mongering*. It is characterized by exaggerating and repeating certain contents to influence the public sentiment. "Jack the Ripper" was the first serial killer to trigger a worldwide media hysteria, and motivated the establishment of his own literary genre and historical discipline: "ripperature" and "ripperology."[21] As the prototype of the *über*-criminal who can strike anywhere and at any time, he has an enormous impact on reporting about sensational crimes even to this day. And such reporting has an impact. Forensic psychiatrist Dr. Park Dietz, who has analyzed the media's handling of mass murderers for twenty years, points out that "I have repeatedly told CNN and other media if you don't want to propagate more mass murderers don't start the story with sirens blaring. Don't have photographs of the killer. Don't make this 24/7 coverage. Do everything you can not to make the body-count the lead story. Not to make the killer some kind of anti-hero. Do localize the story to the effected community and make it as boring as possible in every other market. Because every time we have intense saturation coverage of a mass murder we expect to see one or two more in the next week."[22]

Not sensationalizing crimes is good media advice in the case of rape as well—and is just as routinely disregarded. Media coverage of the Cologne incident was rife with Ripperisms. Mayor Henriette Reker made international headlines for advising women to keep an arm's length away from any stranger. Reker apologized a few days later. But she was by no means the only one who'd speculated whether public space or sexuality were safe for women at all. Even the vigilante committees had a comeback, only now they were called Home Guard. The subliminal and not-so-subliminal message was that sex benefits men and harms women, that men are safe and women are not—that danger has a gender.

Now we know that our society constructs women as objects of violence and men as subjects of violence: *A man (subject) hurts a woman (object)*. Less well known but in no way less relevant is that women are presented as subjects of fear and men as objects of fear: *A woman (subject) fears a man (object)*. Sharon Marcus writes:

> Even though women in fact are neither the sole objects of sexual violence nor the most likely targets of violent crimes, women constitute the majority of fearful subjects; even in situations where men are empirically more likely to suffer from violent crimes, they express less fear then women do and tend to displace this fear into concern for their mothers, sisters, wives, daughters.[23]

She calls the rules and regularities that assign each of us our position in these narratives the "gendered grammar of violence," noting that "to take male violence or female vulnerability as the first and last instances in any explanation of rape is to make the identities of rapist and raped preexist the rape itself."

When making political demands, it seems necessary to postulate the special vulnerability of women (and children) and by extension their special need for protection. But this is a double-edged sword: by defining a political subject as vulnerable (and thereby worthy of protection, but at the same time needing protection) we take away their status as subject and make them into an object to be protected. "To experience the body as itself essentially weak is to necessitate placing it under constant surveillance,"[24] Ann Cahill points out: a catch-22.

But, after all, human bodies are vulnerable. It's the shock of noticing one's own vulnerability, and realizing that protection is always relative and never absolute, that has historically led to the allocation of this universal vulnerability only to certain bodies—bodies perceived as female, or racialized bodies that have to be "saved" (from their primitive state, from their oppressive fathers/husbands, etc.) and so on. This opens up a difference between bodies in need of protection (vulnerable) and protecting/controlling bodies (invulnerable), as if it were impossible to be both at the same time, whereas humans are always everything: needy and self-determining, autonomous and dependent, and everything in between.

That's why philosopher Judith Butler calls for a redifinition of vulnerability: to stop seeing it as a characteristic of the other, but rather as an integral part of the self—a self that, by recognizing its own vulnerability, becomes able to have empathy for other people's vulnerability without turning them into objects (of protection). In an analogy to the platitude that "you can only truly love other people when you love yourself," Butler declares that we can only truly feel empathy for others when we are allowed empathy with ourselves. This turns vulnerability from a weakness into a resource that makes us profoundly human.[25]

Missing Victims

This book started with the numbers that everybody knows: 90 percent of all rape victims are female and 90 percent of perpetrators are male. But what do these figures really tell us when we look at them more closely?

Until the 1970s, surveys didn't even ask men if they had ever been sexually harassed or raped. When these questions were first included, a surprisingly high number of men reported they had experienced sexual violence. But that is so alien to our worldview that an internet image search for "rape victim" produces solely images of female victims. Only after scrolling down for a long, long time do images of men start appearing—that is, images of perpetrators, potential perpetrators, and politicians—but still no male victims.

In 1988, a study examined gender bias in rape cases. The researchers told the subjects they were testing to what extent a jury's decision was informed by the evidence, then related a "true case" of a student who had been raped at gunpoint while hitchhiking. When the police apprehended the car, they found the gun and arrested the driver. At the trial, the driver admitted there had been sexual intercourse but claimed it had been consensual.

The test subjects were asked to fill out a "jury questionnaire" and rate the probability of the driver forcing the student or whether it was the student who initiated sex, how pleasurable the act might have been for the driver and the student respectively, what length of prison sentence they'd find appropriate, and so on. What they didn't know was that they had been divided into four groups, each of which had been told a different version of the same "case": in the first group the driver ("rapist") was male and the student ("victim") female, in the second group both were male, in the third both female, and in the fourth the driver was female and the student male.

Almost all subjects agreed that the driver was guilty, but when the student was female the crime was assumed to have been a lot more serious than when the student was male. The fourth group (thinking the driver was female and student male) was the most likely to assume that the student had initiated sexual contact, enjoyed it more than in any other combination, and was least traumatized by it (versus most traumatized if the student was female). In accordance with these judgments, they asked for the highest sentences when the victim was female and the lowest when the victim was male.[26] Another study found that 40 percent of male test subjects presumed that if a man was raped by a woman, he "was to blame for being careless or for not escaping."[27] That research also found that 35 percent of men and 22 percent of women were convinced that a man didn't mind being raped by a woman.

But even experts can be caught in the gender trap. Clinical psychologists Guy Holmes and Liz Offen did a study with psychiatrists and psychologists, whom they divided into two test groups. Both groups were given the same detailed description of symptoms associated with sexual abuse. One group was told they were diagnosing a female patient and the other a male patient. While Holmes and Offen had expected their subjects to recognize post-traumatic stress disorder (PTSD) as a result of sexual abuse in the case of the "woman" more often than in the case of the "man," they hadn't counted on the ratio being twice as high.[28] Narratives determine our perception of sexual violence to a large extent, as media historian Frank Tomasulo explains: "People generally do not come to believe things *after* seeing them; they see things only when they *already* believe them."[29]

Changing laws to acknowledge the existence of male victims is one such narrative. So where are the others?

As it turns out, they are mainly missing. The most famous literary account of the rape of a man—the man in question being Thomas Edward Lawrence, better known as Lawrence of Arabia—is also nearly the only internationally renowned account. Even though it is the key scene in his memoir *The Seven Pillars of Wisdom*, the rape stays invisible, like a ghost always at the edge of vision but never spotted—except when new research is published to "prove" that the rape that can't be true isn't true after all.[30]

Social media has noticed the existence of male victims but when the hashtag #metoo trended after the allegations of sexual harassment, assault, and rape surfaced against Hollywood film producer Harvey Weinstein, men's voices were conspicuous by their absence, except for those who spoke out to support women who spoke out. Such a pattern perpetuates the unspoken assumption that victims are women and perpetrators are men. Before the case of Jimmy Bennet accusing Asia Argento turned the debate for a while on its head, when men have been addressed in the context of #metoo, it is mainly in that role and the idea was that they should reflect why "they" did "things like that." One man wrote in the *Independent* that, although he had been sexually harassed himself, that didn't give him or any other man the right to join in with #metoo—or #hetoo—because the hashtag "was meant to highlight the structural oppression women face and the sexual violence that goes hand-in-hand with it. That is something men, as a class, cannot possibly understand—even if we are sometimes the victims of sexual assault too."[31] His German colleague Gero von Randow went so far as to proclaim that male rape victims who tweeted #metoo "haven't understood anything at all." Because the hashtag is about patriarchy and not "just bad behavior or sexual delinquency, but specific violence against women. Men aren't victims of that."[32]

So what are men victims of? Each year the US Bureau of Justice Statistics asks approximately 90,000 households about the frequency, characteristics, and consequences of crimes they have experienced and publishes the results in the National Crime Victimization Survey.

In 2012, 38 percent of sexual violence victims were male—while up until then the numbers had stayed in the 10 percent zone.[33] How could this be explained? Largely, this was due to drastic changes to definitions of rape. It took the FBI until 2012 to change the definition from "the carnal knowledge of a female forcibly and against her will" to "the penetration, no matter how slight, of the vagina or anus with any body part or object, or oral penetration by a sex organ of another person, without the consent of the victim."[34] While victims could now be any (recognized) gender, they still had to be penetrated—preferably, though no longer exclusively, with a penis. This posed lots of difficulties: for example if a rapist performed oral sex on a victim, it was rape if the victim was female (if the tongue penetrated the vagina, however slightly), but not rape if the victim was male (because his penis presumably couldn't be penetrated).

That was the reason the 2011 National Intimate Partner and Sexual Violence Survey by the Centers for Disease Control, one of the most comprehensive surveys of sexual victimization conducted in the United States to date, included "being made to penetrate" into their list of "nonconsensual sex." Suddenly the difference between the numbers of female and male victims—those were the only genders listed in the survey—shrank to less than 1 percent: 1,270,000 women and 1,267,000 men had been victims of unwanted sexual intercourse in those twelve months.[35]

Those numbers are not only shockingly high but also shocking, full stop. They go against everything we have learned about sexual violence. What do they tell us? Are the numbers equal after all? Can we compare male rape and female rape? Can we compare any rape with any other rape? I don't know. Nor do we know whether similar statistics apply to other countries or even other years. What they do show though is that we can't treat male victims as the exception that proves the rule any longer. It might be hard to get our heads around the fact that "being made to penetrate" is a kind of rape, but it has only been twenty years since marital rape was recognized as a crime in Germany and discounting rape by a husband already seems absurd, so it seems likely we can expand our definitions again.

Now, it's clear that statistics have to be taken with a pinch—or a pitcher—of salt. So Lara Stemple and Ilan H. Meyer compiled a meta- study about men as victims.[36] Stemple comes to the conclusion: "through decades of feminist-led struggle, fallacies described as 'rape myths' have been largely discredited in American society, and an alternative narrative concerning female victimization has emerged . . . For men, a similar discourse has not been developed."[37] Among male-rape myths she lists the assumptions: that female-perpetrated abuse is rare or non-existent; that male victims experience less harm (as an example Stemple cites the 2009 CBS News report about a rapist who raped four men; the report finished: "no one has been seriously hurt");[38] that for men all sex is welcome anyway; and that "real men" can protect themselves.[39]

This is important because male-rape myths are as detrimental to male victims as female-rape myths are to female victims. One of the most harrowing letters I received after this book was published in Germany was from a male victim, in which he described that what made healing so difficult for him was that all cultural messages—newspaper articles, TV reports, conversations with friends about the topic—addressed him not as a victim, but as a (potential) perpetrator *because he was a man*.

If we think of male victims at all, we imagine the people raping them to be male as well. Women just don't figure as predators in our societal imagination. Lara Stemple thus followed her study on male victims with a peer-reviewed paper this time on female perpetrators.[40] It is perhaps worth noting that Lara Stemple is a well-known feminist, and that her study includes statistics which are only American and from the years 2008 through 2013. Looking at self-reported perpetrators, Stemple writes: "Of those who affirmed that they had 'ever forced someone to have sex with you against their will,' 43.6 percent were female and 56.4 percent were male."[41] Still, the rest of the statistics seemed to indicate that the majority of rapists are male. Are these unexpected proportions perhaps due to women being more honest about their crimes? Mysterious. But only until one took into consideration the figures for "being made to penetrate" which had been disregarded in the other statistics. However, this is the kind of sexual violence men are most likely to experience and women are most likely to perpetrate. And 79.2 percent of men who had been made to penetrate cited a woman as the perpetrator.

But how is that possible? After all, you need an erection to be able to penetrate and an erection is proof of sexual arousal, isn't it? It isn't. We now know that people of all genders can show signs of physical stimulation without the corresponding emotional arousal. We also know that orgasms can be the nervous system's way to release too much tension and pressure. These facts, combined with general ignorance about arousal, can make it a lot harder for victims, who might feel betrayed by their bodies or unsure whether they have "really" been raped because society (and perhaps the rapist) tells them that their bodies' self-protection reaction is a sign of consent.

Another factor that can impede healing is not one that makes headlines often. A 1996 Alabama case made headlines because SF, a man, had been unconscious during his rape by TM, a woman. Although TM had told a witness after the act that SF's blackout had "saved her a trip to the sperm bank,"[42] a doctor had to be called in to convince the court that it was indeed possible for a man to have an erection and ejaculate while unconscious.[43] Even so, SF was sentenced to pay $120 a month in child support for TM's baby, as well as $7,152.40 retroactive child support and $300 for the paternity test. "By emphasizing the equality of all children and by according illegitimate children an extensive right to parental support, the UPA ensures that illegitimate children will no longer be subject to the social and legal discrimination they traditionally have suffered,"[44] the court ruled, transforming the victim (of rape) into a perpetrator (who discriminates against his illegitimate child) with breathtaking speed.

Lawyer Ellen London observes: "The discourse employed by the courts denies male victimization and ensures that women remain subordinate in the traditional hierarchy, and the underlying assumption of such discourse is that men are responsible for their sexuality, or that they have agency in a way that women do not."[45]

A 2003 study showed that inmates in US prisons who had been victimized sexually by staff were mainly male—and more of them reported female staff members as perpetrators than male ones. These numbers were confirmed by Lara Stemple, who found that female inmates were more likely to be victimized by other inmates. If it had been the other way around, nobody would have raised an eyebrow, but the perpetrators being mainly female, an explanation had to be found that redistributed responsibility:

> First, the fact that the vast majority of prisoners are male naturally leads to more complaints made by men. Second, female staff have relatively low status in correctional settings, and are therefore less likely to receive protection in correctional environments. Third, female staff may experience such harassment and lack of support from their male counterparts that they form alliances with male inmates for protection and support.[46]

A consequence of this incredulity toward male victimhood and female perpetration is that women not only receive shorter prison sentences for the same crime (gender jail gap)[47] but are often sentenced for "lewd and obscene conduct rather than indecent assault, thus muddling statistical comparisons between male and female offending."[48]

When I was doing a reading in Berlin, one person raised their hand and asked: "What about the crimes against sexual self-determination that have been committed completely legally around the corner from here until recently? Why do we not talk about those?" They were referring to operations performed at the nearby hospital (and countless others worldwide) on babies whose genitals are not clearly "male" or "female"—a process that is unethical but also surprisingly arbitrary: surgery is considered necessary if a newborn's clitoris is longer than a centimeter or if the penis was less than 2.5 centimeters (when stretched).[49] And they were right: This *is* a kind of sexual violence. But it is not what we talk about when we talk about sexual violence. Neither do we talk about disabled women being sterilized without their consent in Germany till 1990.[50] (Compulsory sterilization is not restricted to Germany of course. In the US for example sterilization in prisons was only made illegal in 2014) Or that women with drug addictions were put under pressure to have abortions if they didn't want to be thrown out of methadone programs. Or that new contraceptive drugs are tested on so-called Third World women, at the moment mainly in India.[51] Sexual self-determination is so much more than just protection from unwanted touch.

There is good news: things are changing. In 2017, Sweden took a leading role and passed a law granting compensation for trans people who were forced to undergo sterilization in order to be accepted as their real gender. But the discourse around rape still genders us by teaching us how many genders there are, (namely) two—victims and perpetrators—as well as how to act according to our gender and how the genders interact. Rape is by no means the only source of gender information, but nowhere else do we gender so relentlessly.

Masculinity and Its Victims

If we talk about male rape at all, it is nearly exclusively in the context of prison rape.[52] However, such discourse usually includes the information that perpetrators turn their victims into ersatz women by calling them feminizing names like *whores*, *bitches*, *old ladies*, or *punks* (in Shakespeare's time punk was a synonym for a female prostitute), thereby upholding the clear distinction between men, the ones who rape, and the others, who are raped.

The person who put the problem of prison rape on the political agenda is Stephen Donaldson (alias Donald Tucker, alias Robert Anthony Martin Jr.). Having been arrested in 1973 after a nonviolent Quaker pray-in against the US bombing of Cambodia, Donaldson was brutally raped more than sixty times over two days by forty-five inmates in a Washington, DC, jail. When he finally managed to get to two guards, dressed only in a t-shirt, they took him to the hospital—but he was handcuffed during the whole examination and received no treatment for his severe physical injuries nor for the emotional trauma. Donaldson was the first US inmate who went to the press. In his autobiography, *A Punk's Song*, he details how he now faced the horrible decision

> to cooperate in the prosecution of the two young inmates who had led the rapes, to bring suit against the Corrections Department, or to

> drop out of the legal process. The prospect of giving my assailants a still longer prison term went contrary to [my deep convictions]. Yet many who were working to change the penal system felt that the first prosecution of a prison rape case would set a significant precedent and have a real deterrent effect on such situations in the future.[53]

In the end he didn't have the heart to condemn his tormentors to spend more time in an institution where violence and especially sexual violence was par for the course. Donaldson, like Gerlinda Smaus, was convinced that rape was part of the power and control structure of the prison system and that the difference between the legal and illegal violence was only gradual: "There is, ultimately, no prison rape issue. There is only the prison issue."[54]

Dropping the case meant that he either had to pay bail or go back to prison. Donaldson chose prison as a protest against the bail system, which allows privileged, often white offenders to buy their freedom and fills the prisons with poor, predominantly black inmates. But then he was told he had to go back to the *same prison*. He describes what would now be recognized as PTSD: "My conscience tells me I should have gone, but I was shaking all over. It was obvious I just couldn't go through it again."[55] There were no crisis centers for cases like his; nobody had any notion that they existed at all. The women's movement had just started raising awareness about rape, but as a man, Donaldson didn't qualify as a victim. So the treatment he got was a week at the veterans' hospital in Washington, DC: "The government sewed up the tears in my rectum which the government occasioned."[56]

In March 1980, Donaldson went to hospital and demanded help but was sent home. He was unemployed, his apartment had been broken into twice in one day, and he was battling depression, so he took a .25-caliber pistol and repeated his demand. The doctor told him to put his toy gun away. Just to prove that it was real, Donaldson fired a shot through the window. This time he was sentenced to prison for four years and was raped again—but managed to befriend four other inmates who protected him from his rapists. The five of them developed a deep sexual-emotional bond and showed that sexuality within prison didn't have to be a means to oppression, but could also be a way to subvert and escape the devaluation and dehumanization of jail. "I discovered that they could throat me for hours on end—I mean, they were in heaven. It was the most wonderful thing that had happened since they got locked up. And they got very grateful and cherished the experience."[57]

This is where the analogy that it's rape that reproduces the gender order in prison breaks down. Instead, prison is an environment that considers any kind of intimacy as "unmanly," so sexuality—disregarding whether it's forced or consensual—is seen as "female." Donaldson was still a punk, "Donny the punk," but he wasn't an object to be used and abused any longer. "They never said anything to put me down. Never once." Gendering "Donny" as a punk, meant that sex with him wasn't homosexual and didn't endanger their "masculinity" (a trait that was essential for survival in the harshly hierarchical world of incarceration). One of the inmates spent hours with Donny's head in his lap, reading cowboy stories to him and caressing his neck. "And I asked him, 'Why do you do this?' And he said, 'Well, this is what I do with my girlfriend back home. So I reckon if you're gonna be our girlfriend here, I'll do the same thing with you.' "[58]

In the 1990s, Donaldson founded the organization Stop Prisoner Rape, now Just Detention International.

It is an indicator of how little we are sensitized to the plight of victims who don't fit our images of victims that the only rape jokes people tell with impunity are jokes about prison rape.[59] There is even a board game called "Don't Drop the Soap"—designed by art student John Sebelius, son of Obama's Secretary of Health and Human Services, Kathleen Sebelius, and US Magistrate Judge K. Gary Sebelius—where players navigate the perils of a prison sentence and try to avoid being raped. There are many theories about why we treat prison rape in such a cavalier fashion: that the majority of victims are male and that they are supposed to be "bad" guys are surely part of it, but most people also don't know the extent of the problem. Sexual victimization studies are restricted to households, so they leave out rapes of inmates and homeless people. The 2003 Prison Rape Elimination Act required the Bureau of Justice Statistics to conduct a corresponding survey of sexual victimization in jail.

Comparing the findings Lara Stemple concludes:

> The examination of data from prisons, jails, and juvenile detention institutions reveals a very different picture of male sexual abuse in the United States from the picture portrayed by the household crime data alone . . . The 2012 NCVS's household estimates indicate that 131,259 incidents of rape and sexual assault were committed against males. Using adjusted numbers from the detainee surveys, we roughly estimate that . . . more than 900,000 sexual victimization incidents were committed against incarcerated males.[60]

Stemple emphasizes, and I emphatically agree, that this in no way suggests that men are the "real" victims, or that they are the more important victims. But it does suggest that we should reconsider how we speak about rape and gender, and stop unthinkingly asuming, it is always something only men do to only women. For example, the important Europe-wide agreement on ending sexual violence, known as the Istanbul Convention, is called in full the Convention on Preventing and Combating Violence Against Women and Domestic Violence, thus embedding gender assumptions into its title. It seems to be easier to think of men as inherently dangerous than to think of them as vulnerable—as human.

To recognize men and people of other genders as victims doesn't detract any recognition from female victims, Stemple stresses: "Compassion is not a finite resource."[61] But money is, so it's important to ensure funding for rape crisis centers for women. But perhaps it is time to campaign for more rape crisis centers that offer services to men as well.

Tell the truth: isn't it a relief, that sexual violence isn't confined to one gender and one gender alone? Because it is only when we understand rape as not genetically or biologically determined that change becomes imaginable—for everyone. bell hooks reminds us,

> Focussing solely on those aspects of male sexual expression that have to do with reinforcing male domination over women, (some feminist activists) are reluctant and downright unwilling to

> acknowledge that sexuality as it is constructed in sexist society is no more "liberating" for men than it is for women . . . Sexual freedom can exist only when individuals are no longer oppressed by a socially constructed sexuality based on biologically determinded definitions of sexuality.[62]

Biologically determined definitions of sexuality purport that "real men" always have agency over their sexuality and are invulnerable: male victims aren't such a discursive minefield because they compete with female victims, but because they endanger the concept of masculinity.

For example, philosopher Keith Burgess-Jackson proposed that *all* men (regardless of whether they have ever committed a sex crime, are victims of sexual violence themselves, or neither) should pay a special tax—a men's tax, so to speak—to finance programs for female rape victims and sexual education courses for men.

> Curfews could be imposed on men living in communities with high levels of violence. Men might even be "required to participate in study groups or consciousness-raising sessions as a condition of receiving certain privileges, such as drinking alcoholic beverages or driving a motor vehicle."[63]

Sadly, this thinking became all too familiar after "New Year's Eve," when the unspoken subtext of the discussions about dangerous Arabic men was that male sexuality was dangerous in general.

"Much of the existing rethoric used to describe and theorize sexual harrassment is unfortunately mired in the concept of 'unilateral sexism'—that is the belief that men are the oppressors and women are the oppressed, end of story,"[64] establishes Julia Serano—a trans woman who thus has a double perspective on the world of embodied gender interactions. Serano understands rape culture not as a set of isolated actions, but as a mindset with consequences for all genders. At the root of this she identifies the *predator/prey mindset.* She explains,

> While many feminists have discussed how the sexual object/prey sterotype creates a double bind for women in which they can only ever be viewed as either "virgins" or "whores," not enough have considered how the sexual aggressor/predator stereotype might create a similar double bind for men.[65]

As a consequence, there are even fewer role models that break with these stereotypes for men than for women. But freeing men from the restraints of gender would be beneficial for all (genders). Another telling example is the often-discussed children's issue. Serano writes,

> When I was male-bodied, I found that if I were to interact enthusiastically with children, women would often give me dirty looks. A trans male acquaintance of mine told me that the greatest loss he experienced upon transitioning from female to male was his ability to interact freely with children. He teaches young children and has found that he's had to modify his whole approach—for example, keeping more distance and not being as effusive or affectionate with his students as before—in order to avoid other adults viewing him as creepy or suspect.[66]

I have done workshops with kindergarten and nursery-school teachers who have been told not to change the toddlers' diapers or were discouraged from taking the children to the toilet—because they were men. In one case, a young nursery-school teacher was suspected of being a pedophile because he cuddled the kids during story time. He eventually left his job. This is, of course, detrimental to men, who are implicitly accused of having a monstrous sexuality and being unsafe to leave alone with children. But it is also detrimental to children, who learn that any kind of physical attention and warmth is reserved for female attachment figures, while men's bodies are dangerous—and so, if they are little boys, their own bodies are dangerous. The centuries-old binary of sex as masculinity versus emotions as femininity makes any display of affection and tenderness toward children by a man suspicious—like he is breaking the gender law.

It is no coincidence that there is no male synonym for "mothering."[67]

This doesn't just apply to cuddling children. Especially in America, but to a lesser degree in Britain and Germany as well, all touch from men is sexualized. "We prove our trustworthiness by foregoing physical touch completely in any context in which even the slightest doubt about our intentions might arise. Which, sadly, is pretty much every context we encounter," observes author Mark Greene.[68] Men not only starve themselves of touch, they also touch their sons less than their daughters. The result is that:

> by the time they are approaching puberty, many boys have learned to touch only in aggressive ways through roughhousing or team sports. When they do seek gentle touch in their lives, it is expected to take place in the exclusive and highly sexualized context of dating . . . Sex takes on the role of fulfilling both sexual and platonic touch needs.[69]

Laurie Penny observes:

> The big secret about the Golden Age of Masculinity, of course, is that it never really existed. There have always been men who were too poor, too queer, too sensitive, too disabled, too compassionate or simply too clever to fit in with whatever flavour of violent heterosexuality their society relied upon.[70]

Men who behave like human beings rather than gender stereotypes face being called "wimps," being "like a girl" or "a bunch of old ladies," "pussy-whipped," or, most blatantly, "beta males."

Gender trainer Jason Schultz explains,

> It's up to straight men to change these assumptions. Gay men and lesbians have engaged in a cultural dialogue around sexuality over the last twenty-five years, straight women are becoming more and more vocal. But straight men have been almost completely silent. This silence, I think, stems in large parts from fear: our culture tells us that being a "real" man means not being feminine, not being gay, and not being

> weak. They warn us that anyone who dares to stand up to these ideas becomes a sitting target to have his manhood shot down in flames.[71]

It is well known that in a culture that objectifies women, (some) women will (to some extent) take on this role to be considered sexually attractive—or just to be identified as female. "By the same token, in a world where men are only ever viewed as sexual aggressors, some men will take on that role in order to gain attention and to feel desirable."[72] One effect of this situation is that these roles aren't just performed but internalized. "Just as hetero women are often forced to choose between the images of the virgin and the whore, modern straight men are caught in a cultural tug of war between the Marlboro Man and the Wimp."[73]

And the Marlboro Man has a certain role in the dance of seduction, as we are told from the get go by every fairy tale, rom-com, action movie, and advertisement, as author and gender trainer Alyssa Royse notes, "we see example after example of men having to pull huge gestures to lure women into sex, or catch them, or trick them."[74] In films, sexual behavior that borders on harassment—or crosses that border with impunity—is often rewarded with the hero "getting the girl." Han Solo pursues Princess Leia famously in 1980's *The Empire Strikes Back* and corners her in the empty machine room of his spaceship. He tries to take her in his arms; she pushes him away. He takes her hand. She tells him to stop. He replies that she likes him because he is a scoundrel. She disagrees. He kisses her—and instead of giving him a black eye, she realizes that he is the love of her life. Cue the swelling romantic music—or, in this case, the robot C-3PO bustling in with news that he has "isolated the reverse power flux coupling."

This is the other side of the if-a-woman-doesn't-say-no-he-thinks-she-is-easy-to-get coin; it's the message that men have to "wear her down," to pursue and to "pull," because without the extra effort who'd want them (a woman that is easy to get, that's who). Men aren't supposed to be honest about their desires or emotions any more than women are. Because: just as femininity is a performance, so is masculinity. Even if we break these patterns, there are certain rules for rule-breaking. For example, when women talk about sexuality, it's sexy, because women are in the cultural position of "the desired." But when men do the same, it can very easily be threatening or creepy, because this is a doubling of their cultural position of "the pursuer," and too much pursuing is harassment. The same goes for emotions, only the other way around: women who talk about love are seen as needy, while men who talk about love are adorable.

The process that teaches men from boyhood to feel and express only half of the full range of human emotions and repress and deny the other half has been called "toxic masculinity."[75] It starts before children are even born. Study after study has shown that as soon as parents know the sex of their child-to-be, they project gender characteristics on the fetus's every kick and turn. A study demonstrates that parents, when asked for the weight and general appearance of their newborn children, judge their sons to be more robust and lively than their "delicate" and "gentle" daughters even when the infants in question were exactly the same in weight, length, alertness, and strength.[76] In another study, psychologists showed 204 adults a video of a crying baby. "Some were told the baby was male, others in the group were told it was female. The adult subjects saw the crying 'girl' baby as frightened, but when they thought they were watching a boy, they described 'him' as angry."[77] It seems logical to assume that "frightened" babies are picked up and comforted more often and for longer than "angry" babies. "Studies indicate that from the moment of birth, boys are spoken to less than girls, comforted less, nurtured less."[78] Even the language used to communicate with little boys is less flowery and less rich in metaphors and similes. All while parents are convinced that they would never dream of differentiating between the sexes.[79]

What has all this got to do with rape? A lot, as it turns out. Studies found out that people who believe in stereotypical gender roles are more likely to transgress sexual borders.[80] A belief in traditional gender sex roles is even one notch on the Pryor scale to measure the "likelihood to sexually harass."[81]

In 2017, the BBC aired an "experiment": Dr. Javid Abdelmoneim asked parents to swap the pink dresses and blue shirts and trousers of toddlers Marnie and Edward, so that Marnie became "Oliver" and

Edward became "Sophie." He then gave the children some toys and asked volunteers to play with them. Unsurprisingly "Sophie" was offered "a dolly" and soft toys, while "Oliver" was given a robot, a car, and a spatial-awareness-puzzle.[82] When Abdelmoneim revealed the real sex of the children they had played with, the adults were shocked, mainly because they had prided themselves on not buying into gender stereotypes. The show then went on to explain: "When children play spatial awareness games frequently, their brains change physically within just three months."[83] Which is important information, but it also implies that only girls are harmed by these stereotypes. But while boys do learn all that useful spatial awareness and hand-eye co-ordination, girls learn—via those dolls and tea sets and kitchens—social skills, like empathy, care-taking, emotional expression, and connection. And both sides of this equation are missing out on vital, valuable skills.

Analyzing the effects of gender on boys and men is a relatively new field of research, but—together with the effects of gender generally—it is vital for an understanding of gendered violence. One of those effects is surely that boys are being cut off from their emotions, and thereby from parts of their personality (just as girls are cut off from the corresponding parts of their personalities). "The cliché about men not being in touch with their emotions says nothing about inherent markers of maleness. It instead identifies behavioral outcomes that have been rigorously taught, often by well-meaning parents and society at large,"[84] establishes writer Kati Holloway.

A 2015 study found that even the five-year difference in life expectancy between men and women had nothing to do with biology and everything to do with "toxic masculinity." "Men have a cultural script that tells them they should be brave, self-reliant and tough. Women don't have that script, so there isn't any cultural message telling them that, to be real women, they should not make too much of illnesses and symptoms," the researchers explained.[85] This isn't only relevant in the case of life-threatening illnesses. Men don't learn to look after themselves in the same ways that women do. They don't ask for help as often, which leads to them developing more stress-related illnesses and dying by suicide three times more often than women. Astonishingly, they are also being *struck by lightning* four to six times more often. How is that possible? Lightning is not sexist, as far as we know. For a long time, it was thought that had to do with men doing dangerous jobs, like working on scaffolds. But in most places health and safety rules wouldn't allow workers onto a scaffold in a thunderstorm. In fact, men are struck by lightning while playing golf or similar activities, because they have learned from childhood that they are not "made of sugar" and "a little bit of rain won't hurt." As it turns out, it does.

In the discourse of sexual violence, it is important to not disregard how men are disenfranchised from their emotions and feelings, because people who are in contact with their feelings—and that includes "unmanly" feelings of sensitivity and neediness and fear—are better able to notice feelings in others and consequently respect their boundaries. And even though I've said this before, it can't be repeated often enough: The saying that one can only love somebody else if one is able to love oneself goes for empathy as well. It is impossible to really have empathy for anybody if one is constantly denied empathy for oneself. The discourse shouldn't be about which gender is the biggest victim, but what we can learn from each other's experiences.

If femininity isn't a biological constant, neither is masculinity.

6

Missions: Yes Means Yes

Perpetrators

Recently, a friend who was preparing a workshop on consent asked me what she should suggest to people who had transgressed sexual borders and wanted to take responsibility for their actions. What can they do when the harm is already done, but they don't want to enhance it by pretending nothing has happened? I was surprised to realize I couldn't think of a single answer. Before asking me, she had posed the same question on Facebook, and her otherwise exceedingly supportive community reacted with comments like: "All rapists are assholes—always!" "Tell the rapists to stop bawling," and "We don't want rapists on this forum." Author, performer and social worker Kai Cheng Thom had a similar experience:

> Seven years ago, when I first started training as a support worker for survivors of intimate partner violence, I was sitting in a training workshop when someone asked what our organization's policy was on taking requests for support from people who were abusing their partners and wanted help stopping. The answer was brusque and immediate: "We don't work with abusers. Period."[1]

But aren't these valid questions? Shouldn't we want abusers to face the consequences of their actions? Shouldn't they do the best they can to repair—or at least minimize—the damage, if they get the chance? Or, as Thom puts it: "Doesn't the feminist saying go, 'We shouldn't be teaching people how not to get raped, we should be teaching people not to rape?' "[2]

Dealing with perpetrators seems to be an even bigger taboo than all the other loaded questions around the minefield that is rape. When Joanna Bourke wrote her book about rapists in 2010, she decided not to call it that: "Would you have picked up this book if it was called *Rapists* rather than *Rape*? Most of my friends were honest enough to say 'no.'"[3] And nothing made Samantha Geimer more unpopular than her insistence that "no matter what his crime, Polanski was entitled to be treated fairly; he was not."[4]

The case of Welsh footballer Chedwyn "Ched" Evans, who was convicted of raping a nineteen-year-old waitress in 2012, throws up similar questions. The media followed the trial with hungry interest—beginning with the identity of the complainant being leaked, first on Twitter, then "accidentally" on Sky News, and more than six thousand times since. A drunk woman accusing a prominent footballer of rape is the stuff shitstorms are made of, and this was no exception. She was called all manner of names and threatened until she had to be relocated and given a new identity by the police. But what had been her actual claims? She had woken up naked in a hotel bed without any recollection of the previous night, uneasy about the possibility that someone might have spiked her drinks. The police found out the hotel room had been paid for by Evans, and ten days later he and his friend and fellow footballer Clayton McDonald were charged with rape. Evans and McDonald maintained that the three of them had had consensual sex. McDonald, who had chatted the young woman up in the street, was acquitted; Evans, who had joined the two later in a hotel room, was sentenced to five years in prison. Judge Merfyn Hughes explained that the claimant had been extremely drunk (by her own account, she had two glasses of wine, two double vodkas, and a Sambuca before meeting McDonald): "CCTV footage shows, in my view, the extent of her intoxication when she stumbled into your friend. As the jury have found, she was in no condition to have sexual intercourse. When you arrived at the hotel, you must have realized that."[5] With this decision, Hughes anticipated the Crown Prosecution Service's new Rape and Sexual Offence Guidelines (which would come into effect three years later, in 2015), to implement *yes means yes* rather than *no means no*.

In October 2014, Evans was released after two and a half years and Sheffield United tried to re-sign him, but a petition with 150,000 signatures argued: "He continues to protest his innocence and for him to walk back into a high-profile job where he's seen as a role model as if nothing happened is just really appalling."[6] Sponsors threatened to withdraw their support and the club finally withdrew its offer. This is noteworthy, as neither judge nor jury had requested a ban from his career as part of the sentence.

But that was just the beginning of Evans's extrajudicial punishment. After Sheffield, Hartlepool United also tried to sign him, but had to back down because of massive public pressure. Ditto Hibernians. Ditto Grimsby Town. And when Oldham Athletic tried, death threats—and, weirdly, even rape threats—against fans, sponsors, and staff put a stop to it.[7] Columnist Caitlin Moran wrote in the *Times*:

> Perhaps young, rich, fit, unrepentant men who have raped do need to see their lives reduced to ash—without prospect of forgiveness, employment or absolution—until the day they die. I'm starting to see the sense in choosing, say, a hundred rapists and making their lives publicly, endlessly awful—unrelentingly humiliating, without prospect of absolution . . . So that men become terrified of raping, in the same way women are terrified of being raped. So that rapists spend their lives dealing with the night they raped in the same way women currently do.[8]

How come an otherwise incredibly clever and liberal author like Moran is falling back on Old Testament ideas about evil and never-ending punishment? From there, the next step could only be reintroducing the death penalty.

My theory is this: because we lack social scripts for victims' healing after rape, we also lack scripts for rapists to reform and reenter society. "*Rape* is a potent word, a word laden with emotive and evaluative significance. To call a sexual act *rape* is to attach to it the harshest sort of condemnation," as philosopher Eric Reitan writes.[9] Rape is a horrible crime, no doubt about it. But this means that rapists remain the Other, inherently evil. The problem with this inside/out politics is that nobody will identify as a perpetrator when we say that "rapists are not like us." Or shorter that rapists are *not us*, not part of our society any longer. We project all the things we, as society, are not or don't want to be onto rapists. Cultural studies professor Sabine Sielke calls this the "othering of sexual violence."[10]

There is a sequel to the Ched Evans story: In 2016, Ched Evans appealed his conviction. The court had allowed two witnesses to testify that they'd had sex with the claimant around the same time as Evans and McDonald had. There was some justification for this—after relatively little alcohol, she couldn't remember anything the next morning—but it meant that the "woman was subjected to a grilling about her morality and sexual behaviour that was a throw-back to the 1980s."[11] The claimant's new identity was leaked, leading to a repetition of the vicious cycle. There still seems to be no other way of dealing with rape apart from the he-is-evil/she-is-a-slut dichotomy.

Evans was pronounced not guilty. Not being a rapist any longer, he had no difficulty rejoining Sheffield United. But what exactly is a rapist? Under German law Evans wouldn't have been convicted in the first place, because in Germany the victim must say "no" explicitly. Still in 2012, the German press was just as shocked by Evans as the British press, even though he would have been considered innocent there. Once the label "rapist" is attached, that person is a social leper. Reitan notes that changes in law over the last few decades "have redefined rape beyond its ordinary use, but have preserved its traditional emotive meaning."[12]

That is especially true of the Sexual Offenders Register in the United States, which lists more than 800,000 offenders, including "people convicted of nonviolent crimes such as solicitation, public urination, streaking and consensual sex with teenagers (even teenagers they subsequently marry)."[13] Other possible offences are sexting (in twenty states), not registering for consensual sex if you are a teenager (thirty states), or drawing pictures of children engaged in sex. Once a person is on the registry, they must live further than 2,500 feet from any school, day-care center, or playground and report regularly to the police. If they fail to do so, they can face prison. If they apply for a job, potential employers can find them on the registry; in some cases their lovers are informed as well. Is that the price we have to pay for the safety of our children? Filmmaker and former public defender David Feige writes:

> Study after study show that our sex offender registries are utterly ineffective at reducing sexual violence, and that public notification about sex offenders may actually increase recidivism by making reintegration into society nearly impossible . . . Rather than narrowly target a very few dangerous offenders and allow them to be monitored by law enforcement, we have morphed our registry into a massive instrument of public censure and marginalization, while utterly failing to advance the purpose for which it was created.[14]

Likewise, hardly anybody knows the ins and outs of the Swedish laws governing sexual offenses, but everybody knows that Julian Assange is a rapist. Or isn't, depending on which camp you belong to. True, the political activist and hacker has—if the accusations are correct—done something extremely reprehensible: saying he would use a condom and then removing it secretly or, stealthing.[15] But that isn't the reason we condemn him (if we condemn him). We condemn him for the ideas associated with the word *rapist*.

Still, the two Swedish women went to the police in August 2010 not to report that the WikiLeaks founder had raped them, but to oblige him to submit to an HIV test. The officer on duty informed the shocked women that their case was dealt with under rape law and that Assange would be arrested.[16] The next day the proceedings were stopped, only to be started again after Assange applied for residence and work permits with the Swedish immigration authorities. This time, though, it was Interpol searching for him with "red alert." One doesn't have to be a cynic to conclude that they were less concerned about rape than the fact that Assange was the man responsible for leaking secret US government documents, videos, and war logs, mainly about the wars in Afghanistan and Iraq, to the press. In December 2010 he surrendered himself to UK police in London. The

Magistrate's Court there decided he was to be extradited to Sweden, which in all probability would have extradited him to the US, where he faced a long prison sentence, possibly the death penalty, and right-wing media and politicians openly calling for his assassination.[17] "A dead man can't leak stuff. This guy's a traitor . . . so if I'm not for the death penalty, there's only one way to do it: illegally shoot the son of a bitch," demanded political commentator Robert Beckel on Fox News, and Republican politician Sarah Palin recommended the secret service should hunt down and execute Assange like an al-Qaeda terrorist.[18] After the UK Supreme Court rejected Assange's appeal for a retrial, he entered the Ecuadorian embassy in London and was granted political asylum. He hasn't left the embassy since.

"We can agree that the legal response to what Assange allegedly did reeks of politically-motivated prosecution without passing judgment on the merits of the allegations against him," comments investigative journalist Lindsay Beyerstein.[19] Nor is the British government guarding the embassy of Equador at all times—to arrest Assange the moment he steps outside (which has cost the taxpayers more than 13 million pounds so far)—out of concerns over sexual self-determination. When Chilean dictator Augusto Pinochet was arrested in 1998 in London, Margaret Thatcher refused his extradition to Spain, even though it was proven that Pinochet was responsible for the murder of thousands and torture of tens of thousands. His internment camps were infamous for their brutal use of rape as a means of breaking detainees, with rats and dogs specifically trained for that purpose.

"Which would you rather have—women's rights or freedom of speech? Standing outside the Ecuadorian embassy on Sunday, listening to various venerable activists give rousing speeches, that's the choice that seemed to have been placed before the international left," writes Laurie Penny. "Julian Assange should be held to account, and the system to do so fairly while protecting the work of WikiLeaks does not exist, and anyone who believes in freedom needs to fight for both."[20]

Rape is a political issue. At the same time, rape is also used as a justification for all sorts of policies, and we make that misuse possible when we take rape out of the context of human actions, opening ourselves up to political and emotional manipulation.

The Right to Forgive

Even when there is no political agenda, rapists are the antithesis to everything we believe in and know how to deal with. The reflex is to shut them out and hope they'll simply disappear.

Thordis Elva and Tom Stranger learned this the hard way. Elva is a well-known feminist in Iceland. In 2009, she has advised the Icelandic government on rape prevention and sexual education for schools. But when she and co-author Stranger came to London in March 2017 to talk about their book *South of Forgiveness* at the Women of the World Festival, the event had to be cancelled after thousands of protesters signed a petition against it. They were protesting because Stranger had raped Elva twenty years previously. The book dealt with Elva's and Stranger's efforts to come to terms with the rape and leave it behind them.

Just about every article about the book started with the question: Do I have the right to forgive my rapist? The answer seems obvious, but Elva answered it patiently again and again: "My forgiveness is not selfless, not sacrificial, and certainly not heroic. It doesn't come with an angelic chorus and a fuzzy feeling, nor does it offer the other cheek … its purpose is to … let this go once and for all … self-preservation at its best."[21]

Far from being a human doormat, it was Elva who decided to contact Stranger and to confront him about the rape. It had happened in Reykjavik when she was 16 and he was 18 on his school exchange in Iceland. She drank rum for the first time, too much rum. After bringing her home from a school dance because she was so drunk she was incapacitated, the exchange student from Australia had sex with the half-conscious Elva for two hours. He was her first boyfriend and two days later he dumped her.

"The rape tied me to a block of cement and the following rejection pushed me over the edge,"[22] analyzed Elva in the book. It took her a long time to realize that what had happened had been rape, because

Tom didn't fit the monster-rapist-stereotype. When she finally mustered up the courage to speak to a teacher, the teacher told Elva she couldn't deal with the situation and sent her to a psychologist, where Elva couldn't say a word but still had to pay for the consultation. She didn't talk about it again, until she wrote him an e-mail eight years later.

To her surprise Stranger answered immediately: "Whatever I can do or offer you, I am more than willing. The question is where to go from here. You tell me."[23] That was the beginning of an eight-year-long correspondence, until they couldn't get any further because there were things that just had to be said face to face and she suggested a meeting. Halfway between Reykjavik and Sydney is South Africa. The two met up in Cape Town for a challenging and intense week during which they managed to break out of the victim perpetrator pattern. Stranger still had the responsibility for the crime but they met on an equal footing, as Elva had demanded: "If you talk about your fears or make yourself vulnerable this week, I do the same."[24]

For this, feminist groups like the "Women's Death Brigade" accused her in London of being a rape apologist.[25] Similar concerns were voiced by protesters when the two were invited to speak at the Bristol Festival of Ideas.

"We are not proposing a formula," Elva said in every interview as a kind of disclaimer. Her critics, on the other hand, did have a formula. Australian lawyer and human rights activist Josephine Cashman stated it: "If someone rapes you, the best place to go is the police."[26] (That's a stance that the rape crisis center in Düsseldorf doesn't share: "It is not our job to tell women what to do but to support them with what they think is right for them. That can mean reporting the rape, but not necessarily so."[27]) Cashman might have understood being wary of going to the police, but not talking to the rapist. She asked, "Are we opening the floodgates for rapists to contact their victims?"[28] An odd concern, given that Elva was the one to contact Stranger and to suggest both their meeting and the book project. It would indeed be alarming to encourage rapists to contact their victims. What is also alarming is that most victims don't know that in most Western countries they are entitled by United Nations law to restorative justice, which is basically what Elva and Stranger did: settling the matter out of court.[29] Had they done so officially, a mediator would have helped them with the process. This is possible in all criminal cases, even with rape. "In Germany the police have to inform you about the possibility of restorative justice when you report a crime, but hardly any police service does so," explains Theresa Bullmann, editor of *TOA Magazin*, the journal for victim-offender mediation in Germany. "They still don't trust this instrument."[30]

As a matter of fact, restorative justice preceded modern justice systems. The Sumerian and Babylonian codes of law included rules for making amends. Until the Middle Ages, there were sophisticated regulations around Europe to restore the social balance after a crime. These were superseded by modern legal systems based on retribution rather than reparations, which changed the perception of law and social order fundamentally. Now it was the law, represented by the state, that was violated, not the rights of an individual person. So it is no longer the person that is paid back in material goods—or by the perpetrator's labor—but the state, either by fines or imprisonment (which usually involves labor). The result is that even when the guilty party is convicted, there is no compensation for the injured party.

This is one of the reasons why conversations about rape convictions often end with the exhausted feeling that there is no justice—*regardless* how long the prison sentence in question is. In fact, one of my lectures started with a young woman from the audience complaining about the low conviction rates for perpetrators. And wherever one stands on the usefulness of prisons, those numbers do seem frivolously low. But however long we talked about the subject, she wasn't satisfied. After a while it transpired that she had been the victim of abuse herself, at the age of nine, by a cousin. Her parents had cut off contact with the cousin's family but refused to talk about it, and the abuse/rape had never been reported. A higher conviction rate or longer sentences wouldn't have changed anything for her. What would have made all the difference, though would have been if her parents had been willing to confront the matter properly. It often seems that we are asking the judicial system to serve an emotional and social purpose it was not created for, and seems unlikely to be able to satisfy.

As understandable as the idea is that rapists should just disappear from the face of the earth, it is not realistic. Even if they go to jail, they will be released eventually. Therefore, it is important to look at perpetrators as well as victims, points out Katie J.M. Baker, "because as a journalist who has covered sexual violence for most of my career, I've seen what happens when we pretend that these guys can simply disappear once they've been pushed out. In my experience, they resurface elsewhere, often to prey on others."[31] Baker was writing after #metoo had toppled careers and even brought about convictions like in the case of Bill Cosby that had hitherto seemed unfathomable. People really were disappearing—if not from the face of the earth, at least from cinema and TV screens. Some tried to stage comebacks, like former CBS anchor Charlie Rose—who after less than six months proposed a TV show in which he would talk with other men who had been #metoo-ed, not about what they had learned from the process but rather about why #metoo was going too far. As outrageous as this is, it was also his only way to get back on TV. Baker had previously profiled young men who had been sent down from their universities for sexual misconduct and observed that

> many had grown increasingly resentful and closed off to change. "At first I thought they didn't want me to participate in campus activities," one told me. "Then I thought they didn't want me to graduate. Now they don't want me to have a job or be part of society. Do they want me to commit suicide? Is that what they want me to do? What is the endgame?"[32]

If we make it impossible for them to return to normal life, eventually they will drift toward extremist viewpoints—because far right men's rights activists are the ones who will welcome them with open arms. At it is, universities and businesses tend to just "pass the trash," as Baker puts it. People accused rightly—and in some cases wrongly—of sexual transgression learn to hate their victims, not to understand them and their own deeds. All that can result is a vicious cycle.

"Because to tell men to sit down, to stay quiet, to disappear—cathartic as it may be—is its own form of looking away, and it is likely to come at someone else's expense."[33]

This is why the wording of the petition against Elva and Stranger is so instructive: it argues that their appearing to talk about their book would "inevitably encourage the normalisation of sexual violence instead of focusing on accountability and root causes of violence."[34] But how can Stranger focus on accountability if he isn't allowed to account for his crime? Even more strangely, Stranger was attacked *because* he took responsibility for his actions. If he had denied everything, he would have been in the clear. Elva never reported the rape. In the eyes of the world he would have been an innocent man. As it was, demonstrators blocked the entrances to the Royal Festival Hall and shouted: "This is a crime scene—there is a rapist inside."[35] As if "rapist" were his profession.

"It is a fallacy that has caused an incredible amount of pain: to equate people with their crime. People perpetuate crimes but they themselves are not these crimes," Bullmann shows. Contrary to the demonstrators' demand that "rapists should not be given a platform," it seems to me that there is a lot to be gained by listening to those that are willing to talk—like Stranger—because these are the stories we desperately lack: the gaps, the blanks, the dark corners of our collective narratives, the inexplicable and unexplainable.[36]

One revelation to be gleaned from Stranger's story is that the rape massively impacted his life as well as hers. After the rape Stranger started having panic attacks and couldn't stay in a relationship for longer than two months before he had to flee from himself. "I thought my certificate of humanity would be burned."[37] Bullmann confirms, "Nobody tells you that, yes, what you have done has awful consequences on somebody else's life, but you are still allowed to love yourself. Because only when we love ourselves are we able to take responsibility for our actions—and only then can we change."

What Elva and Stranger did in Cape Town was in essence narrative therapy: they told each other their life stories—their whole life stories, not just the story of the trauma that bound them to each other—so that the rape was integrated into the context of a whole life, changing it from *the* formative experience into *one* formative experience. One example: every article about their book made a lot of the fact that Elva developed an eating disorder as a result of the rape. But by the time she met Stranger she had already been anorexic for five years. Her older sister had been an alcoholic when Elva was a teenager; her younger brother was born with a cleft lip. Elva's solution was to become the perfect child, excellent at school, modest, and above all pretty which, in this logic, meant thin. Her using alcohol was unthinkable, which made it impossible for her to tell her parents about the rape. "No more worries on my family's already full plate. Telling them that I'd gotten drunk and danced with the devil felt like the ultimate act of betrayal."[38]

Without knowing this, it is impossible to understand why the rape had the impact it did on Elva's life—and not another impact. Only the whole story leads to forgiveness. It was not a matter of just having to say sorry: and that's the end of the matter. Elva and Stranger tried for years, and nearly 300 pages, for forgiveness. When it finally arrives in the book, it is startling and cathartic (even though the readers knew from the beginning that she would forgive him).

"Stories like this are so moving because something really changes," Bullmann stresses. "It can be incredibly healing to hear what went on in the other person, because the fantasy is always worse than reality. And to hear that one didn't deserve what had happened, that the reasons lay in the other person, that is such a relief." For Thordis this meant that she could stop going back to her teenage room in her mind and replaying the rape.[39]

The changes for Stranger were no less immense. He is still the person that perpetrated the crime, but he's not *just* that person any more. A few weeks after his return from Cape Town he met his present wife, Cat.

The rape crisis center in Düsseldorf cautions that in many cases when women attempt to confront their rapist they are raped or humiliated again. This is a real danger. But they did tell me of one case where the perpetrator reacted like Tom Stranger and accepted full responsibility. Of the many, many people talking and writing to me, two told similar stories. And a third person shared that the perpetrator had denied everything, but the act of confronting him had been healing for her.

In each case, the forgiveness couldn't be forced, but when it was right for the erstwhile victims, they could also let go. This is not a formula, to quote Elva; sometimes we can't or won't forgive, and that can be valuable too. Sometimes it is the right decision to let the courts deal with the perpetrator or never to deal with them again. But wherever one stands on this, there are still things to be learned from stories like Elva's and Stranger's. For example, that rape doesn't just affect the victim and the perpetrator but also their environment (one of the most moving scenes is when Tom visits Thordis and her husband a year later in Iceland); that change is possible; and that this specific rape could have been prevented by education about consent.

"We live in a culture that demonizes and oversimplifies abuse, probably because we don't want to accept the reality that abuse is actually commonplace and can be perpetrated by anybody,"[40] Kai Cheng Thom adds:

> When we are able to admit that the capacity to harm lies within ourselves—within us all—we become capable of radically transforming the conversation around abuse and rape culture. We can go from simply reacting to abuse and punishing 'abusers' to preventing abuse and healing our communities.[41]

This proposal has the potential to transform our thinking about sexual violence into a spectrum, rather than invariably something "evil" people do willfully to hurt other people—thereby excluding the percentage of sex offenders who either genuinely don't know they are crossing borders or are in denial about it.[42] (There is the sweet and telling anecdote—though it is not one about rape—told by author and professor Jacqueline Rose, who was attending a dinner party where another guest kept filling her glass with wine, disregarding her repeated assertions that she didn't want to drink any more. In the end, she put her hand over her glass but he was not deterred, so the red wine ran over the back of her hand onto the white table cloth, still he kept pouring.[43]) At the far end are horrific cases of rape and sexual torture but there are also all the other cases on the spectrum. They are not the same but they are all visible. The advantage of this spectrum framing is precisely that it doesn't separate sexual violence from other experiences of transgression in our life. That doesn't mean that sexual transgression can't be experienced as more harmful than other forms of transgression, but that the way we deal with it is informed by the way we deal with damage done to other boundaries in our life.

This is where rape culture comes back into play once more. We live in cultures that tell us we are "difficult" if we complain when we feel neglected, ignored, hurt, or otherwise infringed upon—unless it is our bodies that are infringed upon, and even then only sexually. In other words: It's fine to insult a woman for getting on a full bus with a pram, but not to wolf-whistle at her. But if we are taught to ignore any kind of hurt and not make a fuss, how are we suddenly supposed to know about boundaries—our own and other people's—as soon as the topic is sexuality, and deal with them appropriately, respectfully, and considerately?

"There is an awful, pervasive myth out there that people who abuse others do so simply because they are bad people—because they are sadistic, or because they enjoy other people's pain," Thom posits. "In my experience as a therapist and community support worker, when people are abusive, it's usually because they have a reason based in desperation or suffering."[44] This is no excuse; people still have free will and agency over their actions. But it is at least an explanation that considers rape as a crime and not an identity. It doesn't reduce human beings to nothing more than their crime. The method of "shaming" rapists, on the other hand, blocks change, because denying their humanity denies the very quality they need in order to look at what they have done and recognize that they have harmed other people.

Thom offers her own suggestions for perpetrators, nine of them. The final two in her list are:

> Don't expect anyone to forgive you. But . . . forgive yourself. You do have to forgive yourself. Because you can't stop hurting other people until you stop hurting yourself. If you believe that you are an abuser, a bad person who hurts others, then you have already lost the

> struggle for change—because we cannot change who we are. If you believe that you are a fundamentally good person who has done hurtful or abusive things, then you open the possibility for change.[45]

Rape is an awful crime, but rapists are still human beings. Which is good news, because only human beings can learn from their mistakes.

Consent

In this book I have looked at the discourses that affect how we understand rape. I have questioned a variety of beliefs and convictions concerning sexual violence, including some held by the feminist movement to which I proudly belong.

So what is the truth about rape?

The answer is: there isn't one authoritative narrative about rape, but always many truths and many perspectives. My aim is to open up windows to diverse narratives, in the knowledge that there is always more to say and to reflect upon. But, this being the final chapter, here is an attempt at a balance sheet.

Rape is deeply entangled with the way our society thinks about and creates gender, but it is not straightforwardly gendered in itself. Although much of our discourse suggests it, rape isn't only committed by one gender against another, and being female doesn't mean one is more rapeable. We should try to reflect this in our thinking and speaking. Some people severely lack empathy and humiliate other human beings using sexual acts; some people misunderstand sexual communication and some perform their sexual gender roles to the detriment of other people and themselves. Rape takes place in the vast field between these poles—and sometimes beyond them.

Now, I am not qualified to deal with evil. Fortunately for me, evil isn't relevant for this book. What we mean when we say "evil" is usually psychopathic rapists who have no feeling for their victims whatsoever. Luckily, these kinds of perpetrators are rare. Usually rape is not a sign of evil, but of the banality of, well, not even evil but *dysfunction*, in its sexual variation. Sex isn't disconnected from all other spheres of human existence; sexuality is woven into the fabric of our cultural reality and can't be imagined without it, just as gender, health, happiness, communication, etc., are embodied realities. And so how we imagine our sexuality is always open to negotiation.

I grew up in the 1970s and 1980s, when being a girl meant being expected to flirt with every man you encountered as a matter of politeness, even if you were not attracted to him. I have no idea why. It was just one of the things we learned, together with the fact that you had to look hot but shouldn't *feel* hot—and, above all, that you should never, ever show a "boy" you fancied him, because that was cheap. The boys didn't fare much better. While we had to smile nonstop, they had to do all the running and wooing, whether they wanted to or not. They learned that girls—and later women—weren't friends but more like dog owners; boys had to jump through hoops and beg before they got a pat on the head or penis. The result was that girls like me were most friendly when we weren't sexually interested, which boys saw as a message that they should try harder. Other gender options weren't available.

Welcome to rape culture! Which doesn't mean—as I've tried to show—that anybody still seriously believes that it is okay to drag a crying and flailing woman to bed and tear off her clothes. That's not where it starts. It starts with truisms, like "all's fair in love and war," and gender myths, like the one that our partners will be bored by us if we show them how much we love them, because that would make them too secure. There's also the tiresome and neverending debate about "whether men and women can 'really' be friends with each other 'without sex getting in the way,' " as Laurie Penny notes:

> The truly telling part of this perennial non-controversy is not just that it is entertained as a serious prospect, but that sexuality is assumed to destroy any possibility of friendship. Thus, any person who you might want to see naked is on fundamentally hostile territory, to be conquered rather than understood.[46]

And that brings us back to Susan Brownmiller's argument that rape has nothing to do with sex and everything to do with violence. This formulation was important because it made clear that rape wasn't just a variety of sex—heterosexual, homosexual, nonconsensual—but a crime. All the same—and there is huge anxiety about speaking about this, for fear of letting rapists off the hook—there *are* grey areas where comfortable sexuality ends but rape hasn't yet started. They have a lot to do with sex, or—to be more precise—with sexual illiteracy. Fortunately, these areas are the easiest to change. It's not the solution to demand longer prison sentences, because as Sharon Marcus reminds us:

> Quite literally, the rape has already occured by the time a case comes to court; a verdict of guilty can in no way avert the rape itself, and no one has proven a direct link between increased penalties and convictions for a crime and a decreased incidence of that crime.[47]

The antidote to rape is consent, which has become the gold standard for all things sexual. And that's great—or, at least, it would be, if it weren't for the fact that most of us know precious little about consent.

In 2014, the UK's Home Office called for mandatory education about consent at schools. This is where education should start, at schools, treating children like human beings and not as parts of two vastly diverging gender groups. But the title of its statement follows a familiar script: "End Violence against Women and Girls." So it is not really about consent or happy and confident sex lives. Norman Barker, the Minister for Crime Prevention, described the campaign as "targeted at boys and young men to help them identify and challenge abusive behaviour." In other words: it is about teaching girls to say no, and boys to accept the no. And that's it.[48]

"If the construction of 'the rapist' as a persona is recent, so too is the notion of 'consent,' "[49] Joanna Bourke reminds us. The modern understanding of consent is rooted in the European Enlightenment and Western liberalism,[50] and thereby based in the idea of property—just as the original understanding of rape was. According to philosopher and "father of liberalism" John Locke, a nation's power depends on its citizen's' consent to be ruled by that state; in return for this consent the state protects the citizen's' property. Locke explains:

> Men therefore in society having property, they have such a right to the goods, which by the law of community are their's, that no body hath a right to take their substance or any part of it from them, without their own consent: without this they would have no property at all; for I have truly no property in that, which another can by right take from me, when he pleases, against my consent.[51]

Property, in Locke's sense, means not just landed property and valuables but also one's own labor, and especially one's own body: "Though the Earth, and all inferior Creatures be common to all Men, yet every Man has a Property in his own Person. This no Body has any Right to but himself."[52] This is why the body (like the soul in Christianity) is the only human property that can't be bought or sold, and that stays one's own to the end of one's life. Therefore, the right to self-determination over one's own body is (supposed to be) one of the most fundamental rights of liberalism. It unambigously answers philosophical questions, like whether it is justified to kill one person if by doing so you save the lives of hundreds of others: no, a citizen's right to his own body is inalienable.

But the words "man" and "citizen" give away the fact that, to be a subject of consent, one must first be a political subject. Locke believed in the equality "of all people," but that didn't stop him investing heavily in the Royal African Company and thereby in slavery. Furthermore, he played a major part in the drafting of the constitution of the British colony of Carolina (today the US states of North Carolina, South Carolina, Georgia, Alabama, Tennessee, and Mississippi), which not only codified the slavery system of the plantations—"every freeman of Carolina shall have absolute power and authority over his negro slaves"—but also facilitated the eviction of Native Americans from their land.[53] Nor were women citizens. "So who is human?" Bourke asks, noting that "Debates about who is allowed to engage in consent are fundamentally about the point at which a person becomes a full subject under the law."[54]

Moreover, consent in this sense only meant to give or withhold permission for someone to use one's property or body. That this was by no means enough became glaringly clear with the Tuskegee syphilis experiment, conducted from 1932 until 1972, in which the US Public Health Service in Tuskegee, Alabama, observed the disease's natural progression of untreated syphilis in black men, based on the racist assumption that venereal disease progresses differently in black people.The participants were neither informed that they had syphilis—they were told they had "bad blood"—nor were they treated, for syphilis—even though penicillin had been known to be an effective cure since the 1940s. Their spouses weren't even warned that the disease could be transmitted to them. Insidiously, the doctors could claim they had the obtained "consent," because they offered participants a free meal during examinations—and a free funeral later—and camouflaged the dangerous and painful bone-marrow biopsies as "free treatment."

In the 1960s, a couple of doctors tried to stop the study, but the Centers for Disease Control declared the project would only end with the death (and autopsy) of the last patient. In 1972, epidemiologist Peter Buxtun finally went to the press. Three months later, the study was terminated. In 1974, the National Research Act was passed. Together with the Nuremberg Code and the World Medical Association's Declaration of Helsinki, the National Research Act forms the basis for our understanding of "informed consent"—meaning simply that in order to consent to something, one must have all the relevant information.

Consent is currently the best tool we have to interact as equals. But it is not a cure-all, and it is more complex than it may initially seem. Because consent is always bound up with other social norms. It becomes particularly ambiguous when it comes to people suffering from dementia or other cognitive impairments. Is it more important to protect a person's right to consent to sex or their right to be protected from sexual transgressions?

The implications of this question became apparent in 2015, when a married couple seeking fertility treatment in the UK were told by local authorities to stop having sex, because the husband had Down Syndrome and was not considered able to consent. They warned his wife that disregarding this instruction would be a serious criminal offense. They ordered the husband to attend a sex education course, but despite regular requests, the course was never provided. After a year, the husband's sister took the matter to court. The man finally took and passed the course, and a judge granted him ten thousand pounds in damages, commenting,

> The impact at the time must have been profound, not only for the loss of sexual relations, but . . . he would have been unable to understand why what was happening should be so. And secondly, in order as she put it "not to lead him on," the wife understandably and foreseeably withdrew to another bedroom and withheld much physical affection.[55]

But the damages were only for the delay in delivering the sexual education course, and the judge also ruled that the authorities' decision to bar a married couple from having sex with each other in the first place had been lawful, arguing: "perhaps it is part of the inevitable price that must be paid to have a regime of effective safeguarding."[56]

Consent doesn't mean free will: it *means free will under certain given social circumstances*. Ideally, the two (or more) partners entering into consent are not just willing but equal—but making this a requisite for consent would be absurd, because we can't deny economically or otherwise disadvantaged people the ability to consent. At the same time, we know full well that not all decisions are free. So it seems obvious that preventing abuses of power must involve reducing inequality. This means understanding that policies we might not ordinarily associate with sexual violence may have far-reaching consequences—for instance, granting people a living wage, access to education, health care, and safe living conditions increases their access to self-determination and allows them to make freer choices.

The bad news is that this can only be achieved through fundamental social change. The good news is that every step to reduce inequality is a direct step toward the prevention and reduction of sexual violence. And this is not restricted to questions of gender.

It is important to remember that there are societies and contexts that hardly know rape—like the Minangkabau in West Sumatra—as well as contexts, like the US prison system and military, where sexual violence is unimaginably common. Anthropologist Peggy Reeves Sanday calls these *rape-free* versus *rape-prone societies* and concludes that the more equal a society and the higher its opportunities for participation, the lower its rape rate: "The value placed on mutual respect in personal relations extends to sexual relations."[57]

bell hooks has argued that the ability to love—ourselves and others—is a vital step to decolonize our bodies and psyches. "Indeed, all the great movements for social justice in our society have strongly emphasized a love ethic,[58] hooks emphasizes, referring less to Jesus' Sermon on the Mount and more to Martin Luther King's and Mahatma Gandhi's love politics. After all, to oppress people, it is essential to make them believe that they aren't worth the same—rights, empathy, love—as others. In this framework, self-loathing, neglect, shame, emotional blackmail, and gaslighting[59] are also constituents of rape culture—according to hooks—not as items on the list of potential future (criminal) offenses, but in the sense that we should stop seeing them as inevitable parts of the adventure of romantic love, and instead view them as forms of harm and self-harm that we need to replace and heal with more cooperative interactions.

At the beginning of the millennium, consent trainings, as they were implemented at many American universities, were ridiculed for making sexual partners ask for affirmative consent at every step: "May I touch your hand?" "May I kiss you?" "May I kiss you again?" For want of other models, though, the concept has been taken on widely by now, including by the Thames Valley Police. In their educational movie *Consent—It's Simple as Tea*, an animated stick figure tries to offer another stick figure a cup of tea. A voiceover explains:

> You say, "Hey, would you like a cup of tea?" and they go, "OMG, I would *love* a cup of tea! Thank you!" Then you know they want a cup of tea. If you say, "Hey, would you like a cup of tea?" and they're like, "Uh, you know, I'm not really sure," then you can make them a cup of tea, or not, but be aware that that they might not drink it.

> And if they don't drink it, then—and this is the important bit—don't make them drink it. And if they say, "No, thank you," then don't make them tea. At all.[60]

Consent in words that an eight-year-old would understand.

The problem is that most people who are struggling with consent aren't eight years old, and that conversation isn't always all that unambiguous, for various reasons: because people don't want to hurt other people's feelings, because these other people are their bosses, because people aren't sure what they want themselves, and the list goes on. The yes-means-yes guidelines advise in these cases: that if you are unsure, don't do it. The underlying message is that the absence of unwanted touch equals a happy sexuality. Therefore, the focus is on avoiding unwelcome contact, not on teaching people how to navigate a self-determined sexual life.

But this is by no means the only way to understand consent. Studies have shown repeatedly that people who know what they want and need are a lot better at respecting other people's desires and boundaries as well as their own.[61] That's why Sexologist Betty Martin trains people to get in touch with their own longings. She explains,

> People often say they want to trust the other person. What most people mean is: *I want to trust the other person will not do anything that will upset me*. Well, there is a problem with that: it's impossible. There is no way for you to know how I want to be touched at every moment. If I have the skill to swim, I can trust the water. If I haven't got the skill to swim and say, "Well, I'll just trust the water," then I will drown. The point is to notice what your limits are and trusting them and communicating them and feeling entitled to communicate them and not having to get angry with the other person that they didn't read our mind. When I have the skill to speak up for myself, to say yes, to say no, then I can trust myself.[62]

When I teach consent, the biggest step for my students of all genders usually is to give themselves permission to feel the way they feel—horny, uninterested, adventurous, jealous, appalled, appealed, attracted, distracted—and stop thinking about the "right way" to feel. While there is no right way to *feel*, there are certainly better or worse ways to *act*. Sometimes this even opens the discussion to transgression being not just something a person *does* but something they *neglect* to do—like not speaking with their sexual partner after a one-night stand. But that would be another book. Suffice to say that a healthy sexual culture is not only about permission but about respect, in a far broader sense. It's about changing a sexual culture.

Of course, teaching people to be in touch with their own desires won't stop all rapes! But transforming our sexual conversations so that people can talk honestly about the diversity of experiences and responses to them is a good basis for a less rape-prone society.

Sex is not destiny. Neither is rape. We are all human beings, and *we* decide how to write and rewrite our own narratives, with all their flaws and flukes and contradictions, precisely because they are our stories and they have to make sense to us. As Betty Martin says, "The worst kind of disempowerment is not knowing that you have the power that you actually have."[63]

Afterword: Notes from the Road

"That's brave," was the usual reaction when I told people I was writing a book about rape. This from people who earned their livings by juggling burning torches and butcher's knifes at medieval markets or had survived anorexia, when all I had to do was hit the keyboard on my laptop that didn't hit me back.

Of course, it was not brave to write this book. But it was brave to publish it.

My German publisher and I assumed a handful of university libraries would put in an order and that would be it. But then I was interviewed on TV before the manuscript was finished and later even on the news. Something had made this topic suddenly hot.

What had happened was obviously "New Year's Eve" in Cologne, but that wasn't all. German reality-TV star Gina-Lisa Lohfink was making headlines with a court case that divided the nation. At the outset, there were striking similarities between her case and the Ched Evans trial: Lohfink had no recollection of the incident and only found out about it when the two guys she had been with tried to sell a "sex video" to the press. After seeing the video, Lohfink suspected she had been given Rohypnol.

In both cases the court and the public were highly biased; only this time, the bias was against Lohfink. The media made much of Lohfink's breast implants and the fact that she had performed in a *real* sex video—as opposed to the one that was shot against her will (and shown in court against her will, too). The case ended with Lohfink being ordered to pay a 24,000-euro fine for wrongly accusing the two men of rape. Feminists started demonstrating against the ruling. Lohfink declared she'd rather go to prison and donate the money to charity. She lodged an appeal, inviting politicians to come along and see for themselves how rape victims were treated in court. This immense public attention on top of the Cologne incidents led to Germany's rape laws finally being changed in summer 2016. Curiously, neither of these cases would have been affected by the new law, but there was no denying that public opinion had turned.

Under the old German law, there had to be force for a case to be considered rape. Where British law tries to implement *yes means yes*, Germany didn't even accept *no means no*, except in cases where the victim was "helplessly at the mercy" of the perpetrator.

Yet even what that meant was debatable. For example, cases could be dismissed if the rape had taken place in a block of flats and the victim hadn't shouted for help—because someone somewhere, in another flat, might have heard. The law also made exceptions for threats with imminent danger to life or limb. The problem was that the threat had to concern the sexual act specifically; if it was more general, it didn't count. As Christian Rath reported incredulously in the German newspaper *Taz*,

> What this means becomes clear in a case the Federal Supreme Court had to decide in 2012: A man came to his ex-wife to force a reconciliation. At her place, he shot a visitor and threatened her she "would be next" if she didn't come with him. She followed him to his hotel, where he demanded sex and, fearing for her life, she complied. The court didn't see this as rape—because the threat had concerned her following him to the hotel and not the sexual act.[1]

But why was a conviction for rape so central? After all, the visitor-shooting ex-husband was going to prison for murder. The answer is that it is about recognizing people's perceptions of reality. First and foremost, calls for changes in law indicate that we long for shared values, such as: It is not okay to have sex with another person against their will. "Often women report a rape not because they want the perpetrator to be punished, but because they want him to see that he has done them a wrong and to make sure he won't do it again," stresses lawyer Christina Clemm. "If the result is that the police or the court tell her what she'd experienced as rape was fine by law, that's a catastrophe for the victim's self-esteem."[2]

Similar problems were apparent after "Cologne," because even though everybody was outraged by the assaults, by law they were mere "insults." "This is a profound problem for a state under the rule of law," Ulrike Lembke points out. "The state gets its authority from the promise to protect its citizens from assault by other people or states. This isn't a theoretical obligation but embedded in our constitution."[3] This sounds great, but it doesn't say who is considered a citizen and what is worthy of protection.

What's more, as it is very often word against word in rape cases, the hearing of evidence tends to center on the victim and their conduct. This is a strain for victims because the motivation behind going to court is usually the exact opposite: to be seen and heard and not to have to explain and defend and prove anything. What they hope for, usually, is for a higher power—the judge/common opinion—to tell the perpetrator: What you have done wasn't right, this is a person to respect, you can't treat them like this.

The problem is that courts are not made for that purpose, not just regarding rape cases. They are a very blunt instrument for a very intricate operation. Criminal proceedings are about executability and levels of penalties, and not about relief and reconciliation, nor even symbolic justice. But lacking other instances to publicly recognize injustice—which would lift the burden from individual victims and transform it into a collective pain that can be mourned and let go of collectively[4]—this fundamental social desire weighs down every rape trial in court. This isn't supposed to imply that judges should be biased toward the claimant or that democratic values like the presumption of innocence should be surrendered, but merely to acknowledge that this is a legitimate social desire that, like any other desire, needs space and recognition somewhere.

An example of how this desire can work out successfully is the International Criminal Court's decision to recognize the rapes during the war in former Yugoslavia as war crimes and a serious contravention of the Geneva Convention. In 2008, this led to the United Nations Security Council Resolution 1820, which determined that "rape and other forms of sexual violence can be punished as war crimes, crimes against humanity or as components of genocide." This didn't change the fact that people had been raped; what it did change though was how people dealt with it collectively. The first international conflict in which rape was condemned publicly in this manner was the war in Bosnia. Sociologists Cheryl Benard and Edit Schlaffer recount:

> In our interviews with refugees of ethnic cleansing, the way the women talked about their rapes was striking. Instead of highlighting them, they put them on a par with other brutal experiences. They perceived them in a desexualized manner, as part of the aggression against their overall group: children were frightened with gunshots, men beaten up, women raped, all part of the same violent procedure. The rapes were put in a scale of aggressions—a lot worse than just being robbed or terrorized, but a lot less bad than losing one's relatives. They talked without ambivalence, in the certain knowledge that the perpetrators were wrong. This wasn't about sex it was about war. The world's reaction was helpful here ... The victims didn't have to hide their experiences in shame; instead, a wide international public accused the perpetrators.[5]

The psychological relief is immense when one's own perception is confirmed by an authority on interpreting reality—whether that is a judge or the public at large. For this reason, negotiations about laws are always negotiations about reality. The law doesn't just define what is forbidden but also what is permitted, what is allowed to be, and what is allowed to be thought. If the law says that "no means no" and this has to be respected, that changes the social contract. And just as the German edition of this book was about to go to press, the social contract *was* changed in Germany.

It was only changed to *no means no,* mind, not to *yes means yes*, because lawyers were worried that the law would become "an instrument to uphold the 'right' social norm."[6] Britain was the archetype (and anti-type) for the new German law. Lawmakers in Germany studying the British Sexual Offences Act with the 2015 Rape and

Sexual Offence Guidelines asked questions like: Why are teenagers in Britain under the age of sixteen not allowed to have sex at all, not even with each other? Why is a boy who sleeps with a girl younger than sixteen a rapist, while a girl who sleeps with a boy younger than sixteen is only guilty of "sexual coercion"?[7] Why are children as young as ten years old being convicted of rape?[8]

As a result the German law is very careful to leave enough space for consenting adults (and consenting teenagers, if *both* parties are teenagers) so as not to criminalize "socially adequate behavior when initiating sexual contact."[9] This was mainly to prevent men who were fearful of being accused of rape from infantilizing women in future—telling them not "I know you want it too" but rather "I know you don't want it"—and putting them in a taxi for their own good. That's why in Germany people don't have to make sure the other person gives informed consent; as long as their partner doesn't say no and is able to do so, they are in the clear. So drunken sex is legal, but drugging others with Rohypnol or cases where the claimant is asleep or passed out are not.

All 601 members of Parliament present at the hearing voted for the new law, which would have been a rare first—had the right-wing Christian Democratic Union/Christian Social Union parties not added in a passage at the last minute so the vote was split: unanimous for "no means no" but with a lot of dissent for the new passage that makes it possible to deport sex offenders more quickly if they had been seeking asylum in Germany. Since the new act included sexual harassment—which could include minor sexual transgressions, like touching without consent—one MP warned, "This could mean that forcing a kiss on someone could now lead to a person being deported to a war zone." Now, it's against the German constitution to deport someone to a war zone, but *which* countries are considered war zones is a matter of definition. So every time I read about refugees being deported to Afghanistan—even though the Foreign Office warns travelers not to go there because of the bombs—I am reassured by the news that they are sexual offenders. Knowing about the wording of the law that is not very reassuring.

Another contentious part of the new legislation involved "offences committed out of a group," which basically determined that if a member of a group (not in a legal but in a colloquial sense) committed a sexual transgression, *all other members of that group* were perpetrators in the eyes of the law, whether or not they had seen or noticed the assault at all. Collective punishment is against the German constitution and the UN's Universal Declaration of Human Rights, both of which clearly state that a person can only be charged for individual and not collective wrong doings. It is doubtful whether that part of the law will ever be implemented, although similar laws for "gang-related" crimes have been controversially implemented in the UK. Nonetheless, in the heated debate after "Cologne," this law was passed.

But that wasn't all from the sex crime front. Shortly after, at the height of the United States presidential election, the *Washington Post* released a video of Republican nominee Donald Trump bragging that he couldn't help himself: when he saw a beautiful woman, he just had to kiss her. The tape culminated in Trump's statement that he could do anything with women, including "grab them by the pussy."[10]

Trump retorted that the recording had been made without his knowledge, and anyway it was ten years old and nothing more than "locker-room banter."[11] This might have worked, if it weren't for the sixteen (or more) women who subsequently came forward and accused him of sexual harassment. If he had been a refugee in Germany, he would have been on the next plane home. As it were, a month later he was elected the forty-fifth president of the United States.

In the weeks following the election I was asked about Donald Trump in every interview. I was too stunned to give an exhaustive answer, apart from pointing out that Germany's ideas of gender and sexuality were significantly different from America's—and that we shouldn't give up hope.

Since then, a lot of pussy hats have been knitted and been carried down the streets on countless demonstrators' heads; and one very lovely woman even made one for me after I mentioned on the radio that I wasn't very good at knitting. Donald Trump's gender politics, meanwhile, have stayed true to their promise. In February 2017, he rescinded Barack Obama's decree about granting some rights to transgender people. The part of the debate that made it into the news most often was the wrangling over the quaintly named "bathroom bill," aimed at forbidding trans people from using the toilets and changing rooms of their gender, and forcing them to use the ones that corresponded to the gender they had been assigned at birth. Most of the feminist movement stood with the trans movement, which was no small achievement since the argument to restrict trans rights was premised on safeguarding women's safety from "men who said they were women" in order to enter women-only spaces and rape them. This is not a tendentious reading of the law; it was the official explanation—although there is not a single documented case of a trans woman attacking a cis woman in a public toilet,[12] while there are quite a few cases of Republican politicians being arrested for sex offenses in bathrooms.[13]

The bathroom bill failed in nearly every state; even in North Carolina, where it was approved, parts of it had to be repealed. It is now known as one more moral panic. Nevertheless, the same arguments were brought forward when Britain announced in 2017 that it would change its Gender Recognition Act so that people didn't have to undergo sex reassignment surgery to have their gender officially accepted (they still can if they want, but don't have to)—in other words, people would be allowed to self-declare their gender. After all, who knew better? Quite a lot of people, it seemed. Columnist Janice Turner took it upon herself to speak for "30 million women" in Britain when she told the chair of the Women and Equalities Committee, Maria Miller, "You propose changes that will affect women's safety, privacy, sports."[14] And by "affect" she meant: affect negatively.

The idea that people perceived as male are inherently dangerous, even when they self-identify as female, is still rife. So is the idea that rape laws are there to protect women and women alone, as CDU politician Elisabeth Winkelmeier-Becker showed when she declared in 2016 that the new law was "a milestone for women's rights."[15] No, it isn't. It's a milestone for everybody's right to sexual self-determination.

Early in 2017, the German newspaper *Taz* invited me to do a reading at its premises in Berlin. Quite soon, it became apparent that many of the people present had experienced sexual violence in one way or another. The discussion finally centered around the word *victim*, which most of them saw as restrictive. A group of young women said they felt it put them in a box that they were never allowed to get out of. The term *survivor* was deemed problematic, too, because in Germany it usually describes survivors of the Holocaust. "And, also, it wasn't a question of life or death for me," explained one of them.

They suggested transforming the German word for "survivor," *Überlebende*, by taking away the prefix *über-* and replacing it with the more neutral prefix *er-*. *Erlebende sexualisierter Gewalt* translates as "people who have experienced sexual violence." This self-designation wasn't for use in court—because the term *victim* carries legal rights—nor was it intended as an umbrella term for all "people who have experienced sexual violence." It was simply an alternative collective noun to *victims*.

The feminist movement worldwide has had similar discussions since the 1990s, coming up with terms like "situational victim" and obviously the best known "survivor." So, I suggested to the women in Berlin that I could write an article for *Taz* about their suggestion and duly did so together with my colleague Marie Albrecht.[16] A week later, *Taz* editor Simone Schmollack wrote a counterpoint, arguing that *victim* was the best of all possible words. And that would have been it, if a feminist blog, hadn't published an open letter accusing me of victim-blaming because "the new term suggested that rape was a great experience, like going to the swimming pool."[17] (Even though I had never mentioned swimming pools and the German for experience has the same connotations as the English: it is neutral until it is qualified by an adjective.) Obviously, they were entitled to their opinion; the problem was that they sent the letter not to me but to every newspaper and radio station I was writing for. The letter didn't just blow the argument out of proportion, it also misquoted us. We had explicitly written: "Of course, *Erlebende* is not supposed to replace *victim*. If you decide *victim* or *survivor* is the right way to describe yourself, then that's what we will call you."[18] Still a couple of days later feminist magazine *EMMA* published an article titled "Victims Aren't Allowed to Be Called Victims Any Longer."

And then the e-mails started arriving.

The first one asked: "Now, how are you 'experiencing' the shitstorm?" What shitstorm? This question was answered by the next thousand or so which threatened: "I will make you 'experience'—a lot" or "Maybe you need surgery and a nice stretch in hospital after an 'experience' "—and those were the more restrained ones.

As surprising as it was that the outraged protectors of victims threatened me with rape, it was even more surprising that my biggest crime hadn't been the proposal of a new term but the countries my parents had been born in: "Daughter of a Pole and an Indian. We don't need such an ethnic mix." (Only in the original German, the words for "ethnic mix" had been misspelled.) And, completely out of context, "Islam doesn't belong to Germany." Nobody went for my white German co-author. The tenor was clear: "*Somebody like you is the proof that integration doesn't work*."

Numerous fake-news websites pulled my photo from the *EMMA* article and decorated it with captions like: "Do-gooder tells victims: rape can be an experience. Have fun!"[19] They reasoned that I "came from" a country where rape was "legal" and so I'd tell German women they should enjoy being raped by refugees—disregarding the fact that the country I "came from" was Germany. But even if we look at India, the country my father comes from, rape is by no means legal there; on the contrary, India has reintroduced the death penalty for rapists if the victim dies. But why use facts if you can have fakes?

A right-wing website ended an article about me with the exclamation: "Welcome to Rapefugeestan."[20] Others featured my address or my telephone number. The founder of the nationalist far-right movement Pegida (Patriotic Europeans Against the Islamization of the West), Lutz Bachmann, together with the extreme right-wing party AfD (Alternative for Germany), Sachsen, discovered feminism and criticized me using the same words as *EMMA*. Laurie Penny commented, "When right-wing extremists start quoting you, you should start rethinking your statements."[21] Meanwhile, I shoveled hate mail into a specially designated folder and reported messages like "you stupid xxxx piece of xxx, I hope you will get raped to death" to Facebook, which answered politely that this didn't contravene its guidelines.

So what have I learned from all this?

That solidarity really is the tenderness of the people. Apart from the shitstorm, there was a veritable lovestorm. People I didn't even know wrote me supportive messages, stood up for me online, and told the trolls to piss off. Journalist Marion Detjen published an article in *Die Zeit* detailing her own experience with sexual violence and how helpful it had been that she hadn't been called a "rape victim" back then (she wasn't called anything; the rape was referred to as "it" if it was referred to at all).[22] And Hannah C. Rosenblatt wrote:

> Mithu Sanyal has talked to people who are called victims and asked them what they wanted to be called themselves. She has brought their wish to determine what they are called themselves into the media. As a person who has been the victim of sexual violence this is what I have longed for for years.[23]

I have to admit I cried. The debate made a lot of things clear, such as that language is by no means irrelevant—otherwise nobody would have been upset by the proposal. Also that some people are determined to link rape and refugees rhetorically, come hell or high water.

And that whenever we talk about rape someone will soon start calling for censorship.

Maybe some readers will remember the "butter controversy." The debate was triggered by an interview with director Bernardo Bertolucci at the Cinemathèque Francaise that had been widely ignored back in 2013, but went viral when it was posted on Facebook in late 2016. It concerned the rape scene in *The Last Tango in Paris,* where Paul (Marlon Brando) uses a piece of butter to anally rape his film partner Jeanne (Maria Schneider). In reality, Brando and Bertolucci hadn't used the butter to enter Schneider's body. But the scene wasn't in the script and Schneider was only told at the last minute, without the option of protesting. The theory that actors act more convincingly when they really live the story—method acting—was much in vogue in the 1970s when *The Last Tango* was shot. Nobody thought it was unethical, maybe a little pretentious. As when Dustin Hoffman prepared for his role in *Marathon Man* by fasting and through sleep deprivation and arrived in LA a nervous wreck. Laurence Olivier looked at him and gave him his famous advice: "My dear boy, why don't you just try acting?"[24]

In fact, the butter scene was so convincing that Schneider was deeply unsettled and has hated Bertolluci ever since. In a 2007 interview, she'd felt "a little raped."[25] What do you do when what you thought was a brilliant idea turns out to be a brilliant disaster that causes someone significant harm? Correct, ignore the problem and do nothing to make things better. At least that's what Brando and Bertolluci did. Maybe because they were unsettled themselves. Marlon Brando has also said the shooting traumatized him. We don't know the ultimate reasons. But we do know that Bertolucci said in the famous 2013 interview at the Cinemathèque Francaise he felt guilty for what he had done to Maria Schneider.

There are a lot of sad things about the whole story: nobody believed Schneider until Bertolucci had confirmed her account, but also that it was this confession that he still felt guilty that started the shitstorm. What would have happened if he had denied it? Probably not very much. The butter scene made him famous, but his human reaction—to feel guilty because he had harmed another human being—earned him contempt. This doesn't mean we have to feel sorry for him. That's not what this is all about. But it would be great to create a climate of candor, where people can say that they have made a mistake and learn from it.

Admittedly, Bertolucci went on to declare that he stood by his decision on "artistic" grounds, because he'd wanted Schneider's reaction "as a girl, not as an actress."[26] Her "real anger" and "real humiliation" had been more important to him than not humiliating her. All the same, the suggestion that no one should ever watch Bertolucci's films wasn't a solution. It is rarely helpful to make an example of anybody; Bertolucci would merely be a pawn sacrifice that wouldn't change anything about the film industry's handling of rape. In the end Bertolucci wasn't shunned, as Harvey Weinstein would be a year later.

Rape on film has by no means a glorious history. The first time a mainstream Hollywood film showed a naked female breast, after the moral guidelines of the Hays Code had forbidden nearly all sexuality, was in 1964 in *The Pawnbroker*. The reason that scene got past the censors was that the breast was shown in the context of a rape—and, even more cynically, a rape in a Nazi concentration camp. Did director Sidney Lumet want to show the horror of fascism? Definitely. But in the scene, he wanted to show the breast. Otherwise he could have shot it from behind as his camera team suggested. Sex sells and so does violence. When I was thirteen, the sexiest women on German TV were rape victims with torn red dresses and enormous pupils in their terror-stricken eyes. Even when a film is about the horror of rape, the language of its imagery more often than not says something else completely.

That's why it's so difficult to make an anti-rape film. In October 2016 the rape crisis centers in Baden-Württemberg, Germany, worked with the film academy Konstanz to produce an informational film titled *Stop Rape*. The title was very much the message of the film. The team comprised of more women than men; the rape that was shown happened at home and not in a dark street. Still, many cinemagoers said they were (re)traumatized by being confronted with the film without any warning, among the advertisements before another film.

Maybe it isn't about a "right" or "better" way to show rape in film. Maybe it is about why we show rape with such monotonous regularity, as if we didn't have scores of other ways to create emotional drama on screen. Because by showing a rape we reproduce it—at least on the visual plane. Yes, sometimes rape is central to the plot. But according to Joanna Bourke, every eighth Hollywood movie boasts—and I use the verb advisedly—a rape scene. Now, it is obviously important not to hush up rape, but it is also important not to purport that rape is just part of everyday life. It isn't—or it shouldn't be. But that's what it looks like in the cinema.

Therefore, I would like to propose the Sanyal test, grandiosely analogous to the Bechdel test—which a film passes if (1) two women who both have names are (2) shown having a conversation about (3) something other than a man. My version checks three simple points as well: 1 Does the film have one—or more than one—rape scene? 2 If so, is the scene simply a code for the raped character's emotional backstory and not essential to the plot? 3 Is there a more original way to drive the plot? If the answer to these three questions is yes, the scene should be cut from the script and the writers should think more creatively.

Still things are changing in Hollywood. As a rule, rape scenes are now shot with a "rape choreographer" to make sure the actors aren't traumatized in the process.

Then came #metoo. In the wake of the allegations of sexual abuse against Hollywood mogul Harvey Weinstein, actor Alyssa Milano tweeted: "If you have been sexually harassed or assaulted write 'me too' as a reply to this tweet." And the replies poured in.

Soon there was a deluge of similar and disparate experiences on the internet, highlighting the ubiquity of the problem. Though Milano was widely seen as the originator of the hashtag, she'd never claimed she'd started it. In fact, it was a black activist ten years earlier, Tarana Burke, who coined it as a means to assist healing—what Burke called "empowerment by empathy."[27] And #metoo has created a lot of empathy. It's given stories and experiences the public space and attention they had been denied. It's a bit like the people writing to me, only on a global scale. It's what the courts couldn't deliver. These stories need to come out; they need a community and collective mourning. And it hasn't just happened online. People are calling into talk shows on the radio and even on TV in the sudden, safe knowledge that they will be believed and welcomed.

The downside is that the discussion—like many discussions of sexism in the media—tends to reproduce the same old stereotypes: hunter/prey, active/passive, powerful/powerless. Reading the newspapers one gets the impression that women are endangered no matter how rich and famous they are and that the world is a dangerous place for them. On one call-in show, a woman described how she had been attacked while out jogging. The perpetrator came up behind her and put his hand over her mouth. She took his little finger and pulled it away, breaking his grip, and escaped. The shocked presenter replied, "That must have been traumatizing"—completely overlooking the fact that she had defended herself successfully.[28] For Laura Kipnis, this omission is part of the problem: "Gender is a system: male aggresion and female passivity are *both* social pathologies that are, to varying degrees normalized. Changing any element (including reducing female passivity) is going to alter the dynamics of the system."[29]

The other disconcerting factor is that—again like in most public outrages—the first impulse seemed to be "who is to blame." At least it looked that way in Hollywood, and then in the British Parliament, which soon had to deal with their own allegations of sexual transgressions. It's a bit like a game of musical chairs; every time the music stops, a few more careers have been terminated.

Judith Butler told an audience at the University of Zurich that she was concerned about the vehemence with which Weinstein was degraded. It gave her a ghostly feeling of déjà vu: *If we haven't managed to prevent Trump, at least we can take down another powerful white man.*[30] The words "witch hunt" soon crept into the conversation. While nobody doubts that serious misconduct has been perpetrated, it is still worrying that people are punished before an investigation, and even more so that the public should applaud this jettisoning of democratic rights. After all, there is only a gradual difference between treating victims without empathy and treating potential perpetrators without empathy.

It should go without saying that #metoo is still incredible, and incredibly important. As we talk about it endlessly on every channel, new social values and norms are being negotiated and communicated widely. #Metoo is the most resounding possible PR campaign for socially acceptable behavior. "Think of Harvey Weinstein" has become shorthand for: *Be careful, you are transgressing sexual boundaries*. Where before people were considered spoilsports when they opened their mouths, suddenly they are simply normal. The time seems to be ripe for a new negotiation of the treacherous territory that is sexual violence.

In 2018, Sweden again decided to be a trailblazer by passing a bill that sex without consent constitutes rape. On its face, this seemed to be the same as the new German law—and the Swedish government pointed out that it is only the tenth country in Europe to recognize that sex without consent is rape (the others are England, Wales, Scotland, Northern Ireland, the Republic of Ireland, Belgium, Cyprus, Luxembourg, Iceland, and Germany). Only Sweden didn't choose *no means no* but *yes means yes*. Under the new law, a person must now consent to sexual activity with words or clear body language: "If a person wants to engage in sexual activities with someone who remains inactive or gives ambiguous signals, he or she will therefore have to find out if the other person is willing."[31]

International media sneered: "Sweden is now the least romantic country on earth."[32] German news magazine *Der Focus* was so shocked that it claimed Swedish men had to get their sexual partners to sign a contract before engaging in sex at all. It issued a correction after Swedish diplomat Nina Rölke explained that nobody had to sign any contract if they didn't want to, just as nobody had to have sex if they didn't want to: "It's not rocket science that sex has to be consensual, but when you put that into law people seem to be very upset. I don't know why, but the fact that there is all this outcry about it shows that consent isn't self-evident."[33]

But not only Germans seemed to be wary about the new law. Swedish defense attorney Baharak Vaziri launched a sexual consent app with the telling name Libra. She was deluged with complaints that the app not only made a mockery of the new law but also ignored the fact that people might change their minds halfway through. Still, the app is set to launch in Germany, Austria, and Switzerland. And in England, a growing number of teenagers record a kind of "contract" on their phones before having sex: *Do you want it? Yes. Yes.* This shows that there is real fear and insecurity about the new law and the nature of consent in general. That has to be addressed, too. And in a more meaningful way than the usual quibs: In sex everything is okay except sexism.

Since the new law was approved, I've asked Swedish lawyers and law professors: What will it mean for sexual interactions? How will it affect court cases? Will the interpretation of the law reflect gender stereotypes? Their answers were cautious: the new law is more of a message to society then an instrument to gauge consent and punish nonconsensual sex, since the absence of consent will still have to be proven.

As a message it has definitely worked. Sweden has got a new debate about consent. The question remains whether this can best be debated by laws or for example by sex education. Luckily, Sweden's Crime Victim Compensation and Support Authority has simultaneously been given the task to produce information and education campaigns.

But what about gender stereotypes? "Everybody is responsible for making sure whether there is consent or not. That goes for men, women, and other genders," emphasizes Rölke. The Swedish government, however, insists, "The responsibility of men and boys must be clarified."[34] Sex educator Rona Torenz comments, "When speaking about *yes means yes*, we operate with a very antagonistic and gendered giver-receiver model. The receiver of consent—imagined as male—has to ask and the receiver—imagined as female—is then supposed to say yes or no. That is not a good model for relationships, sexual or otherwise."[35]

Also in 2018, the Swedish Academy postponed the Nobel Prize for Literature to 2019 following sexual-abuse allegations. #Metoo had arrived in the book world. One of the most controversial cases involving writers was that of author Junot Diaz of Pulitzer Prize fame, because it blurred the boundaries between victims and perpetrators. In April 2018, Diaz had published an essay in the *New Yorker* revealing he had been raped when he was eight years old by "a grown up" he'd "truly trusted."[36] In May, when Diaz was on a panel at the Sydney Writers' Festival, author Zinzi Clemmons went to the microphone and accused him of having written his essay as a "cover" to protect against allegations that were going to come out against him. She later clarified on Twitter that Diaz had cornered and "forcibly kissed"[37] her six years earlier, when she had been a student and had invited him to do a workshop at her university. In the wake of

Clemmons' revelation, author Alisa Valdes detailed her relationship with Diaz:

> I thought we were soul mates. Two bright rising star Latino writers. Similar politics. Similar styles. I told him this. He said he agreed . . . He also had a girlfriend he had never told me about and, once he *did tell me*, said wasn't a big deal because he cheated on her all the time and she put up with it.[38]

After that, he'd asked Valdes to clean his kitchen because he was too depressed to do it himself.

> He had just told me about the girlfriend, and thought I would still want to clean his kitchen. When I asked him about this, he laughed and called out from his futon on the floor in his bedroom: "Sweetie, you can take the man out of the D.R., but you can't take the Dominican out of the man."[39]

In answer to Clemmons' tweet, author Carmen Maria Machado wrote: "When I made the mistake of asking him a question about his protagonist's unhealthy, pathological relationship with women, he went off on me for twenty minutes."[40] The protagonist in question is Yunior de Las Casas, Diaz's alter ego and the narrator of his 2008 novel *The Brief Wondrous Life of Oscar Wao* as well as a returning character in his books. So it wasn't a hundred miles away to imagine that he also shared some of his author's flaws. Likewise in his *New Yorker* piece Diaz had described the repercussions of his childhood abuse on his life—depression, addiction, suicide attempts—and on his love life—continual cheating and general mistreatment of women.

That made him an awful boyfriend. But did it make him unsuitable to be the chairman of the Pulitzer committee? He stepped down from the chair less than a week after the allegations. And what about his books: Is it appropriate that several bookshops announced they would not stock his novels any longer? The case is fascinating on so many levels because it shows that #metoo isn't just about sexual crimes but about a much wider discussion of sexual ethics.

Undoubtably, Diaz behaved unethically. But he wasn't the only one. Accusing someone without listening to their reaction—as Clemmons did at the Sydney Writers' Festival, again with good reason—is unethical. Calling his own abuse story a "preemptive strike"—as not only Clemmons but loads of people have done since—is unethical. Sure, Diaz's *New Yorker* piece is uncomfortable reading, especially for the women he'd cheated on, because he didn't so much ask for their forgiveness as bestow it upon himself. The text also functions to build him up: *See, all these gorgeous women loved me and I treated them badly*. But narcissism isn't a crime. Kissing someone without their consent is though, albeit a minor one. And raping an eight-year-old child is a major one.

So where does this leave us? With the realization that sexual and relationship ethics are an integral part of the discussion about sexual violence, but they are not the same thing. We must address them both if we really want to change our sexual and emotional culture, but behaving like an asshole doesn't warrant being shunned from society. The reason why all these stories are coming up now is that, for too long, that was just the way relationships/the job market/the book world worked. Now it's time to talk about alternatives. The problem with speaking about sexism is that the language we have to do so is in itself sexist. This shouldn't dishearten us, but it should make us humble when attempting that challenge.

This afterword was written mainly on the road. Coming home on the train after a reading in Frankfurt, I sat opposite two highly intoxicated young men who were keen on conversation. They asked me what I had done in Frankfurt.

"A reading," I told them.

"A reading?"

"Yes, a reading."

Eventually I told them the title of my book. To my surprise, the one who was the most drunk immediately called out, "I'm sure you think that only women can be raped! Let me tell you, I was raped regularly by my ex-girlfriend for half a year." The other one looked at him with bleary eyes and retorted: "Well, if you hadn't wanted it, you could have left her."

It was a magical moment to be able to tell them that of course men can be raped and that we know by now how hard it is to leave an abusive relationship. The nature of the conversation swiftly changed. The friend asked his drunken mate, "Do you think I wasn't enough of a friend? Should I have supported you more?"

I was awed, as I am every time people share their stories with me after lectures and workshops. This book is for you.

Bibliography

Abrahamsen, David. *The Psychology of Crime*. Columbia University Press, 1960.

Adamczak, Bini. "Po auf Finger." *Missy Magazine* March/April/May 2016, p. 102.

Alcoff, Linda Martin and Gray-Rosendale, Laura. "Survivor Discourse: Transgression or Recuperation?" *Signs* 18:2 (1993), p. 281.

Allen, Mike. "Bush Reverses Abortion Aid: U.S. Funds Are Denied to Groups That Promote Procedure Abroad." *Washington Post* January 23, 2001.

Appleton, Tom. "Bei den Affen: Mit Tarzan im Dschungel der Städte und Bücher." *Telepolis* February 4, 2012.

Arendt, Hannah. *Macht und Gewalt*. Piper, 1970.

Aristotle. De Generatione Animalium Arnsperger, Malte: Der Triumph des Missmutigen. *Stern* October 5, 2011.

Ashbrook, Penny. "Rape on Screen." *SpareRib* April 1989, p. 38.

St. Augustine. *The City of God* (Book 1, Chapter 19). Library of Nicene and Post-Nicene Fathers, 2005.

Baker, Katie J. M. "What Do We Do With These Men?" *New York Times* April 27, 2018.

Beckford, Martin. "Sarah Palin: hunt WikiLeaks founder like al-Qaeda and Taliban leaders." *The Telegraph* November 30, 2010.

Benedict, Helen. *Virgin or Vamp: How the Press Covers Sex Crimes*. Oxford University Press, 1992.

Benard, Cheryl and Edith Schlaffer. *Die Emotionsfalle: Vom Triumph des weiblichen Verstandes*. Krüger, 1999.

Benetar, David. *The Second Sexism: Discrimination Against Men and Boys*. Wiley-Blackwell, 2012.

Beyerstein, Lindsay. "A Feminist Lawyer on the Case Against Wikileaks' Julian Assange." bigthink.com.

Bianco, Marcia. "Statistics Show Exactly How Many Times Trans People Have Attacked You in Bathrooms." *Mic* April 2, 2016.

Blakely, Mary Kay. "New Bedford Gang Rape: Who were the men?" *Ms* July 1983, p. 51.

Bonger, William. *Criminality and Economic Conditions*. Little Brown, 1916.

Bordo, Susan. *The Male Body: A New Look at Men in Public and Private*. Farrar, Strauss & Giroux, 1999.

Bourke, Joanna. *Rape: A History from 1860 to the Present*. Virago, 2007.

Bower, Elisabeth. *Ladie's Night*. Seal Press, 1993.

Brenssell, Ariane. "Trauma als Prozess – Wider die Pathologisierung struktureller Gewalt und ihrer innerpsychologischen Folgen." Lecture, Trauma und Politik, Frankfurt am Main January 24, 2013.

Brenssell, Ariane. "Trauma politisch verstehen." Ansätze aus der kritischen Psychologie. Abstract from her lecture with *aufgetaucht. Kritische Psychologie in Halle* February 12, 2015.

Brenssell, Ariane. "Traumaverstehen." In *Störungen: texte kritische psychologie* 4. eds. Brenssell, Ariana and Klaus Weber, Argument Verlag, 2016, p. 123–50.

Brenssell, Ariane and Klaus Weber (eds.). *Störungen: texte kritische psychologie* 4. Argument Verlag, 2016.

Brown, Wendy and Janet Halley (eds.). *Left Legalism/Left Critique*. Duke University Press, 2002.

Brownmiller, Susan. *Against Our Will: Men, Women and Rape*. Simon and Schuster, 1975.

Buchwald, Emilie, Pamela Fletcher, and Martha Roth (eds.). *Transforming a Rape Culture*. Milkweed Editions, 2005.

Burroughs, Edward Rice. *Tarzan of the Apes*. Create Space Independent Publishing, 2017.

Butler, Judith. "Endangered/Endangering: Schematic Racism and White Paranoia." in *Reading Rodney King/Reading Urban Uprising*. ed. Robert Gooding-Williams, Routledge, 1993, p. 17.

Butler, Judith. "Vulnerability And Resistance Revisited." Lecture, Trinity College, February 5, 2015.

Cahill, Ann J. *Rethinking Rape*. Cornell University Press, 2001.

Campbell, Beatrix. "The Accused on Release." *Marxism Today* March 1989, p. 43

Cauterucci, Christina. "Why It's Reasonable to Feel a Queasy Mix of Emotions About the 'Shitty Media Men' Spreadsheat." *Slate.com* October 12, 2017.

Chancer, Lynn S. "The Before and After of a Group Rape." *Gender & Society* 1:3 (1987), p. 248f.

Chivers, Meredith L. et al. "A Sex Difference in the Specificity of Sexual Arousal." *Psychological Science* 15:11 (2004), pp. 736–44.

Clark, Anna. "Why Does Popular Culture Treat Prison Rape As a Joke?" *Alternet*, August 16, 2009.

Cleaver, Eldridge. *Soul on Ice*. Dell/Delta, 1991.

Cleese, John and Connie Booth. "Fawlty Towers: The Kipper and the Corpse." *BBC* March 12, 1979.

Clemm, Christina and Tanja Mokosch. "Das Sexualstrafrecht basiert auf Mythen." *Süddeutsche Zeitung* August 13, 2014.

Clendinen, Dudley. "Barroom Rape Shames Town of Proud Heritage." *New York Times* March 16, 1983.

Connell, Noreen and Wilson, Cassandra (eds.) for New York Radical Feminists. *Rape: The First Sourcebook for Women*. New American Library, 1974.

Cosens, Claire. "Polanski wins libel case against Vanity Fair." *The Guardian* July 22, 2005.

Clover, Carol. *Men, Women, and Chainsaws*. Princeton University Press, 1992.

Condry, John and Sandra Condry. "Sex Differences: A Study of the Eye of the Beholder." *Child Development* 47:3 (1976), pp. 812–19.

Corbin, Alain. *Die sexuelle Gewalt in der Geschichte*. Wagenbach, 1992.

Coveney, Lal et al. *The Sexuality Papers. Male Sexuality and the Social Control of Women*. Hutchinson Educational, 1984.

Crenshaw, Kimberley. "Mapping the Margins: Intersectionality, Identity Politics, and Violence Against Women of Color." *Stanford Law Review*, 43:6 (1991), p. 1269.

Daly, Mary. *Gyn/Ecology: The Metaethics of Radical Feminism*. Beacon Press, 1978.

Dane, Gesa. "Frauenraub-Entehrung-Notzucht." in *Unzucht – Notzucht – Vergewaltigung: Definitionen und Deutungen sexueller Gewalt von der Aufklärung bis heute*. ed. Christine Künzel, Campus, 2003, pp. 89–204.

Dane, Gesa. *"Zeter und Mordio:" Vergewaltigung in Literatur und Recht. Wallstein*, Göttingen 2005.

Dargent, Ralf. "Die Bloßstellung von 'Wetterfuzzi' Kachelmann bei Jauch." *Die Welt* October 15, 2012.

Darwin, Charles. *The Descent of Man and Selection in Relation to Sex*. 1871. Prometheus Books, 1998.

Darwin Correspondence Project, University of Cambridge.

Davidson, Julie. "Victim's Voice—*Rape: My Story* by Jill Saward and Wendy Green." *London Review of Books* 13:2 (1991).

Davis, Andrew Jackson. *The Genesis and Ethics of Conjugal Love*. Progressive Publishing House, 1874.

Davis, Angela Y.. *Women, Race & Class*. Vintage Books (Random House), 1983.

Despentes, Virginie. *King Kong Theory*. The Feminist Press, 2010.

Deutsch, Helene. *The Psychology of Women, Vol. II*. Grune & Stratton, 1945.

Díaz, Junot. "The Silence: The Legacy of Childhood Trauma." *The New Yorker* April 16, 2018.

Diederichsen, Diedrich and Florian Cramer. "Verknüpfung, Markt und Medien", Lecture, Kulturwissenschaftliches Institut Essen, Café Central,

Grillo Theater, Essen, December 15, 2009.

Diski, Jenni. "Diary." *London Review of Books* 31:21 (2009), p. 53.

Dietz, Dr. Park, appearing on "Charlie Brooker's Newswipe." *BBC* March 25, 2009.

Doblhofer, Georg. *Vergewaltigung in der Antike: Beiträge zur Altertumskunde*. De Gruyter, 1994.

Donaldson, Stephen. "Jim Goad: The Punk who wouldn't shut up." *ANSWER ME!* Vol. 4 (1994) p. 28.

Dubois, Ellen Carol and Linda Gordon. "Seeking ecstasy on the Battlefield: Danger and Pleasure in Nineteenth-century Feminist Sexual Thought." In *Pleasure and Danger. Exploring Female Sexuality* ed. Vance, Carole S., Routledge & Kegan Paul, 1989, pp. 31–49.

Dunant, Sarah. *Transgressions*. Random House, 2005.

Dworkin, Andrea. *Letters from a War Zone*. Secker and Warburg, 1988.

Dworkin, Andrea. *Pornography: Men Possessing Women*. Penguin, 1989.

Eckert, Penelope and Sally McConnell-Ginet. *Language and Gender*. Cambridge University Press, 2013.

Ehrhardt, Christoph. "Wo sexuelle Belästigung Alltag ist." *Frankfurter Allgemeine Zeitung* January 15, 2016.

Ellis, Havelock. *Das Geschlechtsgefühl: Eine Biologische Studie*. Curt Kabitzsch, 1909.

Elsner, Erich and Dr. Wiebke Steffen. *Vergewaltigung und sexuelle Nötigung in Bayern. Zusammenfassung der Untersuchungsergebnisse und kriminologische Wertung*. Bayerisches Landeskriminalamt, 2005.

Elva, Thordis and Tom Stranger. *South of Forgiveness*. Scribe, 2017.

Estrich, Susan. *Real Rape*. Harvard University Press, 1988.

Fae, Jane. "Trans or otherwise, it's time to overhaul the law on 'rape by deception.'" *The New Statesman* June 30, 2013.

Fagot, Beverly I. "The Influence of Sex of Child on Parental Reactions to Toddler Children." *Child Development* 49:2 (1978), pp. 459–65.

Farr, James. "So Vile and Miserable an Estate: The Problem of Slavery in Locke's Political Thought." *Political Theory*, 12:2 (1986), pp. 263–89.

Feige, David. "Shawna: A Life on the Sex Offender Registry." *The Marshall Project* September 17, 2017.

Fein, Ellen and Sherrie Schneider. *The Rules: How to Capture the Heart of Mr Right*. Grand Central Publishing, 1995.

Fein, Ellen and Sherrie Schneider. *The Rules II: More Rules to Live and Love By*. Thornsons, 1997.

Fein, Ellen and Sherrie Schneider. *The New Rules: The Dating Dos and Don'ts for the Digital Generation*. Piatkus, 2013.

Feller, Stephen. "Study: Acting tough may be bad for men's health." *upi.com* March 23, 2016.

Ferguson, Margaret W., Quilligan, Maureen and Nancy J. Vickers. *Rewriting the Renaissance: The Discourse of Sexual Difference in Early Modern Europe*. University of Chicago Press, 1986.

Ferguson, Sian. "3 Reasons Why Saying 'Real Men Don't Rape' Reinforces Rape Culture." *everydayfeminism.com* February 28, 2015.

Fichte, Johann Gottlieb. "Deduktion der Ehe. §§ 3 und 4." In *Fichte: Werke in sechs Bänden*. 1796. Felix Meisner, 1911.

Filipovic, Jill. "Is the US the only country where more men are raped than women?" *The Guardian* February 22, 2012.

Firestone, Shulamith. *The Dialectic of Sex: The Case for a Feminist Revolution*. Bantam Books, 1972.

Firma, Terry. "More Republican Politicians than Trans People Have Been Arrested For Sex Acts in Bathrooms." *Patheos* April 11, 2016.

Fiske, John. *Media Matters: Everyday Culture and Political Change*. University of Minnesota Press, 1994.

FlightScarlet. "Does Rape Culture Exist?" *BLOGHER* February 12, 2016.

Foucault, Michel. *The Archaeology of Knowledge*. Pantheon, 1972.

Foucault, Michel. *Politics, Philosophy, Culture: Interviews and Other Writings: 1977–1984*. Routledge, 1988.

Foucault, Michel. *The History of Sexuality, Volume I: An Introduction*. Trans. Robert Hurley. Gallimard, 1978.

Franck, Sebastian. *Weltbuch: spiegel und bildtnis des gesantzen Erdtbodens*. Morhart, 1542, p. 228.

French, Marilyn. *The Women's Room*. Virago, 1997.

Freud, Sigmund. *Three Contributions to the Theory of Sex*, 1905.

Friedman, Jaclyn. "Toxic Masculinity." *The American Project* March 13, 2013.

Friedman, Jaclyn and Jessica Valenti (eds.). *Yes Means Yes: Visions of Female Sexual Power & a World Without Rape*. Seal Press, 2008.

Friedrichsen, Gisela. "Die Angst der Richter vor dem klaren Wort." *Der Spiegel* June 1, 2011.

Frommel, Monika. "'Nein heißt nein' und der Fall Lohfink." *Novo* June 27, 2016.

Frus, Phyllis. "Documenting Domestic Violence in American Films." in *Violence and American Cinema*. ed. David J. Slocum, Routledge, 2001, pp. 226–44.

Fusco, Coco. *A Field Guide for Female Interrogators*. Seven Stories Press, 2008.

Fusco, Coco. "Invasion of Space by a Female." In *Yes Means Yes: Visions of Female Sexual Power & a World Without Rape*. eds. Friedman, Jaclyn and Jessica Valenti, Seal Press, 2008, pp. 127–40.

Gadan, Ralph. "Migration importiert archaisches Frauenbild." *Die Welt* February 1, 2016.

Gehmacher, Johanna,, Gabriella Hauch and Marie Messner (eds.). *Bodies/*

Politics. Österreichische Zeitschrift für Geschichtswissenschaften, January 2004.

Geimer, Samantha. "Judge the Movie, Not the Man." *Los Angeles Times* February 23, 2003.

Geimer, Samantha and Judith Newman. *The Girl*. Simon & Schuster, 2013.

Gender Initiativkolleg (ed.). *Gewalt und Handlungsmacht: Queer Feministische Perspektiven*. Campus, 2012.

Gensing, Patrick. "Rechtsextreme Reaktionen nach Köln: 'Rache für unsere Frauen'." *tagesschau.de* January 12, 2016.

Gibbon, Edward. *The History of the Decline and Fall of the Roman Empire, Band IV*. 1788. Baudry's European Library, 1840.

Gray, Norma B., Gloria J. Paileo and G. David Johnson. "Explaining rape victim blame: A test of attribution theory." *Sociological Spectrum* 13:4 (1993) pp. 377–92.

Grieger, Katja et al. "Was Ihnen Widerfahren Ist, Ist In Deutschland Nicht Strafbar."

Griffin, Susan. *Made From This Earth: Selections from her Writing*. Women's Press, 1982.

Griffin, Susan. "Rape: The All-American Crime." in *Rape: The Power of Consciousness*. Harper & Row, 1979, pp. 3–22.

Grimm, Jacob. "Über die Notnunft an Frauen." In *Zeitschriftt für Deutsches Recht und deutsche Rechtswissenschaft, Book* 5, 1841, pp. 1–29.

Groth, Nicholas A, and Ann Wolbert Burgess. "Sexual Dysfunction during Rape." *The New England Journal of Medicine* October 6, 1977, pp. 764–6.

Hall, Edith. *Joe Queenan: A Brief History of Shame*. *BBC Radio* 4 June 27, 2015.

Hallinger, Etta and Mithu Sanyal. Interview. *Missy Magazine* April 2011.

Hans, Barbara and Johannes Korge. "BKA-Studie: Ein Drittel aller 'Ehrenmord'-Opfer sind männlich." *Der Speigel*, August 5, 2011.

Hartmann, Heidi and Ellen Ross. "Comment on 'On Writing the History of Rape'." *Signs* 3:4 (1978), pp. 931–35.

Hegel, Georg Wilhelm Friedrich. "Vorlesung über die Philososphie der Geschichte." In *Hegel: Werke in 20 Bänden, Book 12*. Suhrkamp, 1970.

Heller, Zoe. "Pride and Prejudice." *The New York Review of Books* November 27, 2012.

Hentig, Hans von. "Remarks on the Interaction of Perpetrator and Victim." *Journal of Criminal Law and Ciminal Behaviour* 31 (1940), pp. 303–9.

Higgins, Lynn A. and Brenda R. Silver (eds.). *Rape and Representation*. Columbia University Press, 1991.

Higgins, Lynn A. "Screen/Memory: Rape and Its Alibis in Last Year at Marienbad" in *Rape and Representation*. eds. Higgins, Lynn A. and

Brenda R. Silver, Columbia University Press, 1991, pp. 303–21.

Hildebrandt, Antje. "Gina-Lisa Lohfink vor Gericht als 'Hure' beschimpft." *Die Welt* June 1, 2016.

Holloway, Kati. "Toxic masculinity is killing men: The roots of male trauma." *salon.com* June 12, 2015.

Holmes, Guy and Liz Offen. "Clinicians' hypotheses regarding clients' problems: are they less likely to hypothesize sexual abuse in male compared to female clients?" *Child Abuse & Neglect* 20:6 (1996), pp. 493–501.

Hommen, Tanja. "'Sie hat sich nicht im Geringsten gewehrt:' Zur Kontinuität kultureller Deutungsmuster sexueller Gewalt seit dem Kaiserreich." In *Unzucht – Notzucht – Vergewaltigung: Definitionen und Deutungen sexueller Gewalt von der Aufklärung bis heute*. ed. Künzel, Christine, Campus, 2003, p.119–136.

hooks, bell. *All About Love*. Harper, 2000.

hooks, bell. *Feminist Theory: From Margin to Center*. South End Press Classics, 2000.

Horek, Tanya. *Public Rape: Representating Violation in Fiction and Film*. Routledge, 2004.

Howson, Nick. "Ched Evans: Oldham Athletic move off after club officials' families subjected to rape and death threats." *International Business Times* January 8, 2015.

Huie, William Bradford. "Killer's Confession: The Shocking Story of Approved Killing in Missisippi." *Look Magazine* January 24, 1956. Irwin, Mary Ann. "'White Slavery' As Metaphor: Anatomy of a Moral Panic." *Ex Post Facto: The History Journal* Vol. 5 (1996).

Jervis, Lisa and Andi Zeisler (eds.). *BITCHfest: Ten Years of Cultural Criticism from the Pages of Bitch Magazine*. Farrar, Straus & Giroux, 2006.

Joel, Daphna and Anne Fausto-Sterling. "Beyond sex differences: New approaches for thinking about variation in brain structure and function." *Phil. Trans. R. Soc. B.*, 371:20150451 (2016).

Johnson, Dominic. "Sarkozy befremdet Afrika." *Die Tageszeitung* August 1, 2007.

Jüttner, Julia. "Kachelmann-Talk bei Maischberger: Freie Bahn für Schwarzer." *Spiegel Online* June 1, 2011.

Kachelmann, Jörg. *Recht und Gerechtigkeit: Ein Märchen aus der Provinz*. Heyne, 2012.

Kästner, Sibylle. "Rund ums Geschlecht. Ein Überblick zu feministischen Geschlechtertheorien und deren Anwendung auf die archäologische Forschung." In *Vom Knochenmann zur Menschenfrau: Feministische Theorie und archäologische Praxis*. eds. Karlisch, Sigrun M., Sibylle Kästner and Eva-Maria Mertens, Agenda Verlag, 1977, pp. 13–29.

Kampusch, Natascha. "Anfeindungen seltener." *ORF.at* March 24, 2015.

Kanin, Eugene J. "False Rape Allegations." *Archives of Sexual Behaviour* 23:1 (1994), pp. 81–92.

Kant, Immanuel. *Die Religion innerhalb der Grenzen der bloßen Vernunft. Die Metaphysik der Sitten.* 1793. Akademieausgabe von Immanuel Kants Gesammelten Werken, digitalised at Universität Duisburg.

Karlisch, Sigrun M., Sibylle Kästner and Eva-Maria Mertens (eds.): *Vom Knochenmann zur Menschenfrau: Feministische Theorie und archäologische Praxis.* Agenda Verlag, 1977.

Kelley, Abby. *An Anti-Slavery Album: Or Contributions From Friends of Freedom.* Western Anti-Slavery Collection, Library of Congress.

Kellor, Frances Alice. "Sex in Crime." *International Journal of Ethics* October 1898, pp. 74–85.

Kelly, Liz, Jo Lovett and Linda Regan. "Home Office Research Study 293. A gap or a chasm? Attrition in reported rape case." Home Office Research, Development and Statistics Directorate February 2005.

Kerner, Susanne. "Warum ich meinen Vergewaltiger nicht angezeigt habe." *Huffington Post* January 22, 2016.

Kieler, Marita. "Tatbestandsprobleme der sexuellen Nötigung, Vergewaltigung sowie des sexuellen Missbrauchs widerstandsunfähiger Personen." Dissertation, Juristische Reihe TENEA, Book 52, 2002.

Kimmel, Michael. "An Unnatural History Of Rape." In *Evolution, Gender And Rape.* ed. Travis, Cheryl Brown, MIT Press, 2003, pp. 221–34.

King, Larry. Interview with Samantha Geimer. *CNN Larry King Live.*

Kitchens, Caroline. "It's Time to End 'Rape Culture' Hysteria." *Time* March 20, 2014.

Klindienst, Patricia Joplin. "The Voice of the Shuttle is Ours." In *Rape and Representation.* eds. Higgins, Lynn A. and Brenda R. Silver, Columbia University Press, 1991, pp. 35–64.

Kluin, Katharina. "Vergewaltigt im Flüchtlingsheim." *Stern* March 28, 2016.

Koch, Angela. "Die Verletzung der Gemeinschaft: Zur Relation der Wort- und Ideengeschichte von 'Vergewaltigung'." In *Bodies/Politics.* eds. Gehmacher, Johanna, Gabriella Hauch and Marie Messner, Österreichische Zeitschrift für Geschichtswissenschaften, 2004, pp. 37–56.

Kotynek, Martin, Stephan Lebert and Daniel Müller. "Die Schlechterungsanstalt." *Die Zeit* August 16, 2012.

Krafft-Ebing, Richard von. *Psychopathia Sexualis: Mit besonderer Berücksichtigung der Conträren Sexualempfindungen.* Verlag von Ferdinand Enke, 1894.

Krischer, Markus. "Die Phantasien des Lawrence von Arabien." *Focus* August 2, 2008.

Künzel, Christine (ed.). *Unzucht – Notzucht – Vergewaltigung: Definitionen und Deutungen sexueller Gewalt von der Aufklärung bis heute.* Campus, 2003.

Lady Bitch Ray (Sahin, Reyhan). *Die Bedeutung des muslimischen Kopftuchs: Eine kleidungssemiotische Untersuchung Kopftuch tragender Musliminnen in der Bundesrepublik Deutschland.* Lit Verlag, 2014.

Lagouranis, Tony and Allen Mikaelian. *Fear Up Harsh: An Army Interrogator's Dark Journey Through Iraq.* New American Library, 2007.

Langhans, Daniel. *Von den Lastern, die sich an der Gesundheit rächen.* Bey Emanuel Haller, 1773.

Laqueur, Thomas. *Auf den Leib geschrieben: Die Inszenierung der Geschlechter von der Antike bis Freud.* Campus, 1992.

Lauret, Maria. *Liberating Literature: Feminist Fiction in America.* Routledge, 1994.

Law Center to Prevent Gun Violence. "Statistics on Domestic Violence & Firearms." January 1, 2012.

Lembke, Ulrike. "Vis haud ingrata – die 'nicht unwillkommene Gewalt'." Lecture. *Die kulturellen Wurzeln sexualisierter Gewalt und ihre rechtliche Verarbeitung,* 11:18 (2008).

Lembke, Ulrike. "Der derzeitige Zustand ist nicht hinnehmbar." Interview. *Missy Magazine* September 23, 2011.

Lembke, Ulrike. "Bundesrichter Fischer pöbelt gegen die Reform des Sexualstrafrechts." *Missy Magazine* June 28, 2016.

Leonhard, John. "It's not whether you can or can't forgive; it's whether you will or won't." *The Telegraph* March 8, 2006.

Leonard, John. Obituary. *The Telegraph* August 14, 2002.

Linning, Stephanie. "'I'd rather have been raped by a man,' says woman, sexually assaulted by female friend who used bandages and a sex toy to pretend she was male." *Mail Online* September 8, 2015.

Liszt, Franz von. *Lehrbuch des deutschen Strafrechts.* De Gruyter, 1932.

Livius, Titus. *Ab Urbe Condita: Römische Geschichte.* Friedrich Vieweg, 1821.

Locke, John. *Zweite Abhandlung über Regierung.* Welcker online, 2010.

Locke, John. *The Works.* Thomas Tegg, 1823.

Loewenfeld, Leopold. *Über das Eheliche Glück: Erfahrungen, Reflexionen und Ratschläge eines Arztes.* Verlag von J. F. Bergnabb, 1919.

Lohaus, Stefanie and Anne Wizorek. "Die Rape Culture wurde nicht nach Deutschland importiert – sie war schon immer da." *Vice Magazine* January 6, 2016.

Lombroso, Cesare and Guglielmo Ferrero. *Das Weib als Verbrecherin und Prostituierte: Anthropologische Studien.* J.F. Richter, 1894.

London, Ellen. "Comments: A Critique of the Strict Liability Standard for Determining Child Support in Cases of Male Victims of Sexual Assault and Statuatory Rape." University of Pennsylvania Law Review 152, pp. 1957–99.

Lorenz, Maren. "'... da der anfängliche Schmerz in Liebeshitze übergehen kann': Das Delikt der 'Nothzucht' im gerichtsmedizinischen Diskurs des 18 Jahrhunderts." In *Unzucht – Notzucht – Vergewaltigung: Definitionen und Deutungen sexueller Gewalt von der Aufklärung bis heute*. ed. Künzel, Christine, Campus, 2003, pp. 63–88.

Lutz, Martin. "Das Phänomen 'taharrush gamea' ist in Deutschland angekommen." *Die Welt* January 10, 2016.

Maas, Heiko. "Wenn sich eine solche Horde trifft, war das abgestimmt." *Die Tageszeitung* January 10, 2016.

MacKinnon, Catharine. *Feminism Unmodified: Discourses on Life and Law*. Harvard University Press, 1987.

MacKinnon, Catharine. "Sexuality, Pornography, and Method: Pleasure under Patriarchy." *Ethics* 99:2 (1989), pp. 314–46.

Magnanti, Brooke. "Myth: When it comes to sexual attraction, men are visually stimulated and always interested in sex – and women aren't." In *The Sex Myth: Why Everything We're Told is Wrong*. Magnanti, Brooke, Phoenix, 2012, pp. 9–32.

Magnanti, Brooke. *The Sex Myth: Why Everything We're Told is Wrong*. Phoenix, 2012.

Malkin, Bonnie. "Last Tango in Paris director suggests Maria Schneider 'butter rape' scene not consensual." *The Guardian* December 4, 2016.

Mansour, Ahmad. Interview. *Süddeutsche Zeitung* January 9, 2016.

Marcotte, Amanda. "RAINN Denounces, Doesn't Understand the Concept of 'Rape Culture'." *Slate* March 18, 2014.

Marcus, Sharon. "Fighting Bodies, Fighting Words." In *Gender Struggles: Practical Approaches to Contemporary Feminism*. eds. Mui, Constance L. and Julian S. Murphy, Rowman & Littlefield, 2002, pp. 166–85.

Marinic, Jagoda. "Befreiung von der Scham." *Die Tageszeitung* June 3, 2011.

Marriott, Trevor. *Jack the Ripper: The 21st Century Investigation*. John Blake, 2005.

Matussek, Matthias. "Der neue Mann aus dem Dschungel." *The European* February 3, 2013.

May, Tanja and Stefan Blatt. "Jetzt redet sie!" *Bunte* June 15, 2011.

Mendelsohn, Tina and Svenja Flaßpöhler. Interview. *3Sat Kulturzeit* June 14, 2016.

Meroney, John. "A Conversation with Gore Vidal." *The Atlantic* October 2009.

Messina-Dysert, Gina. "Rape and Spiritual Death." *Feminist Theology: The Journal of the Britain and Ireland School of Feminist Theology* 20:2 (2012), pp. 120–32.

Meyer, Eugene L. "Pacifist elects to pay fine rather than return to jail." *Washington Post* September 27, 1973.

Meyer, Verena. "Wenn schon das Wort Nein genügt." *Süddeutsche Zeitung* June 12, 2016.

Mill, James. *The History of British India*. Baldwin, Cradock and Joy, 1817.

Miller, Abraham H. "The Arab Rape Game." *Washington Times* February 2, 2016.

Miller, Gerrit. "The Primate Basis of Human Sexual Behaviour." *The Quarterly Review of Biology* Vol. 4 (1931), pp. 380–403.

Mitchell, Juliet. *Psychoanalysis and Feminism*. Penguin, 1974.

Mittal, Aditi. "A Beginner's Guide to India: Episode 1: Women" *BBC Radio 4* December 15, 2016.

Moran, Caitlin. "The limits of redemption." *The Times* December 13, 2014.

Morgan, Robin. *Going Too Far: The Personal Chronicle of a Feminist*. Random House, 1977.

Morgan, Robin. "Theory and Practice: Pornography and Rape." In *Take Back the Night: Women on Pornography*. ed. Lederer, Laura, William Morrow & Co, 1980, pp. 134–49.

Mui, Constance L. and Julian S. Murphy. *Gender Struggles: Practical Approaches to Contemporary Feminism*. Rowman & Littlefield, 2002.

Müller, Johann Valentin. *Aufsätze und Beobachtungen aus der gerichtlichen Arzneywissenschaft*. Mylius, 1779.

Mulvey, Laura and Anna Backman Rogers (eds.). *Feminisms: Mutations and Appropriations in European Film Debates*. Amsterdam University Press, 2015.

Neckel, Sighard. *Status und Scham: Zur symbolischen Reproduktion sozialer Ungleichheit*. Campus, 1991.

Newman, Sandra. "What kind of person makes false rape accusations?" *Quartz* May 11, 2017.

Okin, Susan Muller. *Is Multiculturalism Bad For Women?* Princeton University Press, 1999.

Ovid. *Liebeskunst*. Reclam Verlag, 1992.

Penny, Laurie. "If you really believe in WikiLeaks, you must want Assange to face up to justice." *The Independent* August 22, 2012.

Penny, Laurie. *Unspeakable Things: Sex, Lies and Revolution*. Bloomsbury, 2014.

Pérez, Miriam Zoila. "When Sexual Autonomy Isn't Enough: Sexual Violence Against Immigrant Women In The United States." In *Yes Means Yes: Visions of Female Sexual Power & a World Without Rape*. eds. Friedman, Jaclyn and Jessica Valenti, Seal Press, 2008, pp. 141–50.

Petran, Anna and Johanna Louise Thiel. "Weiterentwicklungen und (neue) Widersprüche – eine Einleitung zu queer_feministischen Gewaltdebatten." In *Gewalt und Handlungsmacht: Queer Feministische Perspektiven*. ed. Gender Initiativkolleg, Campus, 2012, pp. 9–26.

Pettegrew, John. *Brutes in Suites: Male Sensibility in America: 1890–1920*. John Hopkins University Press, 2001.

Piepzna-Samarasinha, Leah Lakshmi. "What it feels like when it finally comes: Surviving incest in real live." In *Yes Means Yes: Visions of Female Sexual Power & a World Without Rape*. eds. Friedman, Jaclyn and Jessica Valenti, Seal Press, 2008, pp. 93–106.

Plummer, Ken. *Telling Sexual Stories: Power, Change and Social Worlds*. Routledge, 1997.

Plutarch. *Moralia*. ed. Vogel, Manuel and Christiane Weise, Marixverlag, 2012.

Politt, Katha. "Naming and Blaming: Media Goes Wilding in Palm Beach." *The Nation* June 24, 1991, pp. 847–52.

Porter, Roy. "Rape – Does it Have a Historical Meaning? In *Rape: An Historical and Social Inquiry*. ed. Tomaselli, Sylvana, Basil Blackwell, 1989, pp. 216–36.

Pusch, Hendrik. "Flüchtling beschützte sie Silvester: Hier bedankt sich Caitlin bei ihrem Retter." *Express* January 18, 2016.

Rath, Christian. "'Nein' heißt endlich 'Nein'." *Die Tageszeitung* January 6, 2015.

Rattansi, Ali. *Multiculturalism: A Very Short Introduction*. Oxford University Press, 2011.

Redfern, Corinne. "Amber Amour: 'I Live-Blogged My Rape'." *Marie Claire* January 6, 2016.

Real, Terrence. *I Don't Want to Talk about it: Overcoming the Secret Legacy of Male Depression*. Scribner, 2003.

Reemtsma, Jan Philipp. *Vertrauen und Gewalt: Versuch über eine besondere Konstellation der Moderne*. Hamburger Edition, 2013.

Reitan, Eric. "Rape as an Essentially Contested Concept." *Hypathia* 16:2 (2001), pp. 43–66.

Reynolds, James Bronson. "Sex Morals and the Law in Ancient Egypt and Babylon." *Journal of Criminal Law and Criminology* 5:1, 1914.

Riekel, Patricia. "Werden Frauen künftig schweigen?" *Bunte* and *Focus* June 1, 2011.

Rivers, Caryl. *Selling Anxiety: How the News Media Scare Women*. University Press of New England, 2007.

Robinson, Bruce. *They All Love Jack: Busting the Ripper*. 4th Estate, 2015.

Roiphe, Katie. *The Morning After: Sex, Fear, and Feminism*. Hamish Hamilton, 1994.

Roiphe, Katie. "Working Women's Fantasies." *Newsweek* April 16, 2012.

Ronson, Jon. *The Psychopath Test*. Picador, 2012.

Rosen, Ellen Israel. "The New Bedford Rape Trial." *Dissent* Nr. 32 (1985), p. 207.

Ross, Deborah. "Class Waugh." *Independent* November 27, 2000.

Royse, Alyssa. "The Danger in Demonizing Male Sexuality." *The Good Men Project* March 28, 2013.

Rückert, Sabine. "Schuldig auf Verdacht." *Die Zeit* June 24, 2010.

Rückert, Sabine. "Zwei blaue Flecken und ein Nullbefund." *Die Zeit* February 24, 2011.

Rupp, H.A. and K. Wallen. "Sex Differences in Viewing Sexual Stimuli: An eye tracking study in men and women." *Hormones and Behaviour* 51:4 (2007), pp. 524–54.

Sahin, Reyhan (Lady Bitch Ray). *Die Bedeutung des muslimischen Kopftuchs: Eine kleidungssemiotische Untersuchung Kopftuch tragender Musliminnen in der Bundesrepublik Deutschland.* Lit Verlag, 2014.

Sampson, Robert J. "Rethinking Crime and Immigration." *Contexts* 7:1 (2008), pp. 28–33.

Sanday, Peggy Reeves. "Rape-Free versus Rape-Prone: How Culture Makes a Difference." In *Evolution, Gender And Rape.* ed. Travis, Cheryl Brown, MIT Press, 2003, pp. 337–62. Sanyal, Mithu. *Vulva.* 2009. Wagenbach, 2017.

Satoshi, Kanazawa and Mary C. Still. "Why Men Commit Crimes (And Why They Desist)." *Sociological Theory* 18:3 (2000), pp. 434–47.

Satrapi, Marjane. *Persepolis: Gesamtausgabe.* Edition Moderne, 2013.

Saward, Jill and Wendy Green. *Rape: My Story.* Pan Books, 1991.

Scacco, Anthony M. Jr. (ed.). *Male Rape: A Casebook of Sexual Aggressions.* AMS, 1982.

Schellong, Julia. "Außer Kontrolle." *The European* February 22, 2013.

Schiller, Friedrich. *Der Spaziergang* (795), verse 95.

Schiller, Friedrich. *Fiesco's Conspiracy at Genoa.* Open Book Publishers, 2015.

Schmieder, Jürgen. "Ein Albtraum namens Polanski." *Süddeutsche Zeitung* September 24, 2013.

Schneeberger, Ruth. "TV-Kritik: Natascha Kampusch 'Ich werde Geächtet'." *Süddeutsche Zeitung* May 17, 2010.

Schneider, S.L. and R.C. Wright. "Understanding denial in sexual offenders: a review of cognitive and motivational processes to avoid responsibility." *Trauma Violence Abuse* 5:1 (2004), pp. 3–20.

Schultz, Jason. "Getting Off on Feminism." In *To Be Real: Telling the Truth and Changing the Face of Feminism.* ed. Walker, Rebecca, Anchor Books, 1995, pp. 107–26.

Schwab, Waltraud and Martina Havernock. "Sensation statt Tabu? Wortmeldungen zum Internationalen Tag gegen Gewalt an Frauen." *Die Tageszeitung* November 25, 2008.

Schwarze, Friedrich Oskar von. *Commentar zum Strafgesetzbuch für das Deutsche Reich.* Fues, 1873.

Schwarzer, Alice. Appell gegen Prostitution. *EMMA.*

Schwarzer, Alice. "Der mutige Auftritt der Ex-Freundin vor Gericht." *Bild* January 6, 2011.

Schwarzer, Alice. "Es geht um viel mehr als um zwei Menschen." *EMMA* Autumn 2010.

Schwarzwaldklinik, Episode "Gewalt im Spiel." *Schwarzwaldklinik/BverwGE* February 1, 1986.

Seidling, Michael. "Wortlaut: Der Freispruch für Jörg Kachelmann." *Frankfurter Allgemeine Zeitung* May 31, 2011.

Senzee, Thom. "Argentina Makes History With Three-Parent Birth Certificate." *Advocate* May 3, 2013.

Serano, Julia. "Why Nice Guys Finish Last." In *Yes Means Yes: Visions of Female Sexual Power & a World Without Rape*. eds. Friedman, Jaclyn and Jessica Valenti, Seal Press, 2008, pp. 227–40.

Sezgin, Hilal. "Deutsche Respektlosigkeiten." *Die Zeit* January 13, 2016.

Shams, Alex. "Neither Taharrush Gamea Nor Sexism Are Arab 'Cultural Practices'." *Huffington Post* January 21, 2016.

Shehadeh, Nadia. "Arabisch Und Nordafrikanisch Aussehende Menschen™." *Shehadistan* January 8, 2016.

Shorter, Edward. "On writing the history of rape." *Signs* 3:2 (1977) pp. 471–82.

Sielke, Sabine. *Reading Rape: The Rhetoric of Sexual Violence in American Literature and Culture 1790–1990*. Princeton University Press, 2001.

Siemens, Ansgar. "Interview with Gina-Lisa Lohfink 'Muss ich erst umgebracht werden?' " *Spiegel Online* June 11, 2016.

Siemens, Ansgar. "Prozess gegen Gina-Lisa Lohfink: Wenn der Gerichtssaal zur Bühne wird." *Spiegel Online* June 27, 2016.

Sigusch, Volkmar and Tobias Haberl. "Ich bin in Rage angesichts unserer Sexualkultur." *Süddeutsche Zeitung Magazin*, 2015.

Simkins, Michael. "Method acting can go too far – just ask Dustin Hoffman." *The Guardian* March 31, 2016.

Sissay, Lemn. Dawn Project. August 28, 2015.

Slocum, David J. (ed.). *Violence and American Cinema*. Routledge, 2001.

Small, Meredith. *Female Choices: Sexual Behavious of Female Primates*. Cornell University Press, 1993.

Smaus, Gerlinda. "Vergewaltigung von Männern durch Männer." In *Unzucht – Notzucht – Vergewaltigung: Definitionen und Deutungen sexueller Gewalt von der Aufklärung bis heute*. ed. Künzel, Christine, Campus, 2003, pp. 221–42.

Smeeth, Mary and Susanne Kappeler. "Mercy: A New Novel By Andrea Dworkin." *Sparerib* 1990, p. 27.

Smith, Brenda V. "Watching me, watching you." *Yale Journal of Law and Feminism* 15:22 (2003), p. 230.

Smith, Ronald E., Charles J. Pine and Mark E. Hawley. "Social cognitions about adult male victims of female sexual assault." *Journal of Sex*

Research Vol. 24 (1988), pp. 101–12.

Snellman, Anja. *Geographie der Angst*. Btb, 2001.

Sobchack, Vivian (ed.). *The Persistence of History: Cinema, Television and the Modern Event*. Routledge, 1996.

Soderlund, Gretchen. *Sex Trafficking, Scandal, and the Transformation of Journalism: 1885–1917*. University of Chicago Press, 2013.

Sontag, Susan. *Kunst und Antikunst: 24 literarische Analysen*. Fischer, 2009.

Starr, Sonja B. "Estimated Gender Disparities in Federal Criminal Cases." University of Michigan Law and Economics Research Paper No. 12–018, August 29, 2012.

Steinitz, Sylvia Margaret. "Der Fall Gina-Lisa Lohfink: Chronik einer angekündigten Schändung." *Stern* June 8, 2016.

Stekel, Wilhelm. *Onanie und Homosexualität (Die homosexuelle Neurose) [Störungen des Trieb- und Affektlebens II]* Urban & Schwarzenberg, 1921.

Stemple, Lara and Ilan H. Meyer. "The Sexual Victimization of Men in America: New Data Challenge Old Assumptions." *UCLA Williams Institute* April 2014.

Stemple, Lara, Andrew Flores and Ilan Meyer. "Sexual Victimization Perpetrated by Women: Federal Data Reveal Surprising Prevalence." *Aggression and Violent Behavior* 34:0 (2017), pp. 302–11.

Struckman-Johnson, Cindy and David Struckman-Johnson. "Acceptance of male rape myth among college men and women." *Sex Roles* 27:3/4 (1992), pp. 85–100.

Subdhan, Abigale. "Vancouver baby becomes first person to have three parents named on birth certificate in B.C." *National Post* February 10, 2014.

Symons, Donald. *The Evolution of Human Sexuality*. Oxford University Press, 1979.

Tacitus. *Des Cornelius Tacitus Werke: Lateinisch mit deutscher Übersetzung und erläuternden Anmerkungen von Wilhelm Boetticher. Book II. Annalen XI-XVI*. Verlag von Wilhelm Engelmann, 1864.

Thal, Max. *Sexuelle Moral: Ein Versuch der Lösung des Problems der geschlechtlichen, insbesondere der sogenannten Doppelten Moral*. Koebner, 1904.

Thom, Kai Cheng. "Nine ways to be accountable when you've been abusive." *everydayfeminism.com* February 1, 2016.

Thornbill, Randy and Craig T. Palmer. "Why Men Rape. *The Sciences* 40:1 (2000), pp. 30–6.

Tomaselli, Sylvana and Roy Porter (eds.). *Rape*. Blackwell Publishing, 1986.

Tomasulo, Frank. "'I'll see it when I believe it.' Rodney King and the Prison House of Video." In *The Persistence of History: Cinema, Television and*

the Modern Event. ed. Sobchack, Vivian, Routledge, 1996, pp. 69–88.
Travis, Cheryl Brown. *Evolution, Gender, and Rape*. MIT Press, 2003.
Travis, Cheryl Brown (ed.). *Evolution, Gender And Rape*. MIT Press, 2003.
Traynor, Luke. "Fake penis woman Gayle Newland to appeal conviction over sex attacks on victim wearing blindfold." *The Mirror* November 17, 2015.
Troppanneger, Christian Gottlieb. *Dicisiones Medico-Forens*. Hilscher, 1733.
Tucker, Donald. "A Punk's Song: View from the Inside." In *Male Rape: A Casebook of Sexual Aggressions*. ed. Scacco, Anthony M. Jr., AMS Press, 1982, pp. 59–79.
Ufer, Steffen. Interview. *Focus* June 7, 2010.
Ulli, Christa. Conversation with directors Philippe Mach and Marc Wolfberger about their documentary *Schuld und Scham wechseln die Seite. SRF.*
Valdes, Alisa. "I Tried to Warn You About Junot Diaz." https://oshuncreative.wordpress.com/ May 4, 2018.
Valenti, Jessica. "What the Assange case reveals about rape in America." *Washington Post* December 10, 2010.
Veselka, Vanessa. "The Collapsible Woman: Cultural Responses to Rape and Sexual Abuse." In *BITCHfest: Ten Years of Cultural Criticism from the Pages of Bitch Magazine*. ed. Jervis, Lisa and Andi Zeisler, Farrar, Straus & Giroux, 2006, pp. 56–61.
Volpp, Leti. "Feminism versus Multiculturalism." *Columbia Law Review* 101:5 (2001), pp. 1181–218.
Vorsamer, Barbara. "Jungs sind halt so." *Süddeutsche Zeitung* November 24, 2017.
Waal, Frans B.M. De. "Bonobo Sex and Society: The behaviour of a close relative challenges assumptions about male supremacy in human evolution." *Scientific American* June 1, 2006, pp. 14–21.
Walker, Janet. "Trauma Cinema: False Memories and True Experience." *Screen* 42:2 (2001), pp. 211–16.
Walker, Rebecca (ed.). *To Be Real: Telling the Truth and Changing the Face of Feminism*. Anchor books, 1995.
Walkowitz, Judith R. "Jack the Ripper and the Myth of Male Violence." *Feminist Studies*, 8:3 (1982), pp. 542–74.
Wan, William. "What makes some men sexual harassers?" *Washington Post* December 22, 2017.
Wells-Barnett, Ida. *On Lynching*. Arno Press, 1969.
Wigmore, John Henry. *Wigmore's Code of the Rules of Evidence in Trials of Law*. Little Brown, 1935.
Williams, Kayle and Michael E. Staub. *Love My Rifle More Than You: Young*

and Female in the U.S. Army. W. W. Norton, 2005.
Wilson, Barbara. *Sisters of the Road*. Virago, 1986.
Winkelmeier-Becker, Elisabeth et al. "Eckpunktepapier zur Reform des Strafrechts – mit dem Grundsatz 'Nein heißt Nein' " June 16, 2016.
Wirtz, Ursula. *Seelenmord: Inzest und Therapie*. Kreuz Verlag, 1989.
Wolf, Gary. "The (Second Phase Of The) Revolution Has Begun." *Wired Magazine* January 10, 1994.
Wolf, Naomi. *Vagina*. Rowohlt, 2013.
Woolf, Virginia. *A Room Of One's Own*. Penguin, 2012.
Yaghoonofarah, Hengameh. "Willkommen in der Hölle, Ladys." *Die Tageszeitung* January 6, 2016.
Young, Cathy. "Crying Rape: False rape accusations exist, and they are a serious problem." *Slate* September 18, 2014.
Ziegler, Martyn. "Ched Evans deal was exed after 'vile and abusive threats, including death threats' reveal Oldham." *The Independent* January 8, 2015.
Zumach, Andreas. "Vergewaltigung jetzt Kriegsverbrechen." *Die Tageszeitung* June 21, 2008.

Notes

Introduction

1. See Anja Snellman, *Geographie der Angst*, Btb, 2001.
2. Wendy Brown and Janet Halley (eds.), *Left Legalism/Left Critique*, p.26.
3. Mithu Sanyal, *Vulva*, Wagenbach Klaus GmbH, 2009.
4. Joanna Bourke, *Rape: A History from 1860 to the Present*, p. 6f.
5. Katie Roiphe, *The Morning After: Sex, Fear, and Feminism*, p. 46.
6. See Nicholos A. Groth and Ann Wolbert Burgess, "Sexual Dysfunction during Rape," *The New England Journal of Medicine*, October 6, 1977, p. 764–6.
7. Kanazawa Satoshi and Mary C. Still, "Why Men Commit Crimes (And Why They Desist)," *Sociological Theory* 18:3 (2000), p. 440.
8. Randy Thornhill and Craig T. Palmer, "Why Men Rape," *The Sciences* (2000), p. 33.
9. Michael Kimmel, "An Unnatural History Of Rape," in *Evolution, Gender And Rape*. ed. Cheryl Brown Travis, MIT Press, 2003, p. 231.
10. Ibid., p. 232
11. Carol Clover, Professor for Media Studies and Linguistics calls that "our ultimate gender story" (Carol Clover, *Men, Women, and Chainsaws*, p. 227.)
12. See the National Institute of Justice report "Victims and Victimization" available atnij.gov.
13. The numbers vary from around 78 percent in the US to 64/68 percent in the UK (for the US see the US Department of Justice Report, "Homicide Trends in the United States, 1980–2008 " available at bjs.gov, for the UK see the "Victims" section of the "Homicide" report by the Office of National Statistics available at ons.gov.uk).

14 This was changed in 2013 to "Penetration, no matter how slight, of the vagina or anus with any body part or object, or oral penetration by a sex organ of another person, without the consent of the victim." The current FBI policy is available atfbi.gov.

15 Article 90 Section 1 of the Swiss Criminal Code. All other forms of forced sexual acts are classed as sexual harassment, though nowadays they carry the same maximum sentence as vaginal rape.

16 Joanna Bourke, *Rape*, p. 213.

17 Ibid.

18 A constitutional complaint that this violated the principle of equality was disregarded by the Bundesesverfassungsgericht on 22 March 1999—2 BvR 398/99.

19 Germany has now committed to creating a third gender possibility for passports and birth registers. India and Pakistan and Bangladesh already have three genders: men, women and hijras (or kinnars).

20 Joanna Bourke, *Rape*, p. 8.

21 Seeug Daphna Joel and Anne Fausto-Sterling, "Beyond sex differences: New approaches for thinking about variation in brain structure and function," 2016.

Sex: No Means Yes, No Means No!

1 Richard von Krafft-Ebing, *Psychopathia Sexualis*, p.13.

2 Lord Byron, *Don Juan*, Stanza 117.

3 Ovid, *The Art of Love (Ars Amatoria)*, Book I Part XVII. Ovid was famous for not recognizing "no" as "no." For example, his main reason for going to the dog races was to press himself against unsuspecting women in the crowd.

4 See Aristotle, *De Generatione Animalium*.

5 Sarah Griffith, "Raping and pillaging? Viking conquests were more like 'romantic breaks': DNA reveals warriors brought their women when raiding British Isles," *Mail Online* December 8, 2014.

6 Charlotte Hedenstierna—Jonson et al. "A female Viking warrior confirmed by genomics," *The American Journal of Physical Anthropology* September 8, 2017; Sibylle Kästner. "Rund ums Geschlecht: Ein Überblick zu feministischen Geschlechtertheorien und deren Anwendung auf die

archäologische Forschung," in *Vom Knochenmann zur Menschenfrau: Feministische Theorie und archäologische Praxis*. eds. Sigrun M. Karlisch, Subylle Kästner, Eva-Maria Mertens, Münster, 1977, p. 24.

7 Havelock Ellis, *Psychology of Sex*, 1910.

8 Charles Darwin, *The Descent of Man and Selection in Relation to Sex*, p. 229f.

9 Susan Sontag, *Styles Of Radical Will*, p. 46.

10 There was also the assumption that a woman who fell pregnant after a rape hadn't been raped at all. Republican senator Todd Akin, still upheld in 2012: "If it's a legitimate rape, the female body has ways to try to shut that whole thing down." This harks back to the idea that women produce the so-called female semen during orgasm, propagated by the Greek physician Soranus of Ephesus in the second century and implemented in law by Emperor Justinian. Interestingly, this conviction, at the same time, put female desire in the center of the sexual act. To be able to conceive a child a woman had to be aroused. See Tanja Hommen, "Sie hat sich nicht im Geringsten gewehrt: Zur Kontinuität kultureller Deutungsmuster sexueller Gewalt seit dem Kaiserreich," in *Unzucht–Notzucht–Vergewaltigung: Definitionen und Deutungen sexueller Gewalt von der Aufklärung bis heute*, ed. Christine Künzel, p. 119–136; Wikipedia Rape and pregnancy controversies in United States elections 2012; Thomas Laqueur, *Auf den Leib geschrieben: Die Inszenierung der Geschlechter von der Antike bis Freud*, Campus, 1992, p. 185.

11 See therulesbook.com.

12 Laurie Penny, *Unspeakable Things: Sex, Lies and Revolution*, p. 108f.

13 Richard von Krafft-Ebing, *Psychopathia Sexualis*, p. 2.

14 Andrew Jackson Davis, *The Genesis and Ethics of Conjugal Love*, p. 28.

15 Doctors presumed that masturbation would cause the spinal cord to rot, as well as leprosy and softening of the brain. See Maren Lorenz: "'. . . da der anfängliche Schmerz in Liebeshitze übergehen kann . . .' Das Delikt der 'Nothzucht' im gerichtsmedizinischen Diskurs des 18 Jahrhunderts," in *Unzucht—Notzucht—Vergewaltigung. Definitionen und Deutungen sexueller Gewalt von der Aufklärung bis heute*, ed. Christine

Künzel, p. 73; See, for example, the writings of Swiss physician Daniel Langhans (Daniel Langhans, *Von den Lastern, die sich an der Gesundheit rächen*, Bey Emanuel Haller, 1773, p. 68ff.).

16 Mailer did follow this statement up with two maybes, but he went on to defend his viewpoint. When the interviewer, Paul Krassner, protested, Mailer elaborated: "one [masturbation] is violence towards oneself; one [rape] is violence towards others. And you don't recognize—let's follow your argument and be speculative for a moment—if everyone becomes violent towards themselves, then past a certain point the entire race commits suicide. But if everyone becomes violent toward everyone else, you would probably have one wounded hero-monster left." "An Impolite Interview with Norman Mailer." *The Realist*, issue 40, December 1962, p. 20–1.

17 See Dr. Ulrike Lembke, "Vis haud ingrata—die 'nicht unwillkommene Gewalt' Die kulturellen Wurzeln sexualisierter Gewalt und ihre rechtliche Verarbeitung," *Vortrag anlässlich des FRI Exchange* 11:18 (2008), p.6.

18 See Matthias Matussek, "Der neue Mannaus dem Dschungel," *The European* February 3, 2013.

19 Richard von Krafft-Ebing, *Psychopathia Sexualis*, p. 13.

20 Helene Deutsch, *The Psychology of Women, Vol II*, Grune & Stratton, 1944/45, p. 79f.

21 Sigmund Freud, *Three Contributions to the Theory of Sex*, Project Gutenberg, 2005 [1920].

22 Idib.

23 See Leopold Loewenfeld, *On Conjugal Happiness*, John Bale, Sons & Company, 1912.

24 Helene Deutsch, *The Psychology of Women.*

25 Katie Roiphe,"Working Women's Fantasies," *Newsweek* April 16, 2012.

26 Laurie Penny, *Unspeakable Things*, p. 114f.

27 Sigmund Freud, *Psychopathology of Everyday Life*, Chapter VIII, note 7, 1914.

28 Peggy Reeves Sanday, "Rape-Free versus Rape-Prone: How Culture Makes a Difference," in *Evolution, Gender, and Rape.* Cheryl Brown Travis, ibid., p. 349.

29 Joanna Bourke, *Rape*, p. 33.

30 Ibid.

31 Cf. John Herny Wigmore, *Wigmore's Code of the Rules of Evidence in Trials of Law*, Little Brown, 1935.

32 Hans von Hentig, "Interaction of Perpetrator and Victim," *Journal of Criminal Law and Criminal Behaviour* Vol. 31 (1940), p. 305.
33 David Abrahamsen, *The Psychology of Crime*, Columbia University Press, 1960, p. 161.
34 Caesar Lombroso and William Ferrero, *The Female Offender*, D. Appleton and Company, 1898, p. 151.
35 William Bonger, *Criminality and Economic Conditions*, Boston, 1916, p. 60.
36 Frances Alice Kellor, *Sex in Crime: International Journal of Ethics* October 1898, p. 85.
37 Joanna Bourke, *Rape*, p. 220
38 Laurie Penny, *Unspeakable Things*, p. 214.
39 The "New York Radical Feminists," also known as "Feminists—A Political Organization to Annihilate Sex Roles" had also proposed similar terms in the 1960s.
40 Bini Adamczak, *Po auf Finger*, *Missy Magazine* March/April/May 2016, p. 102.
41 Donald Symons, *The Evolution of Human Sexuality*, Oxford University Press, 1979, p. 253–4.
42 Bestsellers like Louann Brizendine's *The Female Brain* (2006) claim that women are compelled to say 13,000 words more than men per day, while men only want one thing—or two, if the thing in question is breasts. Brizendine explains neither how she arrived at the very specific number of 13,000 nor what happens to women who don't manage their daily quota of words. They probably can't bear the pressure and explode. This is like the steam-boiler model, only this time it's not men having to ejaculate sperm but women having to ejaculate words.
43 Cf. Polly Vernon, "Stephen Fry shocks feminists by claiming women don't really like sex," *The Observer* October 31, 2010. See also *Attitude Magazine* November 2010.
44 Steve Connor, "The science of women and sex: Is Stephen Fry right after all?" *The Independent* November 2, 2010.
45 See Meredith Small, *Female Choices: Sexual Behaviour of Female Primates*, Cornell University Press, 1993.
46 Frans B.M. De Waal, "Bonobo Sex and Society. The behaviour of a close relative challenges assumptions about male supremacy in human evolution," *Scientific American* June 1, 2006.
47 See Meredith L. Chivers et al., "A Sex Difference in the Specificity of Sexual Arousal," *Psychological Science* 15:11 (2004), p.736–744.

48 See Dr. Brooke Magnanti, "Myth: When it comes to sexual attraction, men are visually stimulated and always interested in sex—and women aren't," in *The Sex Myth: Why Everything We're Told is Wrong,* Dr. Brooke Magnanti, Phoenix, 2012, p. 9–32.

49 H.A, Rupp, K. Wallen, "Sex Differences in Viewing Sexual Stimuli: An eye tracking study in men and women," *Hormones and Behaviour* 51:4 (2007), p. 524–554.

50 The World Association for Sexual Health considers this as a sexual human right. It is number 5 in the Declaration of Sexual Rights from 1999: "The right to sexual pleasure: Sexual pleasure, including autoeroticism, is a source of physical, psychological, intellectual and spiritual well-being."

51 Laurie Penny in an interview with Mithu Sanyal, Cologne, June 11, 2015.

52 Susan Griffin, *Made from this Earth: Selections from her Writing*, London, 1982, p. 4.

53 Heidi Hartmann and Ellen Ross, "Comment on 'On Writing the History of Rape,'" *Signs* 3:4 (1978), p. 932.

54 Susan Brownmiller, *Against Our Will: Men, Women and Rape*, p. 14.

55 Ibid., p. 13f.

56 For a book that is praised as being the first cultural history of rape, *Against Our Will* is surprisingly ahistorical. Heidi Hartmann and Ellen Ross point out: "Although Brownmiller draws evidence from the past, she does not treat rape as a changing social force, as a dynamic in the social, sexual and legal contexts of specific societies." (Heidi Hartmann and Ellen Ross. Ibid. p. 932). See also Roy Porter, "Rape—does it have a Historical Meaning?" in *Rape: An Historical and Social Inquiry*, ed. Sylvana Tomaselli and Roy Porter. Basil Blackwell, 1989.

57 Susan Brownmiller, *Against Our Will*, p. 16.

58 Ibid. p. 14.

59 Ibid.

60 Ibid.

61 Ibid., p. 17.

62 Ibid., p. 15.

63 Juliet Mitchell, *Psychoanalysis and Feminism*, p. 364.

64 Ellen Carol DuBois and Linda Gordon, "Seeking Ecstasy on the Battlefield: Danger and Pleasure in Nineteenth-century Feminist Sexual Thought," in *Pleasure and Danger: Exploring Female Sexuality,* ed. Carole S. Vance, p. 32.

65 Ibid. Obviously not the whole women's movement opposed prostitution: then just as now, there were feminists fighting for better working conditions for sex workers. The word *abolitionist* (in regard to prostitution) was first used by feminists fighting to abandon the laws banning prostitution.
66 Ken Plummer, *Telling Sexual Stories: Power, Change and Social Worlds*, p. 64.
67 Quoted in Lal Coveney et al., *The Sexuality Papers: Male Sexuality and the Social Control of Women*, London, 1984, p. 26.
68 Robin Morgan, *Going Too Far: The Personal Chronicle of a Feminist*, Random House, 1977, p. 164.
69 Ken Plummer, *Telling Sexual Stories*, p. 63.
70 Ibid., p. 68.
71 This is the reason feminists in Germany use the term "sexualised violence"—instead of "sexual violence"—to show that sex may be the weapon of, but not the motivation for, rape.
72 Catharine Alice MacKinnon, "Sexuality, Pornography, and Method: Pleasure Under Patriarchy," *Ethics* 99:2 (1989), p. 323.
73 Discussion with Michel Foucault, David Cooper (psychiatrist and founder of the British anti-psychiatry movement together with R.D. Laing), his colleague Marine Zecca, philosopher Jean-Pierre Faye and Marie-Odile Faye, editor of *Change Magazine*. Michel Foucault, *Politics, Philosophy, Culture: Interviews and Other Writings*, p. 200f.
74 Ibid.
75 Ibid.
76 See Ann J. Cahill, *Rethinking Rape*, p. 143ff.
77 Susan Griffin, *Rape: The Power of Consciousness*, Harper & Row, 1979, p. 3. (Originally published as "Rape: The All American Crime," *Ramparts* 1971, p. 26–35.)
78 Virginia Woolf, *A Room Of One's Own*, p. 54; Marilyn French, *The Women's Room*, p. 46.
79 Marilyn French, *The Women's Room,* Book 5, chapter 19. In fact that sentence is so famous that it was quoted in nearly all her obituaries (cf. A. G. Sulzberger and Herbert Mitgang, "Marilyn French, Novelist and Champion of Feminism, Dies at 79," *The New York Times* May 3, 2009.) It could be argued that French herself didn't agree completely with her famous sentence, as she put it in the mouth of one of her characters, Val the mother of the raped girl, while another character argues against it.

80 Maria Lauret, *Liberating Literature: Feminist Fiction in America*, p. 100.
81 The victim's name is widely known because it was leaked during the court case on TV, which led to her being ostracized and indirectly to her death in a car crash. The case sparked a debate about the naming of rape victims. (See Katha Politt, "Naming and Blaming. Media Goes Wilding in Palm Beach," *The Nation* June 24, 1991, p. 847—852.) For this reason I only use names if the people concerned have gone public on their own accord.
82 See Ellen Israel Rosen, "The New Bedford Rape Trial," *Dissent* Nr. 32 (1985), p. 207f.
83 See Helen Benedict, *Virgin or Vamp: How the Press Covers Sex Crimes*, p. 141f.
84 Helen Benedict, *Virgin or Vamp,* p. 142.
85 Tanya Horek, *Public Rape: Representing Violation in Fiction and Film*, p. 73.
86 John Fiske, *Media Matters: Everyday Culture and Political Change*, p. xix.
87 See Lynn S. Chancer, "The 'Before and After' of a Group Rape," *Gender & Society* 1:3 (1987), p. 248f.
88 Herman Melville's novel Moby Dick is set in parts in New Bedford.
89 Quoted from Dudley Clendinen, "Barroom Rape Shames Town of Proud Heritage," *New York Times* March 16, 1983.
90 Ulrike Lembke, "Der derzeitige Zustand ist nicht hinnehmbar," *Missy Magazine blog "von Recht und Geschlecht"* September 23, 2011.
91 Quoted from Helen Benedict, *Virgin or Vamp*, p. 134.
92 Quoted from Ibid., p. 141.
93 Tanya Horek, *Public Rape*, p.163.
94 Ibid., p. 95.
95 Ibid.
96 Susan Brownmiller, *Against Our Will*, p. 8.
97 Quoted from Beatrix Campbell, "The Accused on Release," *Marxism Today* March 1989, p. 43.
98 Carol Clover, *Men, Women and Chainsaws*, p. 150.
99 Janet Walker, "Trauma Cinema: False Memories and True Experience," *Screen* 42:2 (2001), p. 21.
100 Mary Kay Blakely, "New Bedford Gang Rape: Who were the men?" *Ms* July 1983, p. 51.
101 Penny Ashbrook, "Rape on Screen," *SpareRib* April 1989, p. 38.

102 Ken Plummer, *Telling Sexual Stories: Power, Change and Social Worlds*, p. 72.
103 Susan Griffin, "Rape: The All-American Crime," in *Rape: The Power of Consciousness*, Susan Griffin, p. 3.
104 Mary Smeeth and Susanne Kappeler, "Mercy: A New Novel By Andrea Dworkin," *Sparerib* 1990, p. 27.
105 Katie Roiphe, *The Morning After: Sex, Fear, and Feminism*, p. 9.

A Fate Worse Than Death: Honor and Honesty

1 Or to give them their full name: Sexual and reproductive health and rights (SRHR). In 1999 the 14th World Congress of Sexuality agreed on the Universal Declaration of Sexual Rights.
2 Francis Hodgson, *Merivale*, p. 64.
3 Emperor Justinian revised the law of *raptus* in the sixth century to mean a sexual crime against a woman. Before, *raptus* had mainly concerned the abduction of a married woman, now it included unmarried women and widows as well (though not prostitutes and slaves) and was seen as a crime against the woman herself as opposed to a crime against her husband. It is noteworthy that there was no marital rape exemption, so a husband could be prosecuted for raping his wife.
4 Georg Doblhofer, *Vergewaltigung in der Antike: Beiträge zur Altertumskunde*, p. 6.
5 Cf. Gesa Dane, *"Zeter und Mordio:" Vergewaltigung Literatur und Recht*, Wallstein, 2005, p. 46.
6 Tanya Horek, *Public Rape*, p. 57.
7 See Livius, *Ab Urbe Condita* 38, 24, 2–11.
8 See also Plutarch, *Concerning the Virtues of Women (De Mulierum Virtutibus)* 22. *Moralia* 258 d-e.
9 Elizabeth I had also gone back to England's warrior queen to strengthen the image that a woman on the throne was up to defend her country. Poems like James Aske's "Elizabetha Triumphans" portray her as the reincarnation of a fierce, warfaring Boudica.
10 Tacitus, *Annals*, in *The Complete Works Of Tacitus*, ed. Alfred John Church et al. Perseus/Random House, 1942, 14.35.
11 Edward Gibbon, *The History of the Decline and Fall of the Roman Empire, Band IV*, p. 74.
12 Edward Rice Burroughs, *Tarzan of the Apes*. Quoted from *Brutes in Suits: Male Sensibility in America*, John Pettegrew, p.79.

13 James Bronson Reynolds, "Sex Morals and the Law in Ancient Egypt and Babylon," in *Journal of Criminal Law and Criminology*, 5:1 (1914).
14 Cf. Johann Valentin Müller, *Aufsätze und Beobachtungen aus der gerichtlichen Arzneywissenschaft*, §89.
15 Cf. Christian Gottlieb Troppanneger, *Dicisiones Medico-Forens*, p. 173f.
16 Samantha Geimer on Larry King Live, *CNN Larry King Live* February 24, 2003.
17 For further examination of the role of rape in origin stories see: Margaret W. Ferguson, Maureen Quilligan and Nancy J. Vickers, *Rewriting the Renaissance: The Discourse of Sexual Difference in Early Modern Europe*, University of Chicago Press, 1986, or Patricia Klindienst Joplin, *The Voice of the Shuttle is Ours*. In *Rape and Representation*, Lynn An. Higgins and Brenda R. Silver, p. 35–64.
18 See Gesa Dane, *Zeter und Mordio: Vergewaltigung in Literatur und recht*, p. 46f.
19 Augustine, *The City of God*. Book 1, Chapter 19. The text is the Dods-Wilson-Smith translation from the Library of Nicene and Post-Nicene Fathers, Series 1, Vol. 2.
20 Ibid.
21 According to Augustine, concupiscence—the human capacity for erotic arousal—was God's punishment for original sin. That meant that humans sinned as punishment for sin and so on ad infinitum.
22 It is noteworthy that Martin Luther doesn't use the term rape in his translation of the bible, but uses the literal translation "'disgrace,' to weaken a woman," and to "sleep at a woman's side" (Gesa Dana, *Zeter und Mordio*, p. 36).
23 Ibid. p. 53f.
24 Ibid. p. 170.
25 Kate Harding, "When a Feminist Trailblazer Turns to Victim-Blaming, It's Time to Let Go of a Hero," *Cosmopolitan* September 18, 2015.
26 The controversy had been sparked off by an interview Brownmiller had done with *The Cut* in which she displayed dissatisfaction with anti rape activism at colleges and with the slut walks (Interview by Katie Van Syckle, "Against Our Will Author on What Today's Rape Activists Don't Get," *The Cut* September 17, 2015). The main bone of contention was that Brownmiller disagreed with the claim that women should wear

whatever they liked and drink "as much as men" because Brownmiller saw men as being predatory and therefore didn't think it was safe for the women in question. Brownmiller's comments were seen as being victim-blaming and the debate culminated in feminist Jessica Valenti stating: "It's a reminder for those with their heyday behind them that young people do not make you irrelevant, living in your own bubble does." (Jessica Valenti, "If feminist icons lose their way the movement continues without them," *The Guardian* September 21, 2015); Kate Harding, "When a Feminist Trailblazer Turns to Victim-Blaming, It's Time to Let Go of a Hero," *Cosmopolitan* September 18, 2015.

27 Patricia Riekel, "Werden Frauen künftig schweigen?" *Bunte and Focus* June 1, 2011.

28 Sabine Rückert, "Schuldig auf Verdacht," *DIE ZEIT* June 24, 2010.

29 Ibid.

30 Compare Susan Estrich, *Real Rape*, Harvard University Press, 1988.

31 Joanna Bourke, *Rape*, p. 9.

32 §177 Strafgesetzbuch, "Sexuelle Nötigung: Vergewaltigung" Rape Law. There are exceptions to this requirement of force but only if the perpetrator "exploits a situation where the victim is defenselessly at the mercy of the perpetrator."

33 Catharine MacKinnon, *Feminism Unmodified: Discourses on Life and Law*, p. 82.

34 Eric Reitan, "Rape as an Essentially Contested Concept," *Hypathia* 16:2 (2001), p. 43–66.

35 Quoted from Malte Arnsperger, "Der Triumpf des Missmutigen," *Stern* May 10, 2011.

36 "Dann sage ich, du hast mich vergewaltigt," interview with Steffen Ufer in *Focus* June 7, 2010.

37 Sabine Rückert, "Zwei blaue Flecken und ein Nullbefund," *DIE ZEIT* February 24, 2011.

38 Patricia Riekel, "Werden Frauen künftig schweigen?".

39 See Cathy Young, "Crying Rape: False rape accusations exist, and they are a serious problem," *Slate* September 18, 2014.

40 Ulrike Lembke, "The rate for false accusations in sex crimes is according to recent comparative studies around 3 percent. Older studies by very different researchers estimate it to lie somewhere between 2 percent and 8 percent." (Ulrike Lembke, "Der derzeitige Zustand ist nicht hinnehmbar.")

41 The study by Eugene Kanin was compiled on the basis of reported rapes in Indiana Town between 1978 and 1987. A report was classified as false if the complainant retracted it on this ground. Eugene J. Kanin, *False Rape Allegations. Archives of Sexual Behaviour* Vol. 23 (1994), p. 81–92.

42 Laura Kipnis, *Unwanted Advances: Sexual Paranoia Comes to Campus*, Harper Collins, 2017, p. 167.

43 See The Code for Crown Prosecutors: " False Allegations of Rape and/or Domestic Abuse, see: Guidance for Charging Perverting the Course of Justice and Wasting Police Time in Cases involving Allegedly False Allegations of Rape and/or Domestic Abuse," available at cps.gov.uk.

44 Although law professor Lisa Avalos states that the UK prosecutes false allegations of rape more aggressively than other countries: "In the course of my research I have not found any country that pursues these cases against women rape complainants in the way the UK does. The UK has an unusual approach and I think their approach violates human rights" (quoted from Sandra Laville, "109 women prosecuted for false rape claims in five years, say campaigners," *The Guardian* December 1, 2014).

45 See Claus Peter Müller and Julia Schaaf, "Wie konnte es zu diesem Fehlurteil kommen?" *FAZ* July 25, 2011.

46 The National Registry of Exonerations data shows that since records began in 1989, only 53 men wrongly convicted as rapists had to be exonerated, compared to 790 exonerations for wrongful convictions of murder in the same time period.

47 See Liz Kelly, Jo Lovett and Linda Regan, "Home Office Research Study 293: A gap or a chasm? Attrition in reported rape case," *Home Office Research, Development and Statistics Directorate* February 2005.

48 See Sandra Newman, "What kind of person makes false rape accusations?" *Quartz* May 11, 2017.

49 Chris Ostendorf, "How Conor Oberst became an accidental MRA icon," *The Daily Dot* July 16, 2014.

50 Ibid.

51 Cathy Young, "Crying Rape: False rape accusations exist, and they are a serious problem."

52 Ibid.

53 Alice Schwarzer, "Es geht um viel mehr als um zwei Menschen," *EMMA* Autumn 2010. It is important to note that *EMMA*, being one of the earliest and commercially most successful

feminist magazines in Germany, nevertheless doesn't speak for the majority of the movement. The magazine has been criticized widely as being on the conservative spectrum of feminism, to say the least.

54 Gisela Friedrichsen, "Die Angst der Richter vor dem klaren Wort," *Der Spiegel* June 1, 2011.

55 In 2014 a comparative study by the federal association of women's advice centers and rape hotlines (BFF) evaluated more than 100 cases that ended in an acquittal of the accused or abatement of the action and found considerable problems with the then German rape law that has since been changed. BFF, "Was Ihnen widerfahren ist, ist in Deutschland nicht strafbar."

56 Julia Jüttner, "Kachelmann-Talk bei Maischberger: Freie Bahn für Schwarzer," *Spiegel Online* June 1, 2011.

57 Ibid.

58 Henry de Bracton, *On the Laws and Customs of England*, Cambridge, Selden Society and Harvard University Press (De legibus et consuetudinis Angliae, c. 1235, London, 1569), 4 vols, vol II; p. 415.

59 Article 119, *Straff der nottzucht.*

60 Friedrich Oskar von Schwarze, *Commentar zum Strafgesetzbuch für das Deutsche Reich*, Leipzig, 1873, p. 470.

61 Ibid.

62 Tanja Hommen, "Sie hat sich nicht im Geringsten gewehrt: Zur Kontinuität kultureller Deutungsmuster sexueller Gewalt seit dem Kaiserreich," in *Unzucht—Notzucht- Vergewaltigung. Definitionen und Deutungen sexueller Gewalt von der Aufklärung bis heute*, ed. Christine Künzel, p. 123.

63 Proving one's honor was a difficult procedure as a conviction could only be achieved if the accused confessed or if a witness came forward, who by doing so endangered himself for thus risking being named an accessory because he or she hadn't intervened. The risk for the victim was just as high. If the case didn't result in a conviction, the victim in turn could be accused of committing adultery with the rapist, which was a serious offence often punished by mutilation. Gesa Dane added that in Germany, "If the defendant didn't confess and his guilt couldn't be proved conclusively, he was thus being falsely accused, so the accuser [the rape victim] had to pay compensation to him or was sent to jail herself. With a crime as hard to prove as rape, the risk for the accuser was immense." (Gesa Dane, *Zeter und Mordio*, p. 71f). That the assumed lack of honor was the

reason that prostitutes and non-white women weren't considered as rapeable. Most laws focused on female honor. But there were exceptions: in the Middle Ages, the *Sachsenspiegel* saw sexual freedom as the most important legal right and determined that rape could be committed against reputable and disreputable women alike.

64 Alice Schwarzer, "Der mutige Auftritt der Ex-Freundin vor Gericht," *Bild* January 6, 2011.

65 Tanja May and Stefan Blatt, "Jetzt redet sie!" *Bunte* June 15, 2011.

66 Friedrich Schiller, *Fiesco's Conspiracy at Genoa*, p. 28.

67 Ibid., p. 29

68 Ibid.

69 Berner, "Lehrbuch des deutschen Strafrechts," quoted from *Tatbestandsprobleme der sexuellen Nötigung, Vergewaltigung sowie des sexuellen Mißbrauchs widerstandsunfähiger Personen,* Marita Kieler, Juristische Reihe TENEA 2002, Vol. 52.

70 Though to be more precise only male homosexuality, female homosexuality wasn't recognized as sexuality and was therefore not punished.

71 The total prohibition had ended in 1969 as well but most aspects of the old law became invalid in 1973, but it was only in 1994 that §175 was repealed without replacement.

72 The last time a court in Germany convicted a couple for living together outside the bounds of marriage—and prosecuted their landlord for procuring—was in 1962. That law was repealed in 1969. But even though it is against the law, a state appeals court in California ruled in 1994 that a property owner had the right to refuse to rent an apartment to an unmarried couple.

73 Ulrike Lembke, "Vis haud ingrata—die 'nicht unwillkommene Gewalt' Die kulturellen Wurzeln sexualisierter Gewalt und ihre rechtliche Verarbeitung," lecture on the occasion of the FRI exchange No. 11. 18 April 2008, p. 21.

74 See *EMMA* Summer 2011, p. 22f.

75 See Jessica Valenti, "What the Assange case reveals about rape in America," *Washington Post*, December 10, 2010.

76 Joanna Bourke, *Rape*, p. 11.

77 Michel Foucault, *The History of Sexuality, Volume I: An Introduction*, p. 43.

78 See Claire Cozens, "Polanski wins libel case against Vanity Fair," *The Guardian* July 22, 2005.

79 Quoted from Ralf Dargent, "Die Bloßstellung von 'Wetterfuzzi'

Kachelmann bei Jauch," *Die Welt* October 15, 2012.

80 Quoted from Sabine Rückert, "Schuldig auf Verdacht," *Die ZEIT*, June 24, 2010.

81 Kachelmann and Claudia D. both displayed similar symptoms of PTSD. He couldn't drive through Baden-Württemberg, the county he had been jailed in; she tried to start a self-help group with other ex-girlfriends, explaining that "destiny had made them a community of the emotionally abused" (quoted from Sabine Rückert, "Schuldig auf Verdacht"). In 2016, Kachelmann won a lawsuit against Claudia D., who became subject to a criminal investigation for charges of indirect, aggravated unjust imprisonment. He also obtained a court ruling against Axel Springer Media Group, which publishes tabloids such as *Bild* and *Bunte*.

82 Jane Fae, "Trans or otherwise, it's time to overhaul the law on 'rape by deception,'" *New Statesman* June 30, 2013.

83 *Huffington Post UK* March 22, 2013.

84 Quoted from ibid.

85 See Luke Traynor, "Fake penis woman Gayle Newland to appeal conviction over sex attacks on victim wearing blindfold," *The Mirror* November 17, 2015.

86 Stephanie Linning, "'I'd rather have been raped by a man,' says woman, sexually assaulted by female friend who used bandages and a sex toy to pretend she was male," *Mail Online* September 8, 2015.

87 Quoted from Adrian Blomfield, "Palestinian jailed for rape after claiming to be Jewish," *The Telegraph* July 20, 2010.

The Aftermath: Trauma and Healing

1 Cf. Sighard Neckel, *Status und Scham: Zur symbolischen Reproduktion sozialer Ungleichheit*, p. 51.

2 Christa Ulli in conversation with filmmakers Philippe Mach and Marc Wolfberger about their documentary about rape, "Schuld und Scham wechseln die Seite."

3 Susanne Kerner, "Warum ich meinen Vergewaltiger nicht angezeigt habe," *Huffington Post* January 22, 2016.

4 Julia Schellong, "Außer Kontrolle," *The European* February 22, 2013.

5 Quoted from Amber Amour, "Bloggerin berichtet 'live' im Netz nach ihrer Vergewaltigung," *news.de* March 16, 2016. At that time Amour was in South Africa on her Stop Rape: Educate

world tour. She live-blogged the aftermath of the rape on Instagram before going to the police, triggering an online debate that had supporters and critics up in arms. Amber Amour explained her decision in Marie Claire: "It was almost an intuitive thing. I was still in the bathroom—in the crime scene. I don't even think I'd stood up. I just typed and typed." (Corinne Redfern, "'I Live-Blogged My Rape,'" *Marie Claire* January 6, 2016).

6 Joanna Bourke, *Rape*, p. 425.

7 Vanessa Veselka, "The Collapsible Woman: Cultural Responses to Rape and Sexual Abuse," in *BITCHfest: Ten Years of Cultural Criticism from the Pages of Bitch Magazine,* ed. Lisa Jervis & Andi Zeisler, p. 56.

8 Virginie Despentes, *King Kong Theory*, p. 34.

9 Veselka, "The Collapsible Woman: Cultural Responses to Rape and Sexual Abuse."

10 "'It's not whether you can or can't forgive; it's whether you will or won't,'" *The Telegraph* March 8, 2006.

11 Obituary: Sir John Leonard, *The Telegraph* August 14, 2002.

12 Jill Saward and Wendy Green, *Rape: My Story*, p. 150.

13 Cf. Gina Messina-Dysert, "Rape and Spiritual Death," *Feminist Theology* 20:2 (2012), p. 120–132, or Ursula Wirtz, *Seelenmord: Inzest und Therapie*, Kreuz Verlag, 1989.

14 Ken Plummer, *Telling Sexual Stories*, p. 70.

15 Vanessa Veselka, "The Collapsible Woman," p. 56.

16 Ibid., p. 61.

17 Jill Saward, *Rape*, p. 61.

18 This was the one point that all reviews agreed upon: "Rape victims have at last found a voice." (Julie Davidson, "Victim's Voice: *Rape: My Story* by Jill Saward and Wendy Green," *London Review of Books* 13:2 (1991)).

19 Vanessa Veselka, "The Collapsible Woman," p. 56.

20 Katie Roiphe, *The Morning After,* p. 33.

21 Jagoda Marinic, "Befreiung von der Scham," *taz* June 3, 2011.

22 Prof. Edith Hall in *A Brief History of Shame,* Joe Queenan.

23 Ibid.

24 Vanessa Veselka, "The Collapsible Woman," p. 58.

25 "Kampusch: Anfeindungen seltener," *ORF.at* March 24, 2015.

26 Natascha Kampusch, interview, *ORF* March 5, 2012.

27 Linda Martin Alcoff und Laura Gray-Rosendale, "Survivor Discourse: Transgression or Recuperation?" *Signs* 18:2 (1993), p. 281.

28 Quoted from Virginie Despentes, *King Kong Theory*, p. 33.

29 Ibid., p. 34f.
30 Natascha Kampusch in the documentary *3096 Tage Gefangenschaft*, quoted from Ruth Schneeberger, "TV-Kritik: Natascha Kampusch 'Ich werde Geächtet,'" *Süddeutsche Zeitung* May 7, 2010.
31 Samantha Geimer with Judith Newman, *The Girl*, Simon & Schuster, 2013, p. 9.
32 Michel Foucault, *The Archaeology of Knowledge*, p. 216.
33 Virginie Despentes, *King Kong Theory*, p. 37.
34 Ibid., p. 32.
35 Ibid., p. 38.
36 Vanessa Veselka, "The Collapsible Woman," p. 57.
37 Tanya Horek, *Public Rape*, p. 120.
38 Virginie Despentes, *King Kong Theory*, p. 35.
39 Alain Corbin, *Die sexuelle Gewalt in der Geschichte*, p. 7.
40 Randy Thornhill and Craig T. Palmer, "Why Men Rape," p.181.
41 Gesa Dane, "Frauenraub-Entehrung-Notzucht," in *Unzucht-Notzucht-Vergewaltigung,* ed. Christine Künzel, p. 82.
42 Joanna Bourke, *Rape*, p. 395.
43 Caryl Rivers, *Selling Anxiety: How the News Media Scare Women*, p. 1.
44 For example, being trans was defined as a psychological illness: Gender Identity Disorder Dysphoria. The DSM-5 reclassified it as Gender Dysphoria. This still means that trans people have to get a diagnosis but it now refers to feelings of discontent "resulting from gender identity issues" (Lin Fraser et al., "Recommendations for Revision of the DSM Diagnosis of Gender Identity Disorder in Adults," *International Journal of Transgenderism* 12:2 (2010), p. 80–85.
45 Compare Ariane Brenssell, "Traumaverstehen," in *Störungen: texte kritische psychologie* 4, ed. Ariane Brenssell and Klaus Weber, p. 127.
46 Waltraud Schwab interviewed by Martina Havernock, "Sensation statt Tabu? Wortmeldungen zum Internationalen Tage gegen Gewalt an Frauen," *taz* November 25, 2008.
47 This mail is quoted with the explicit consent of the sender who wishes to remain anonymous.
48 Hannah C. Rosenblatt talking to me in an interview and also in Hannah C. Rosenblatt, "Opfer Diskurs-Zeit für Mut zum Perspektivwechsel!" *Mädchenmannschaft blog* February 21, 2017.
49 Naomi Wolf, *Vagina*, p. 124.

50 Ibid., p. 143.
51 Ibid.
52 Ibid., p. 144.
53 This gendered notion does not only pertain to sexuality. When Theresa May's leadership of the Conservative Party and the UK was called into question in late 2017, the question was "Is she damaged goods?" As far as I know that question has never been asked of a male politician.
54 Ibid., p. 121.
55 Just one example of the many scathing critics is Zoe Heller writing in the *New York Review of Books*: "There is a strange hubris in Wolf's claim to understand how all rape affects all women. It is the same hubris that compels her to instruct us on how all women need to be wooed, and how all women feel when they come." Zoe Heller, "Pride and Prejudice," *New York Review of Books* November 27, 2012.
56 Naomi Wolf, *Vagina*, p. 140.
57 Ibid., p. 137.
58 Vanessa Veselka, "The Collapsible Woman," p. 58.
59 Katie Roiphe, *The Morning After*, p. 73. That is the reason the term survivor hasn't caught on as much in Germany. There, "survivors" are predominantly equated with survivors of the Holocaust and the feminist movement didn't want to risk the accusation of comparing rape to concentration camps. Though in the younger generation there are survivors who choose this term for themselves because they feel it best describes their state of being.
60 Ariane Brenssell, "Trauma politisch verstehen: Ansätze aus der kritischen Psychologie," lecture held on February 12, 2015, *aufgetaucht: Kritische Psychologie*.
61 Jenni Diski, "Diary," *London Review of Books* 31:21 (2009), p. 53.
62 Cheryl Benard and Edit Schlaffer, *Die Emotionsfalle: Vom Triumph des weiblichen Verstandes*, p. 85.
63 Etta Hallenga in conversation with Mithu Sanyal, *MISSY MAGAZINE* April 2011.
64 Vanessa Veselka, "The Collapsible Woman," p. 57.
65 Ariane Brenssell, "Trauma politisch verstehen: Ansätze aus der kritischen Psychologie," p. 131.
66 Ariane Brenssell, "Traumaverstehen," in *Störungen: texte kritische psychologie 4*, ed. Ariane Brenssell and Klaus Weber, p. 123f.

67 Vanessa Veselka, "The Collapsible Woman,"p. 57.
68 Ariane Brenssell, "Trauma als Prozess—Wider die Pathologisierung struktureller Gewalt und ihrer innerpsychologischen Folgen," transcript of a lecture held at the symposium "Trauma und Politik," January 24, 2013, Frankfurt am Main, p. 2.
69 Ariane Brenssell, "Traumaverstehen," in *Störungen: texte kritische psychologie* 4, ed. Ariane Brenssell and Klaus Weber, p. 139ff.
70 Samantha Geimer with Judith Newman, *The Girl*, p. 138.
71 Ibid., p. 176.
72 Samantha Geimer, "Judge the Movie, Not the Man," *Los Angeles Times* February 23, 2003.
73 Samantha Geimer with Judith Newman, *The Girl*, p. 210.
74 Ibid., 242.
75 John Meroney, "A Conversation with Gore Vidal," *The Atlantic* October 2009.
76 Samantha Geimer with Judith Newman, p. 235–6.
77 Ibid., p. 6f.
78 Hannah C. Rosenblatt, "Hilfe annehmen," *Ein Blog von Vielen* September 16, 2017.
79 Ariane Brenssell, "Traumaverstehen," p. 146.
80 "Court denies Polanski victim's dismissal appeal," *ABC News* April 23, 2010. The documents in question refer to the plea agreement.
81 "Polanski's victim is not judge and jury," *Los Angeles Times* October 31, 2009.
82 Samantha Geimer with Judith Newman, p. 229.
83 Jürgen Schmieder, "Ein Albtraum namens Polanski," *Süddeutsche Zeitung* September 24, 2013.
84 Quoted from David Ng, "Judge denies Roman Polanski victim's request to drop statutory rape case," *Los Angeles Times* August 18, 2017.
85 "Samantha Geimer addresses the press after Roman Polanski hearing," published by Jack Flemming on YouTube June 9, 2017.
86 Hannah C. Rosenblatt, "Hilfe ablehnen," *Ein Blog von Vielen* September 16, 2017.
87 Ariane Brenssell, "Traumaverstehen," p. 147.
88 Ibid., p. 134.

Black-and-White Thinking: Racism and Rape Culture

1 Robin Morgan, "Theory and Practice: Pornography and Rape," in *Take Back the Night: Women on Pornography,* ed. Laura Lederer, p. 128.
2 Annie Sprinkle quoted from Laura Mulvey and Anna Backman Rogers (eds.), *Feminisms: Mutations and Appropriations in European Film Debates*, Amsterdam, p. 80.
3 Angela Y. Davis, *Women, Race & Class*, p. 173.
4 His murderers were acquitted by an all-white jury and went free and sold their story with all its gory details for $4,000 to *Look Magazine*. How they fastened a gin fan to his neck before they threw him into the water to prevent the body from floating and that it took three hours for the crepe soles of his shoes to burn (see William Bradford Huie, "Killer's Confession: The Shocking Story of Approved Killing in Mississippi," *Look Magazine* January 24, 1956).
5 Susan Brownmiller, *Against Our Will*, p. 247.
6 Angela Davis, *Women, Race & Class*, p. 179.
7 Shulamith Firestone, *The Dialectic of Sex: The Case for a Feminist Revolution*, p. 110.
8 Ibid., p. 111.
9 Ibid., p. 112.
10 Eldridge Cleaver, *Soul on Ice*, p. 106.
11 Abby Kelley in *An Anti-Slavery Album: Or Contributions From Friends of Freedom*, Western Anti-Slavery Collection, Library of Congress, p. 100.
12 Angela Davis, *Women, Race & Class*, p. 184.
13 Ibid., p. 185.
14 Ida Wells-Barnett, *On Lynching*, Arno Press, 1969, p. 8.
15 Quoted from Angela Davis, *Women, Race & Class*, p. 190.
16 See Joanna Bourke, *Rape*, p. 409.
17 Cf. Ellen Carol Dubois and Linda Gordon, "Seeking ecstasy on the Battlefield. Danger and Pleasure in Nineteenth-century Feminist Sexual Thought," in *Pleasure and Danger. Exploring Female Sexuality,* ed. Carole S. Vance, p. 32ff.
18 Quoted from Joanna Bourke, *Rape*, p. 309.
19 See Mary Ann Irwin, "'White Slavery' As Metaphor: Anatomy of a Moral Panic," *Ex Post Facto: The History Journal* Vol. 5 (1996). When Alice Schwarzer started her petition to get sex work outlawed in Germany in 2014, she

claimed the international term for the "modern slavery" of prostitution would be "white slavery." ("Appell gegen Prostitution," *EMMA*.)

20 Cover, *Focus* January 9, 2016.

21 Cover, *Süddeutsche Zeitung* January 9, 2016.

22 Cover, *wSieci* Nr. 7, 2016.

23 Walter van Rossum, "Silvester in Köln oder Making of Apokalypse 2.0," *Deutschlandfunk* July 15, 2017.

24 Nadia Shehadeh, "Arabisch Und Nordafrikanisch Aussehenden Menschen™," *Shehadistan* 2016.

25 See syrergegensexismus.org. See also "Syrer gegen Sexismus: Flüchtlinge verteilen Blumen," *Süddeutsche Zeitung* January 16, 2016.

26 Quoted from Christoph Ehrhardt, "Wo sexuelle Belästigung Alltag ist," *Frankfurter Allgemeine Zeitung* January 15, 2016.

27 Martin Lutz, "Das Phänomen 'taharrush gamea' ist in Deutschland angekommen," *Die Welt* January 10, 2016.

28 Alex Shams, "Neither Taharrush Gamea Nor Sexism Are Arab 'Cultural Practices,'" *Huffington Post* January 21, 2016.

29 Cf. Christoph Ehrhardt, "Wo sexuelle Belästigung Alltag ist," *Frankfurter Allgemeine Zeitung* January 15, 2016.

30 Patrick Gensing, "Rechtsextreme Reaktionen nach Köln: 'Rache für unsere Frauen,'" *tagesschau.de* January 12, 2016.

31 See ausnahmslos.org. "Cis" being the Latin preposite for "on this side" (in Roman times mainly refering to: on this side of the Alps), while "trans" means "beyond" or "across" (across the Alps). In the 1990s sexologist Volkmar Sigusch coined the term cis(gender) with the rationale: "If we have a concept for transgender, we have to have a concept for cisgender as well, that includes all the people whose understanding of their own sexuality is on the same side as the gender they were assigned at birth." (Volkmar Sigusch in an interview with Tobias Haberl, "Ich bin in Rage angesichts unserer Sexualkultur," *Süddeutsche Zeitung Magazin*, Vol. 21, 2015).

32 Ann J. Cahill, *Rethinking Rape*, p. 153.

33 Quoted from Miriam Zoila Pérez, "When Sexual Autonomy Isn't Enough: Sexual Violence Against Immigrant Women In The United States," in *Yes Means Yes: Visions of Female Sexual Power & A World without Rape,* ed. Jaclyn Friedman and Jessica Valenti, p. 141.

34 Quoted from Katharina Kluin, "Vergewaltigt im Flüchtlingsheim," *Der Stern* March 28, 2016.

35 "Solidarity with the victims of New Year's Eve" was written on the banner that adorned the flowers on the steps to Cologne cathedral.

36 Hilal Sezgin, "Deutsche Respektlosigkeiten," *DIE ZEIT* January 13, 2016.

37 Jan Philipp Reemtsma, *Vertrauen und Gewalt: Versuch über eine besondere Konstellation der Moderne*, p. 106.

38 See "Flucht über das Mittelmeer," *Tagesschau.de* August 4, 2015.

39 E-mail by Uwe Wappler to *Panorama*, quoted from "Diebe, Rauber, Vergewaltiger; Gerüchte über Flüchtlinge," *Panorama* October 29, 2015.

40 "Angebliche Vergewaltigung in Berlin: Lawrow kündigt Telefonat mit Steinmeier an," *Der Spiegel* January 29, 2016.

41 "13-Jährige Lisa missbracht. Vertuschungsversuche. Cousine spricht auf Kundgebung!" available at youtube.com/watch?v=eVkdCm-dRjw.

42 Tanya Horek, *Public Rape*, p. vii.

43 See Divya Talway, "UK attitudes towards Islam 'concerning' after survey of 2,000 people," *BBC Newsbeat* March 23, 2016.

44 See "'Senior member' of English Defence League jailed for sexually abusing 10-year-old girl," *The Independent* February 27, 2018.

45 Susan Muller Okin, *Is Multiculturalism Bad For Women?* Princeton University Press, 1999, p. 16.

46 Leti Volpp, "Feminism versus Multiculturalism," *Columbia Law Review* 101:5 (2001), p. 1196.

47 Ibid.

48 Cf. Lady Bitch Ray, alias of Reyhan Sahin, *Die Bedeutung des muslimischen Kopftuchs: Eine kleidungssemiotische Untersuchung Kopftuch tragender Musliminnen in der Bundesrepublik Deutschland*, Lit Verlag, 2014.

49 Ali Rattansi, *Multiculturalism: A Very Short Introduction*, p. 44.

50 Cf. Anna Petran and Johanna Louise Thiel, "Weiterentwicklungen und (neue) Widersprüche—eine Einleitung zu queer feministischen Gewaltdebatten," in *Gewalt und Handlungsmacht: Queer_Feministische Perspektiven*, ed. Gender Initiativkolleg, p. 16.

51 Ali Rattansi, *Multiculturalism*, p. 56.

52 See Mike Allen, "Bush Reverses Abortion Aid: U.S. Funds Are Denied to Groups That Promote Procedure Abroad," *Washington Post* January 23, 2001.

53 Ben Jacobs, Sabrina Siddiqui and Scott Bixby, "'You can do

anything:' Trump brags on tape about using fame to get women," *The Guardian* October 8, 2016.

54 For example: Ralph Gadan, "Migration importiert archaisches Frauenbild," *Die Welt* February 1, 2016.

55 Leti Volpp, "Feminism versus Multiculturalism," p. 1189.

56 Ibid., p. 1187.

57 Ibid., p. 1192.

58 Sandra Bucerius, "Kriminalität und Migration: Die soziale Integration ist entscheidend," *Mediendienst Integration* July 25, 2016. See also Robert J. Sampson, "Rethinking Crime and Immigration," *Contexts* 7:1 (2008), p. 28–33.

59 Sophie Roznblatt, "Das Problem mit dem Penis," *DIE ZEIT* February 13, 2017.

60 Stefanie Lohaus and Anne Wizorek, "Die Rape Culture wurde nicht nach Deutschland importiert—sie war schon immer da," *Vice Magazine* January 6, 2016.

61 The Indian version of the Slutwalks. The forerunner of the Besharmi-Morcha movement was the Pink Chaddi campaign, in which activists sent pink panties (*chaddi* means underpants) to government officials to protest right-wing violence against people perceived as not in accordance with "Indian values."

62 Noreen Connell and Cassandra Wilson (ed.) for the New York Radical Feminists, *Rape: The first Sourcebook for Women.*

63 Congressional Record 676, "Research into violent behaviors: overview and sexual assaults hearing before the subcommittee on domestic and international scientific planning, analysis and cooperation of the committee on science and technology," U.S. House of Representatives Ninety-Fifth Congress second session, January 10, 11,12, 1878 (No 64).

64 bell hooks, *Feminist Theory: From Margin to Center*, p. 118.

65 Emilie Buchwald, Pamela Fletcher and Martha Roth (eds.), *Transforming a Rape Culture*, p. xi.

66 See Nach Übergriffen, "Köln: Mit nackten Tatsachen gegen Sexismus," *Stern* January 8, 2015.

67 Norman Mailer to an audience at the University of California at Berkeley in 1972.

68 FlightScarlet, "Does Rape Culture Exist?" *BLOGHER* February 12, 2016.

69 rainn.org/news-room/rainn-urges-white-house-task-torce-to-overhaul-colleges-treatment-of-rape.

70 Amanda Marcotte, "RAINN Denounces, Doesn't Understand the Concept of 'Rape Culture,'" *Slate* March 18, 2014.

71 Caroline Kitchens, "It's Time to End 'Rape Culture' Hysteria," *Time* March 20, 2014.

72 Ben Davis, "Columbia Student's Striking Mattress Performance," *Artnet* September 4, 2014.

73 Or so it was understood. Actually the letter stated that it wasn't legally binding. Yet it was de facto treated as if it were the new law and colleges failing to comply with it were investigated by the Education Department.

74 Laura Kipnis, *Unwanted Advances: Sexual Paranoia Comes to Campus*, p. 37f.

75 Cf. Norma B. Gray, Gloria J. Palileo and G. David Johnson, "Explaining rape victim blame: A test of attribution theory," *Sociological Spectrum*, 13:4 (1993), p. 377–392.

76 Laura Kipnis, *Unwanted Advances*.

77 Dana Bolger and Alexandra Brodsky, "Betsy DeVos's Title IX interpretation is an attack on sexual assault survivors," *Washington Post* September 8, 2017. Betsy DeVos's announcement September 7, 2017. (video embedded in Dana Bolger and Alexandra Brodsky. "Betsy DeVos's Title IX interpretation is an attack on sexual assault survivors.")

78 Education Department spokeswoman Liz Hill quoted from John Bowden, "New York AG: Schools have duty to protect trans students," *The Hill* February 28, 2018.

79 Jennifer Doyle quoted from Hanna Stasiuk, "Doyle speaks to Title IX policy, response," *The Miscellany News* April 26, 2017.

80 Jeannie Suk Gersen, "Betsy DeVos, Title IX, and the 'Both Sides' Approach to Sexual Assault," *The New Yorker* September 8, 2017.

81 Laura Kipnis, *Unwanted Advances*, p. 137.

82 Ibid., p. 7–9.

83 Ibid., p. 15.

84 Ibid., p. 19.

85 Roxane Gay, *Bad Feminist*, Harper, 2014, p. 149/152.

86 Ibid., p. 147.

87 Ibid., p. 150.

88 Laura Kipnis, *Unwanted Advances,* p. 157.

89 Quoted from Siobhan Fenton, "Oxford Vice Chancellor Louise Richardson: 'Let extremist groups preach at UK universities:' The new Vice Chancellor has argued that students should engage critically with ideas, rather than be protected from them," *The Independent* January 16, 2016. This is interesting in view of Laura Kipnis's defense of being allowed to have/

make bad experiences. "I got to take risks, which was a training ground for later creative and intellectual risks, precisely because we didn't think of sex as harm. Just to be clear, I'm not trying to say that my generation's story about pleasure was any truer than this one's story about danger. There is no singular true way of thinking about sex and no direct way of experiencing it; how we think about sex is always filtered through whatever shifting set of cultural suppositions prevails." (Laura Kipnis, *Unwanted Advances*, p. 13) And just to be doubly clear, Kipnis is not speaking about rape as bad experience, but about consensual but still bad sexual encounters, about testing out with one's own borders.

90 Gerlinda Smaus, "Vergewaltigung von Männern durch Männer," in *Unzucht-Notzucht-Vergewaltigung*, ed. Christine Künzel, p. 234. See also William Wan, "What makes some men sexual harassers?" *Washington Post* December 22, 2017.

91 Quoted from Joanna Bourke, *Rape*, p. 367.

92 Cf. Jon Ronson, *The Psychopath Test*, Picador, 2012.

93 Joanna Bourke, *Rape*, p. 211.

94 Ibid., p. 237.

95 Kayle Williams and Michael E. Staub, *Love My Rifle More than You: Young and Female in the U.S. Army*, p. 247.

96 Coco Fusco, *A Field Guide for Female Interrogators*, Seven Stories Press, 2008.

97 Coco Fusco, "Invasion of Space by a Female," in *Yes means Yes: Visions of Female Sexual Power & A World Without Rape,* Jaclyn Friedman and Jessica Valenti, p. 134.

98 Ibid.

99 See also Tony Lagouranis and Allen Mikaelian, *Fear Up Harsh: An Army Interrogator's Dark Journey Through Iraq*, New American Library, 2007, p. 17.

100 Coco Fusco, "Invasion of Space by a Female," p. 135.

101 After the famous "Milgram experiment" on obedience to authority figures, which tested the extent to which people were willing to inflict pain on others if a person in a white coat told them to.

102 See Joanna Bourke, *Rape*, p. 359.

103 Gerlinda Smaus, "Vergewaltigung von Männern durch Männer," p. 237.

Omissions: Men, Masculinity, and Myths

1 Sebastian Franck, *Weltbuch: spiegel und bildtnis des gesantzen Erdtbodens*, Morhart, 1542, p. 228.
2 Angela Koch, "Die Verletzung der Gemeinschaft: Zur Relation der Wort- und Ideengeschichte von 'Vergewaltigung'," in *Bodies/ Politics: Österreichische Zeitschrift für Geschichtswissenschaften*, ed. Johanna Gehmacher, Gabriella Hauch and Marie Messner, p. 39.
3 Ibid.
4 See Sharon Marcus, "Fighting Bodies, Fighting Words," in *Gender Struggles: Practical Approaches to Contemporary Feminism,* Constance L. Mui and Julien S. Murphy, p. 166–185.
5 Joanna Bourke, *Rape*, p. 418.
6 Virginie Despentes, *King Kong Theory*, p. 40.
7 Susan Brownmiller, *Against Our Will*, p. 208f.
8 Cf. Hannah Arendt, *Macht und Gewalt*, Piper, 1970, p. 53.
9 Joanna Bourke, *Rape*, p. 415.
10 *Police Illustrated News* September 22, 1888.
11 The famous "Dear Boss" letter, which arrived at the Central News Agency on September 22, 1888 and was released on the first of October after the double murder of Elizabeth Stride and Catherine Eddowes on September 30, 1888.
12 Judith R. Walkowitz, "Jack the Ripper and the Myth of Male Violence," *Feminist Studies* 8:3 (1982), p. 544.
13 Cf. Gretchen Soderlund, *Sex Trafficking, Scandal, and the Transformation of Journalism: 1885–1917*, p. 60ff.
14 Judith R. Walkowitz, "Jack the Ripper and the Myth of Male Violence," p. 545f. Without the Criminal Law Amendment Act the 1895 conviction of Oscar Wilde to two years of hard labour for "indecent acts"—meaning homosexuality—would not have been possible.
15 Ibid., p. 546.
16 Ibid., p. 555.
17 *Pall Mall Gazette* September 10, 1888.
18 *Evening Standard* November 9, 1888.
19 Judith R. Walkowitz, "Jack the Ripper and the Myth of Male Violence," p. 569. Quoting from *The Times* November 16, 1888.
20 Cf. Judith R. Walkowitz, "Jack the Ripper and the Myth of

Male Violence."

21 See Trevor Marriott, *Jack the Ripper: The 21st Century Investigation*, John Blake, 2005, p. 5–7.

22 Dr. Park Dietz on Charlie Brooker's Newswipe, *BBC* March 25, 2009.

23 Sharon Marcus, "Fighting Bodies, Fighting Words," p. 172–3, 177.

24 Ann Cahill, *Rethinking Rape*, p. 154.

25 See Judith Butler, "Vulnerability And Resistance Revisited," Lecture at Trinity College February 5, 2015.

26 See Ronald E. Smith, Charles J. Pine and Mark E. Hawley, "Social cognitions about adult male victims of female sexual assault," *Journal of Sex Research* Vol. 24 (1988), p. 101–112.

27 Cindy Struckman-Johnson and David Struckman-Johnson, "Acceptance of male rape myth among college men and women," in *Sex Roles* 27:3/4 (1992), p. 97.

28 Guy Holmes und Liz Offen. "Clinicians' hypothesis regarding clients problems: are they less likely to hypothesize sexual abuse in male compared to female clients?" *Child Abuse & Neglect* 20:6 (1996), p. 493–501.

29 Frank Tomasulo, "'I'll see it when I believe it:' Rodney King and the Prison House of Video," in *The Persistence of History: Cinema, Television and the Modern Event*, ed. Vivian Sobchack, p. 82.

30 See Markus Krischer, "Die Phantasien des Lawrence von Arabien," *Focus* August 2, 2006.

31 Skylar Baker-Jordan, "I'm a man who has been sexually harassed—but I don't think it's right for men to join in with #MeToo," *The Independent* October 19, 2017.

32 Gero von Randow, "Ich auch? Ich auch: 'Spezifische Gewalt gegen Frauen, die System hat,'" *DIE ZEIT* October 18, 2017.

33 To be more precise, between 5 percent and 14 percent.

34 See "Attorney general Eric Holder announces revisions to the uniform crime report's definition of rape," *US Department of Justice* 2012.

35 "The National Intimate Partner and Sexual Violence Survey: fact sheet," *National Center for Injury Prevention and Control* 2011, p. 18–19.

36 Lara Stemple and Ilan H. Meyer, "The Sexual Victimization of Men in America: New Data Challenge Old Assumptions," *UCLA Williams Institute* April 2014.

37 Ibid.

38 "Male-stalking rapist puzzles experts," *CBS* 2009.

39 Stemple writes: "A related argument for treating male victimization as less worrisome holds that male victims experience less physical force than do female victims, the implication being that the use of force determines concern about victimization. This rationale problematically conflicts with the important feminist-led movement away from physical force as a defining and necessary component of sexual victimization. In addition, a recent multiyear analysis of the BJS National Crime Victim Survey (NCVS) found no difference between male and female victims in the use of a resistance strategy during rape and sexual assault (89 percent of both men and women did so). A weapon was used in 7 percent of both male and female incidents, and although resultant injuries requiring medical care were higher in women, men too experienced significant injuries (12.6 percent of females and 8.5 percent of males)." (Lara Stemple and Ilan H. Meyer, "The Sexual Victimization of Men in America.")

40 Lara Stemple, Andrew Flores and Ilan Meyer, "Sexual Victimization Perpetrated by Women: Federal Data Reveal Surprising Prevalence," *Aggression and Violent Behavior* 34:0 (2017), p. 302–311.

41 Ibid., p. 304.

42 Justitia US Law SF b. State Ex Rel. TM, 695 So. 2d 1186, 1187 (1996), November 22, 1996.

43 Ibid.

44 Ibid.

45 Ellen London, "Comments: A Critique of the Strict Liability Standard for Determining Child Support in Cases of Male Victims of Sexual Assault and Statutory Rape," *University of Pennsylvania Law Review* Vol. 152, p. 1958.

46 Brenda V. Smith. "Watching me, watching you," *Yale Journal of Law and Feminism* 15:22 (2003), p. 230.

47 See the study by law professor Sonja B. Starr, "Estimated Gender Disparities in Federal Criminal Cases," University of Michigan Law and Economics Research Paper No. 12–018, August 29, 2012.

48 Sonja B. Starr, "Estimated Gender Disparities in Federal Criminal Cases," University of Michigan Law and Economics Research Paper No. 12–018, August 29, 2012; Joanna Bourke, *Rape*, p. 212.

49 Cf. Penelope Eckert and Sally McConnell-Ginet, *Language and Gender*, p. 3.

50 Cf. *Zwangssterilisation*, Positionspapier der Staatlichen Koordinierungsstelle nach Art, 3 3 UN-BRK, available at behindertenbeauftragte.de.
51 Cf. Jahel Mielke, "Pharmakonzerne: Gestorben wird anderswo," *Der Tagesspiegel* November 6, 2011.
52 Cf. Gerlinda Smaus, "Vergewaltigung von Männern durch Männer," p. 223.
53 Donald Tucker, "A Punk's Song: View from the Inside," in *Male Rape: A Casebook of Sexual Aggressions*, ed. Anthony M. Scacco Jr, p. 72.
54 Ibid.
55 Quoted from Eugene L. Meyer, "Pacifist elects to pay fine rather than return to jail," *Washington Post* September 27, 1973.
56 Interview with Stephen Donaldson in Jim Goad, "The Punk who wouldn't shut up," *ANSWER ME!* Vol. 4 (1994), p.28.
57 Ibid., p. 29.
58 Ibid., p. 28.
59 Susan Estrich, *Real Rape*; Anna Clark, "Why Does Popular Culture Treat Prison Rape As a Joke?" *ALTERNET* August 16, 2009.
60 Lara Stemple and Ilan H. Meyer, "The Sexual Victimization of Men in America."
61 Lara Stemple quoted in Hanna Rosin, "When Men Are Raped," *Slate* April 29, 2014.
62 bell hooks, *Feminist Theory*, p. 150f.
63 Quoted from Joanna Bourke, *Rape*, p. 437.
64 Julia Serano, "Why nice guys finish last," in *Yes means Yes: Visions of Female Sexual Power and a World Without Rape*, ed. Jaclyn Friedman and Jessica Valenti, p. 227.
65 Ibid., p. 232.
66 Ibid., p. 231.
67 Of course there is "fathering," but that doesn't denote the emotional work of caring and looking after another human being, but the physical act of siring a child.
68 Mark Greene, "When Men Keep Demanding Sex From Their Partners Over and Over," *medium.com* January 24, 2015.
69 Ibid.
70 Laurie Penny, *Unspeakable Things*, p. 75f.
71 Jason Schultz, "Getting off on feminism," quoted in Rebecca Walker (ed.), *To Be Real: Telling the Truth and Changing the Face of Feminism*, p. 112, 120. Even the campaign "Real Men Don't Rape" isn't free of these stereotypes, only the other way

around. Author and activist Sian Ferguson explains on everyday feminism: "We're trying to say 'Hey, you don't need to rape to express or prove your masculinity.' But instead, the phrase unintentionally insinuates that men who conform to the dominant masculinity are incapable of rape . . . Let's think carefully about which men society deems 'normal:' cisgender, able-bodied, neurotypical, heterosexual, white, middle-class men. On the other hand, transgender, mentally ill, physically disabled, non-heterosexual, poor men of color are deemed abnormal." (Sian Ferguson, "3 Reasons Why Saying 'Real Men Don't Rape' Reinforces Rape Culture," *everydayfeminism.com* February 28, 2015.)

72 Julia Serano, "Why nice guys finish last," p. 236.

73 Jason Schultz, "Getting off on feminism," p. 112.

74 Alyssa Royse, "The Danger in Demonizing Male Sexuality," *The Good Men Project* March 28, 2013.

75 The term was (in all probability) coined by psychologist Shepherd Bly to describe negative effects of male socialization on men (and only as a result of this on their nearest and dearest and society as a whole), while nowadays it is mostly associated with the way men's behavior poisons society. Jaclyn Friedman describes toxic masculinity as "a masculinity that defines itself not only in opposition to female-ness, but as inherently superior, drawing it's strength from dominance over women's 'weakness,' and creating men who are happy to deliberately undermine women's power" (Jaclyn Friedman, "Toxic Masculinity," *The American Project* March 13, 2013).

76 Cf. Terrence Real, *I Don't Want to Talk About It: Overcoming the Secret Legacy of Male Depression*, p. 121.

77 Ibid., p. 122.

78 Ibid., p. 110.

79 Cf. John Condry and Sandra Condry, "Sex Differences: A Study of the Eye of the Beholder," *Child Development* 47:3 (1976), p. 812–819; Cf. Beverly I. Fagot, "The Influence of Sex of Child on Parental Reactions to Toddler Children," *Child Development* 49:2 (1978), p. 459–465.

80 See Barbara Vorsamer, "Jungs sind halt so," *Süddeutsche Zeitung* November 24, 2017.

81 See William Wan, "What makes some men sexual harassers?" *Washington Post* December 22, 2017.

82 "No More Boys And Girls: Can Our Kids Go Gender Free?" BBC 2 August 16, 2017.

83 Ibid.
84 Kati Holloway, "Toxic masculinity is killing men: The roots of male trauma," *salon.com* June 12, 2015.
85 Stephen Feller, "Study: Acting tough may be bad for men's health," *upi.com* March 23, 2016.

Missions: Yes Means Yes

1 Kai Cheng Thom, "9 Ways to be accountable when you've been abusive," *everydayfeminism.com* February 1, 2016.
2 Ibid.
3 Joanna Bourke, *Rape*, p. 5.
4 Samantha Geimer with Judith Newman, *The Girl*, p. 232.
5 "Footballer rape trial: Ched Evans jailed five years, Clayton McDonald cleared," *BBC.com* April 20, 2012.
6 "Ched Evans petition: Sheffield United urged not to re-employ rape footballer," *BBC.com* August 13, 2015.
7 Martyn Ziegler, "Ched Evans deal was axed after 'vile and abusive threats, including death threats' reveal Oldham," *The Independent* January 8, 2015; Nick Howson, "Ched Evans: Oldham Athletic move off after club officials' families subjected to rape and death threats," *International Business Times* January 8, 2015.
8 Caitlin Moran, "The limits of redemption," *The Times* December 13, 2014.
9 Eric Reitan, "Rape as an Essentially Contested Concept," p. 43.
10 Sabine Sielke, *Reading Rape: The Rhetoric of Sexual Violence in American Literature and Culture 1790–1990*, p. 2.
11 Sandra Laville, "The Ched Evans trial showed how rape complainants are still put in the dock," *The Guardian* October 14, 2016.
12 Eric Reitan, "Rape as an Essentially Contested Concept," p. 44.
13 Jacob Sullum, "Out of 747,408 Registered Sex Offenders, How Many Are Actually Dangerous?" *reason.com* January 23, 2012.
14 David Feige, "Shawna: A Life on the Sex Offender Registry," *The Marshall Project* September 17, 2017.
15 The nearly 100-page police report is not accessible to the public and summaries of the case are contradictory, but they all agree that the accusations center around the use/abuse of condoms.
16 One of the women tweeted thereupon she had not been raped.

The other sent a text to a friend that she didn't want to accuse Assange of rape: "it was the police who made up the charges." (The tweet was deleted but is archived at archive.is/OTQWI. The text is quoted from a mail by Assange's lawyer and can be viewed at wikileaks.org/IMG/html/Affidavit_of_Julian_Assange.)

17 Martin Beckford, "Sarah Palin: hunt WikiLeaks founder like al-Qaeda and Taliban leaders," *The Telegraph* November 30, 2010.

18 Ibid.

19 Lindsay Beyerstein, "A Feminist Lawyer on the Case Against Wikileaks' Julian Assange," *bigthink.com*.

20 Laurie Penny, "If you really believe in WikiLeaks, you must want Assange to face up to justice," *The Independent* August 22, 2012.

21 Thordis Elva and Tom Stranger, *South of Forgiveness*, Scribe, 2017, p. 30.

22 Ibid., p. 121.

23 Ibid., p. 1.

24 Ibid., p. 158.

25 While she was simultaneously accused of lying about the rape because the pain she described "was just a sign of him giving it to her properly." (One among many deactivated comments under their TED Talk on YouTube.)

26 Josephine Cashman on Australian broadcasting station ABC's Q&A programme, March 6, 2017.

27 Frauenberatungsstelle Düsseldorf in an interview with Mithu Sanyal.

28 Josephine Cashman, March 6, 2017.

29 Since the UN Resolution in 2002, restorative justice is implemented in most Western countries.

30 Theresa Bullmann in an interview with Mithu Sanyal.

31 Katie J. M. Baker, "What Do We Do With These Men?" *New York Times* April 27, 2018.

32 Ibid.

33 Ibid.

34 Petition by Amira Elwakil, "Rapists should not be given platform at Southbank Centre's 2017 Women of the World Festival," *Change.org*.

35 Richard Hartley-Parkinson, "Campaigners storm Southbank Centre to protest talk by 'rapist,'" *Metro* March 15, 2017.

36 Petition by Amira Elwakil, "Rapists should not be given platform at Southbank Centre's 2017 Women of the World Festival," *Change.org*.

37 Thordis Elva and Tom Stranger, "Our story of rape and reconciliation," TED Talk.
38 Thordis Elva and Tom Stranger, *South of Forgiveness*, p. 65f.
39 Ibid., p. 222.
40 Kai Cheng Thom, "9 Ways to be accountable when you've been abusive."
41 Ibid.
42 Cf. S.L. Schneider and R.C. Wright, "Understanding denial in sexual offenders: a review of cognitive and motivational processes to avoid responsibility," *Trauma Violence Abuse* 5:1 (2004), p. 3–20.
43 See Jacqueline Rose, "Who do you think you are," *London Review of Books* 38:9 (2016), p. 13.
44 Kai Cheng Thom, "9 Ways to be accountable when you've been abusive."
45 Ibid.
46 Laurie Penny, *Unspeakable Things*, p. 97.
47 Sharon Marcus, "Fighting Bodies, Fighting Words," p. 169.
48 Home Office, *A Call to End Violence against Women and Girls: Action Plan 2014*, March 8, 2014, p. 6, available at gov.uk.
49 Joanna Bourke, *Rape*, p. 11.
50 Although the concept of consent has been around much longer. There were forms of consent in classical antiquity and a lot of non-Western societies have an understanding of consent that is radically different from ours. But the roots of our use of the word consent go back to the liberalism of the seventeenth and eighteenth century.
51 John Locke, *Second Treatise of Civil Government*, Chapter XI, sec. 138.
52 Ibid., Chapter V, sec. 27.
53 John Locke, *The Works, Book X*, p. 196. Also see James Farr, "'So Vile and Miserable an Estate:' The Problem of Slavery in Locke's Political Thought," *Political Theory* 12:2 (1986), p. 263–289.
54 Joanna Bourke, *Rape*, p. 83f.
55 Sir Mark Hedley quoted from Jack Malvern, "Down's husband barred from sex with wife wins £10,000 damages," *The Times* August 18, 2017.
56 Ibid.
57 Peggy Reeves Sanday, "Rape-Free versus Rape-Prone: How Culture Makes a Difference," in *Evolution, Gender, and Rape*, ed. Cheryl Brown Travis, p. 337.

58 bell hooks, *All About Love*, Harper, 2000, p. xviiif.
59 The psychological term for different forms of manipulation—up to mental abuse—that make victims doubt their own perceptions, coined in reference to the 1938 play and 1944 film *Gaslight*.
60 Thames Valley Poplice YouTube channel, "Tea and Consent," November 16, 2015.
61 Cf. Margarita Tartakovsky, "How to Respect Other People's Boundaries," *Psych Central* November 5, 2014.
62 Manuel Herand YouTube channel, "A talk with Betty Martin," September 16, 2016.
63 Ibid.

Afterword: Notes from the Road

1 Christian Rath, "'Nein' heißt endlich 'Nein,'" *taz* January 6, 2015.
2 Christina Clemm quoted from Tanja Mokosch, "Das Sexualstrafrecht basiert auf Mythen," *Süddeutsche Zeitung* August 13, 2014.
3 Interview with Ulrike Lembke, "Der derzeitige Zustand ist nicht hinnehmbar," *Missy Magazine* September 21, 2011.
4 Andreas Zumach, "Vergewaltigung wird Kriegsverbrechen," *taz* June 21, 2008.
5 Cheryl Benard and Edith Schlaffer, *Die Emotionsfalle: Vom Triumph des weiblichen Verstandes*, p. 88f.
6 Monia Frommel, "'Nein heißt nein' und der Fall Lohfink," *Novo* June 27, 2016.
7 See "BBC Advice Age of Consent," *BBC Radio 1*.
8 "Two boys become youngest convicted of attempted rape," *The Telegraph* May 24, 2010.
9 Elisabeth Winkelmeier-Becker et al., *Eckpunktepapier zur Reform des Strafrechts—mit dem Grundsatz "Nein heißt Nein,"* p. 2.
10 "Transcript: Donald Trump's Taped Comments About Women," *New York Times* October 8, 2016.
11 Ian Johnson, "Trump claims Bill Clinton said 'far worse to me' amid storm over lewd remarks about women," *The Independent* October 7, 2016.
12 Marcia Bianco, "Statistics Show Exactly How Many Times Trans People Have Attacked You in Bathrooms," *Mic* April 2, 2016.

13 Terry Firma, "More Republican Politicians Than Trans People Have Been Arrested For Sex Acts in Bathrooms," *Patheos* April 11, 2016.
14 Janice Turner, "The danger of creating memorials to monsters," *The Times* August 3, 2017.
15 "ARD Umfrage zu 'Nein heißt Nein:' 86 Prozent für Verschärfung des Sexualstrafrechts," *Der Tagesspiegel* June 17, 2016.
16 Mithu Sanyal and Marie Albrecht, "Du Opfer!" *taz* February 13, 2017.
17 Cf. Anneli Borchert, "Im Erlebnisbad der Gewalt—eine Replik auf den Text 'Du Opfer,'" *Ondiestoerenfriedas.de* February 14, 2017.
18 "Opfer sollen nicht mehr Opfer heißen," *EMMA* February 21, 2017; Mithu Sanyal and Marie Alberecht, "Beschreibung sexualisierter Gewalt: Du Opfer," *taz* February 13, 2017.
19 Halle-Leaks blog, "Gutmenschin meint Vergewaltigungs-Opfer sollten mehr Erlebende sein," February 2017, blog.halle-leaks.de.
20 David Berger, "Unglaublich: Opfer von Vergewaltigung sollen ab jetzt 'Erlebende' heißen," *philosophia-perennis.com* February 23, 2017.
21 Laurie Penny talking to Mithu Sanyal in Göttingen, March 7, 2017.
22 See Marion Detjen, "Gewalt ohne Namen," *DIE ZEIT* February 27, 2017.
23 Hannah C. Rosenblatt, "Opfer Diskurs—Zeit für Mut zum Perspektivwechsel," *maedchenmannschaft.net* February 21, 2017.
24 Lawrence Olivier quoted from Michael Simkins, "Method acting can go too far—just ask Dustin Hoffman," *The Guardian* March 31, 2016.
25 Maria Schneider quoted from Elahe Izadi, "Last Tango in Paris: Why the rape scene involving Maria Schneider is only generating such an outcry now," *The Independent* December 5, 2016.
26 Bernardo Bertolucci quoted from Bonnie Malkin, "Last Tango in Paris director suggests Maria Schneider 'butter rape' scene not consensual," *The Guardian* December 4, 2016.
27 Interview with Tarana Burke on *Democracy Now!*, October 17, 2017.
28 "#MeToo—Was muss sich ändern?" *Deutschlandfunk* November 18, 2017.
29 Laura Kipnis, *Unwanted Advances*, p. 203.
30 Cf. Harry Nutt, "Die gespaltene feministische Bewegung,"

Frankfurter Rundschau October 31, 2017.

31 Quoted from Meka Beresford, "Sweden outlaws sex without consent as Europe pushed to tighten rape laws," *Reuters* May 23, 2018.

32 Sandra Saatmann, "Schweden treibt die sexuelle Korrektheit auf die Spitze," *DIE WELT* December 19, 2017.

33 See Margarete Stokowski, "Sterben die Schweden jetzt aus?" *Der Spiegel* December 26, 2017; Nina Rölke quoted from Tim Geyer, "Wir haben die Schwedische Botschaft gefragt, was Deutsche beim Sex nicht verstehen," *Vice* December 22, 2017.

34 "Five things to know about Sweden's new sexual consent law," *The Local* May 24, 2018.

35 Rona Torenz interviewed by Mithu Sanyal in Mithu Sanyal, "Konsens und guter Sex," *WDR Radio 5* February 9, 2018.

36 Junot Diaz, "The Silence: The legacy of childhood trauma," *New Yorker* April 16, 2018.

37 Zinzi Clemmons quoted from Boris Kachka and Devon Ivie, "Junot Díaz's Accuser Confronted Him Publicly During a Q&A at a Writers' Festival," *Vulture* May 4, 2018.

38 Alisa Valdes, "I Tried to Warn You About Junot Diaz," oshun-creative.wordpress.com, May 4, 2018.

39 Alisa Valdes, "I Tried to Warn You About Junot Diaz."

40 Carmen Maria Machado, @carmenmmachado on Twitter May 4, 2018.

Index